Urban Environment: Issues of Poverty

About the Editor

G. Vasant Kumar is a faculty member and Project Coordinator of RCUES-OU, Hyderabad. He did his Ph.D. with distinction from Osmania University in Management. He is a Graduate in Law, Post Graduate in Public Administration, and specialized in leadership and team building from the Brier Crest University, Canada. He is a sociologist working on women and children issues, protection of rights and good governance.

He is a civilian police officer of Andhra Pradesh State Police Service of 36 years experience of working in different assignments. He is winner of Gold Medal in the All Indian Police Duty Meet on Scientific Aids to Investigation (1986) and recipient of UN Peacekeeping Medal during his deputation to United Nation Mission in Bosnia, Herzegovina (1999-2000) where he authored five segments of Police Manual for Bosnian Federal Police and introduced different projects for prevention and rehabilitation of children conflict with society and protection of rights of persons of under priviledged communities.

He is a visiting faculty to many national and international institutions dealing with strategy and change management, leadership, team building, urban issues, urban services, protection of rights of women and children, corporate responsibility, institutional building, empowerment of urban poor, road traffic and transport facilities, legal rights of migrants and displaced personalities, rightful services to the urban poor and secured living.

Urban Environment: Issues of Poverty

ESSAYS IN HONOUR OF PROF. S. BHUPATTHI RAV

Edited by
G. Vasant Kumar

CONCEPT PUBLISHING COMPANY PVT. LTD.
NEW DELHI-110059

ISBN-13: 978-93-5125-183-5

First Published 2015

Published and Printed by

Concept Publishing Company Pvt. Ltd.
A/15-16, Commercial Block, Mohan Garden
New Delhi-110059 (India)
T: 25351460, 25351794, *F*: 091-11-25357109
E: publishing@conceptpub.com, W: www.conceptpub.com
Editorial Office: H-13, Bali Nagar, New Delhi-110 015, India.

Cataloging in Publication Data--Courtesy: D.K. Agencies (P) Ltd. <docinfo@dkagencies.com>

Urban environment : issues of poverty : essays in honour of Prof. S. Bhupatthi Rav / edited by G. Vasant Kumar.
pages cm
Includes bibliographical references and index.
ISBN 9789351251835

1. Urbanization--India. 2. Poverty--Government policy--India. 3. Slums--India. 4. India--Population policy. 5. Environmental impact analysis--India. I. Rav, S. Bhupatthi, honouree. II. Vasant Kumar, G., editor.

HT384.I4U73 2015 DDC 307.760954 23

Dedicated to

Professor S. Bhupatthi Rav

Director

Regional Centre for Urban and Environmental Studies

Osmania University, Hyderabad

Preface

The idea has been conveyed by Dr. K.L.N. Murthy, to felicitate Professor S. Bhupatthi Rav, Director, Regional Centre for Urban and Environmental Studies, Osmania University, Hyderabad on the occasion of 60th year of his birth in honour of scholarship and devotion to the field of Urban and Environmental Studies. His contribution to this branch of knowledge in particular helps to understand urban development is well recognized in the subfield of Health and Planning in urban areas, impact studies (Urban Poverty Alleviation Project) and intensive training imparted to urban local bodies as well as urban functionaries. He has been an acknowledged expert in the field of Public Administration and Policy Studies and a distinguished Public Administrator (Practitioner of Public Administration) who has completed more than 38 years of his active career raising from MA (Public Administration) as student to Director, Regional Centre for Urban and Environmental Studies, Osmania University, Hyderabad, Telangana State. During this period he is an inspired Public Administrator and challenged many students to be real and authentic persons on the staff of Department of Public Administration, Osmania University, Hyderabad. Prof. Rav has also shown by his example what commitment to contribution to the subject as well as dedication to work. Dedication and Devotion are the two faces of a coin and it was felt that a book on Urban Environment—Issues related to poverty is the current content of this book and it is necessary and to mark the occasion, we are proud to release the public action of a festschrift volume with the above title.

This book brings together contribution of 12 chapters of specialists in the field extensively dealt with urban environmental studies. This is prepared not only for the beginners of research but also for seasoned specialists relating to Policy makers, administrators, urban and regional planners. The entire work containing 12 chapters related to the facets of urban environment and issues of poverty. They are sub-divided into the following themes.

1. Urban Environment, Urban Poverty alleviation Human Resources.
2. Urban Poverty Alleviation—An Environmental Impact Assessment Reducing Poverty in urban India and, Social Mobilization.
3. Gender Budgeting—Self-Help Groups and Women Development.
4. Urban Poverty Alleviation related to National and State Government are presented besides. Its status and Structure—Environmental Impact Assessment (EIA)—Government Programmes for Slum Free Cities and 12th Plan Strategy.
5. Slums and Governance, Role of Technology for Slum Improvement and Role of Training and Research Institutions in Improving Urban Environment and Environmental Protection.

The present book has been prepared to study four goals.

1. To analyze Urban Environment and its Patterns particularly urbanization.
2. To provide analysis of issues related Urban Poverty, Urban Slums—Governance and also to exercise the problems that the urban spaces/cities those are facing problems due to rapid growth.
3. To focus on dynamics of population-resource relationship as well to examine the population structure.
4. To provide environmental impact assessment of the impact of Five Year Plans of India.

Hypothesis

1. Increasing population with a decreasing potential population.
2. Increasing population and decreasing comfort.
3. Impact on economic development, if any.
4. Technology as an important input and an agent for creating slum free cities in India.
5. Institutional input for development.

The present book provides an understanding of the structural process of Urbanization in a given environment and leaves an indelible mark for research on the spatial aspects of urban environmental studies with respect to Micro, Meso and Macro-Regions of an administrative hierarchy.

This work would not have been possible without the encouragement and assistance of Prof. S. Bhupatthi Rav, Director, Colleagues and friends of the institute. The editors would like to thank all the authors who have contributed the chapters to this book. The editor would like to extend special thanks to Prof. A.V. Satyanarayana Rao Garu for his continuous support during the preparation and printing of this book in a shortest period of time. Smt. Rajita, who has extended co-operation in bringing out the basic book for making the pre-final shape of the book. Finally, we extend thanks to the Concept Publishing Company Pvt. Ltd., for neat printing and present the book to many researchers for ready reference.

RCUES
Osmania University
Hyderabad
16th January, 2015

G. Vasant Kumar

Contents

List of Contributors

Dr. K.L. Narasimha Murty, Principal (Retd.), Government U.G. and P.G. College (Men), Srikakulam and Consultant, Regional Centre for Urban & Environmental Studies, Osmania University, Hyderabad, Telangana State, India.

Prof. G. Vasant Kumar, Programme Co-ordinator, Regional Centre for Urban & Environmental Studies, Osmania University, Hyderabad, Telangana State, India.

Dr. T. Aishwarya, Research Scholar, Department of Public Administration, Osmania University, Hyderabad, Telangana State, India.

Smt. K.V. Jagadamba, Ex. PG Student, Department of Commerce & Management Studies, Dr. B.R. Ambedkar University, Etcherla, Srikakulam District, Andhra Pradesh, India.

Sri S. Umapathi, IPS, Hyderabad.

Smt. Y. Pentamma, Department of Geosciences, Dr. B.R. Ambedkar University, Etcherla, Srikakulam District, Andhra Pradesh, India.

Smt. Simhadri Kalyani, Infosys, Hyderabad, Telangana State, India.

Sri M. Rama Rao, Research Officer, Regional Centre for Urban & Environmental Studies, Osmania University, Hyderabad, Telangana State, India.

Sri P. Gopal, Technical Assistant, Regional Centre for Urban & Environmental Studies, Osmania University, Hyderabad, Telangana State, India.

PART ONE

1
Introduction

K.L.N. Murty

'Space' is highly competitive but not complementary in the total framework of urban environment and urban land system. The economic activity activates and predominantly dominates by the presence of resources. Resources are the sources for generating the primary, secondary and tertiary activities for development. Urban space is subjected to urbanization process and the elements that are involved may present to evolve a system that is called as urban system. Urban places are considered as important focal points to generate growth in the field of economy upon a geographic place over a period of time. They become service centres, later on become growth centres which vary from one to another and have its impact on the space and people with varying socio-economic, political even cultural life of people for development. The urban service centres may help to generate growth systematically, in short, it creates a good fusion or good environment upon the spatial units. This type of environment has been attracted by many scholars such as economists, geographers, sociologists, public administrators, and their contributions helps to manage the environment which have cut across the boundaries and create an area for new study and research which have been stemmed into an urban environment. Now, this has been gaining momentum to form a new brand entitled broadly as urban environment which is a part and parcel of urban system, having a bearing on people, financial status, and also poverty. According to one scholar, that poverty constitutes a danger to prosperity everywhere.

Methodological dimensions and applied economic, geographic, sociologic, administrative and management problems relating to urban poverty in particular which gradually presents urban slums with varying levels of socio-economic development problems of phenomenon and it is linked-up with an administrative policy. In this volume, chapter 1 deals with urban environment, definitions, classification, protection, and planning process has been presented.

Urban poverty alleviation might be possible only through the Five Year Plans (FYP) for development in India. Urban poverty has been jointly adjoined with prospects and progressive growth such as education, health, sanitation, housing and shelter, livelihoods, skill development programmes, social security and infrastructure facilities. Urban poverty alleviation programmes have been designed in order to cater to the needs of the urban poor, who are living below the poverty line and these programmes have benefited specially women, children, differently abled group and aged people. The above socio-economic groups of people were direct beneficiaries of the urban poverty alleviation programmes in India.

Urban poverty alleviation programme is an important aspect to seek the welfare of people living under BPL in an ideal urban environment. Poverty reduction is an important set goal of the urban policy. Urban growth is the result of culmination of three factors. They are: (1) natural increase in population, (2) net migration from rural areas to urban areas and (3) re-classification of towns. The common notion and notation is that migration largely fuels urban growth is only partially correct. Therefore, it is necessary to view urban poverty as distinct from rural poverty and not as mere transfer of rural poverty into urban areas. The programmes are so designed to reduce urban poverty and also create skillfulness to do the work in a work environment and achieve development at various area levels. They are: (1) Nehru Rozgar Yojana, (NRY), (2) Urban Basic Services of the Poor (UBSP), (3) Prime Ministers Integrated Urban Poverty Eradication Programme (PMIUPEP), (4) Self Employment Component of NRY and PMIUPEP have been jointly framed and formed into a single programme valid for all the urban areas all over the country, (5) Swarna Jayanthi Shahari Rozgar Yojana (SJSRY), (6) Urban Self Employment Programme (USEP), (7) Urban Wage Employment Programme (UWEP), (8) Wider implications for the Twelfth Five

Year Plan beyond the ToR (Terms of Reference), (9) USEP progress—2009-10 to 2013-14, (10) Rajiv Yuva Kiranalu Placements—Consolidated Form, (11) Livelihood skill training reports (12) UWSP—Urban Women Self-Help Programme (Progress Report 2011-12 and 2013) and evaluation, (13) Self Help Groups/State Level Federations (SLFs) and Town Level Federations (TLFs) in Andhra Pradesh and (14) National Urban Livelihoods Mission (NULM).

Human resources are considered as important potential sources of energy to augment 'economic activity using economic resources'. Human growth (Trend of population growth) in various years could be observed and the growth variations may help for designing viable and vulnerable policy studies. The administrator needs the basic statistics relating to demographic situation in different locations and helps to prepare amenable programmes which suits to such an environment to augment/implement a plan for time bound progress for achieving human welfare or human development.

A methodology has been designed for a particular environment to lead the people from poverty and the government is equally responsible to take its decision and execute them in a specified period of time. To understand the concept of urban poverty, one has to read, study and go through the trends of urbanization and economic growth, while doing so, the planner may be able to identify and recognise the urban slums. The historical and economic view of poverty, its ratios and their construction helps to understand the root causes of urban poverty and the existence of poverty in an urban environment. Estimates of poverty ratios, urban poverty ratios and a total poverty ratios, per annum poverty ratio and per annum poverty reduction at the State level may help to understand for designing a suitable policy document. The impact analysis leads further to understand further and further for the furtherance of creating good governance to seek the welfare of the social groups to bring them from BPL to APL.

Reducing poverty at the micro-level is a dire/important need and the planner and the administrator should invariably be able to recognise and identify the patterns of severity and the governance may be able to find solutions for the problems specially related to mounting urban poverty. Through plans, and the plan of action, people who are attached to different and difficult locations and situations, should have to be lifted upwards, according to development plan and its execution from the lowest point of economic growth to the highest point of economic growth taking the norm i.e. the expenditure should be with the least cost factor by the governance.

Poverty is rampant. It is varied and vivid. Planning Commission of India has been paying full attention to eliminate/eradicate poverty through various plans from its inception to the present day and in the Twelfth Five Year Plan also made to form slum free city in order to eliminate slums in different geographic locations of metropolitan cities and also in turn in an hierarchic manner. Various methods have been adopted for the elimination of poverty in urban areas over a period of time by Government of India and respective State governments. They are: (1) Mission for the Elimination of Poverty in Municipal Areas (MEPMA), Government of Andhra Pradesh, (2) Environmental Impact Assessment (EIA), (3) Kudumbasree, Urban CDS, (4) Environmental Impact Assessment (EIA), (5) Livelihood Generation initiatives by Government of Gujarat (UMEED) (6) Environmental Impact Assessment (EIA), and (7) Rajasthan Mission for Skill and Livelihoods (RMOL).

"Reducing poverty in urban India is an urgent task to Government of India. It is deduced that, a common element in these approaches have been the adopting of mission approaches focused on building community structure and integration of skills and livelihoods as central components of the programme.

'Social mobilization' is the process of bringing together all feasible and practical intersectoral allies/partners to raise awareness and demand for a particular programme to assist in the delivery of resources and services and to strengthen community participation for sustainability and self reliance. The process of social mobilization has a definite objective. Following the strategy of social mobilization, SHGs are created with a view to achieve savings mobilization, obtaining credit for immediate requirements, mutual help and economic upliftment through income generating activities. The idea is to address the gap areas and implement the NULM in much more meaningful way so that communities get benefited from the government initiatives. The poverty alleviation paradigm is based on the principles of self help to build sustainable livelihoods and sustainable communities; microfinance often is an integrated part of the strategy for poverty alleviation. The same principle has been adopted by Dr. T. Aishwarya to generate growth and development in a case study. It is visible in her study.

Gender is culturally and socially constructed roles, responsibilities, privileges, and expectations of women and men, boys and girls. Because they are socially constructed, they can change over time and differ from one place to the other. Sex is the biological makeup of male and female people. It is what we are born with and does not change overtime, nor differs from place to place. There is every need to government to think about the gender and sex while making policies and allocating budgets to implement the policies and programmes relating to urban dwellers.

'Gender Budgeting (GB)' its use—priorities—way forward for policy matters has been presented by S. Umapathi. He has stated that gender budgeting to be effective, it is important to look beyond more allocation of resources for women and to track their utilization and undertake analysis of their impact and beneficiary incidence. In essence, the gender budgeting may be defined as addressing gap between policy commitment and allocation and gender sensitive programme formulation and implementation, mainstreaming of gender concerns, in public expenditure and policy gender audit of public expenditure programme implementation and policies relating to public expenditure, fiscal and monetary matters, etc. and stated that "as policy makers we can assess how much budget is required for all the above tasks and the convergence of various departments like department of finance and planning, department of women and child welfare, department of education, department of health and sanitation, department of revenue, department of technical education, department of rural development, department of *Panchayati Raj* and others. A single window for gender budgeting is the need of the hour."

The aggregation of the human development gap by gender disparities explains the need to empower women with information and knowledge besides allowing them to emerge as leaders with confidence to guide their own destinies. The effective training in the extension service may be able to arise from the gradual decrease of urban poverty in urban places, increasing population pressure and ever growing environmental degradation which has a telling effect and implications for food, and nutritive scarcity in future.

Self help groups and bank linkages are in tune with the basic principles of self help groups has been presented by the author.

The governance has to play an important and pivotal role to reduce urban slum dwellers from urban poverty net. And slums are considered to be the major problem in many urban areas including metropolitan cities in a hierarchic way pertinently, special problems posed therein and they are related to transportation, population, health and safety. In view of the above scenario, considering today's poor urban environmental quality in India, the majority families were affected by urban development projects located in slum areas which are under consideration for resettlement or rehabilitation. Slum dwellers constantly deal with issues such as: (1) lack of clean water, (2) constant migration at slums, (3) no sewerage, (4) waste disposal facilities, (5) pollution, and (6) insanitary living conditions.

Geographic information systems and its applications in engineering:

1. GIS is the software used to collect, store and analyse information pertaining to earth's features;
2. GIS stores information in the form of points, lines and polygons;
3. In civil engineering, GIS enables to create 3D models of building, structures, tunnel structure modeling and to measure length and width, area of a pipeline, road, etc. building, plot area, etc. drainage;
4. GIS helps in quick decision-making;
5. The modeling GIS in real world can bring the world into our hands;
6. Currently available is the best available technology for data analysis;
7. DPR explains the following aspects. They are: (a) basic map preparation, (b) proposed water supply, (c) proposed road network, and (d) proposed drainage network.

The technologies prescribed by Ministry of Housing and Urban Poverty Alleviation, (MoHUPA), in RAY guidelines are related to spatial information system, i.e. geographic information system (GIS) and non spatial data management tools via management information system (MIS). These technical applications strengthen the plan preparation process by overcoming challenges like beneficiary identification, boundary delineation, and assessment of infrastructural gaps, etc. There is every need to prepare slum free cities. Rama Rao has presented an article in this direction using RS and GIS techniques for creating urban slum free cities.

Slum free cities—Innovative strategies

The Government of India unveiled an innovative project 'Rajiv Awas Yojana' on the lines of Indira Awas Yojana, under JNNURM to provide affordable housing to the urban poor, thereby achieving slum free cities. The holistic mission of UPA government brought cheers in about 81 millions of urban poor and has become their source of development with property rights, access to a decent and dignified living environment, apart from affordable home. The scheme is also aimed at providing basic amenities like water supply, sewerage, drainage, roads, street lighting, and other social infrastructural facilities involving all stakeholders to alter the existing city planning model and prepare inclusive master plans wherein focus will also be laid for skill development programme of employment promotion through quality training and skill certification by reputed institutions.

The notable task though is being aspired as a great hope of the urban poor, the untold challenges to the urban functionaries to achieve the target of slum free cities by 2014 are not unexpected but definitely needs a systematic and strategic plan. Issues like identification, and evaluation of present slums, feasibility, recognition of beneficiaries, linkage and pooling of financial institutions, granting ownership rights to the beneficiaries, flexibility, for infrastructural development suiting to the local needs, archiving holistic participation of community at large, and involvement of corporate, private and voluntary organizations for contributions of their might are only few to identify but could be more when we focus on the task. The central essence being centred are:

1. To comprehend the tenets of Rajiv Awas Yojana and to formulate planning for implementation.
2. To acknowledge the undercurrents involved and the probable constraints for implementation of the programme

3. To prepare viable strategies for making Rajiv Awas Yojana a reality.[1]

"The ever increasing number of slum dwellers causes tremendous pressure on urban basic services and infrastructure. The major urban concern is the growing gap between the demand and the supply of the basic infrastructure services like safe drinking water, sanitation, sewerage, housing, energy, transport, communication, health, and education. In order to cope with massive programmes that have merged as a result of rapid urban growth it has become imperative to draw up a coherent urbanization policy/ strategy to implement projects in select cities on mission mode".

Evolution and evaluation of the role of training and research institutions in improving urban environment is an urgent need, which helps to give training, skill and development including livelihoods, for the urban poor. The Regional Centre for Urban and Environmental Studies (RCUES-OU), Osmania University, Hyderabad has earned recognition as a world class research and training institutions and constitute a unique model of collaboration and cooperation between Osmania University, the Government of India and the State governments of Andhra Pradesh, Telangana, Karnataka, Kerala, Tamil Nadu and the Union Territory of Puducherry.

The Ministry of Urban Affairs, and Employment, Government of India, has established the RCUES-OU in 1970 to address the research and training needs of the constituent states. Sri P. Gopal concludes that Research and Training Institutes may be able to leave an indelible mark as an asset to eliminate/eradicate urban poverty and thus achieve the desired level of people's welfare from BPL to APL, through innovative research/teaching institutes like RCUES, Osmania University, Hyderabad. The individual efforts lead to the establishment of RCUES, and become nodal centre for South India to augment urban poverty alleviation programmes successfully with utmost sincerity.

NOTE

1. Brochure, Planning Commission, New Delhi (Rajiv Awas Yojana).

2
Urban Environment

K.L.N. Murty

Urban places are considered as important focal points to generate growth in the field of economy upon a geographic place. Cover a period of time, they become the centres, which vary in size and population from one to another and has its impact on the space with different aspects of life such as socio-economic-political and even cultural life. These urban centres may help to generate systematically in short it creates a good environmental network upon the spatial units. This type of environment has been attracted by many scholars such as geographers, economists, sociologists, public administrators, managers and their contributions have cut across the boundaries, which presents and create new study and research stemmed into urban and environmental aspects related to urban poverty issues. Now, this has gained the momentum to form a new brand entitled urban and environmental studies. Geographers and economists have identified seven sub-systems. They are: 1. Evolution of Urban Systems, 2. Functional Classification, 3. Critical Study of Urban Fringe, 4. Urban ecology, 5. Demography and Urbanization, 6. Occupational structure, 7. Methodological dimensions and applied economic, geographic and administrative problems relating to urban poverty in particular, which gradually presents urban slums with varying levels of socio-economic and developmental phenomena and it is linked-up with administrative policy for their progress and well-being. The administrative policy or policy studies by governance have to seek the welfare of the urban society particularly the socio-economic groups belongs to B.P.L. (below poverty line) population and a viable designed administrative policy should have to tackle the problems such as urban slum dwellers to cater to the needs such as shelter, new occupations, skill training, sanitation, health and education, Infrastructure and urban water problems adds to urban environmental spatial organization and spatial structure of the Metro city is more important while tracing out the emerged out problems in an environment such as urban poverty and allied aspects. Urban and environmental problems have to be identified/recognized or sorted-out and plan the development for the area as well as for the people broadly helps to alleviate people from Urban Poverty. The administrative and policy studies helps to create a new paradigm and also seeks for the Constitutional Amendment Act at differential time periods for solving the problems of urban poverty besides the environmental problems through environmental protection methods.

In this study chapter 1 deals with introduction, chapter 2 deals with Urban Environment—Definition-Classification, Protection, Review of Literature and Planning Process. Chapter 3 deals with Urban Poverty Alleviation Programmes—A Macro study, National and State level UPA programmes. Its structure, status and Environmental Impact Assessment (EIA). Chapter 4 deals with Environmental and Population Growth—A case study from India, Andhra Pradesh and Telangana States. Chapter 5 deals with Urban Poverty Alleviation and Environmental Impact Assessment and Methodological perspective. Chapter 6 deals with Reducing Poverty in Urban India: Select State level approaches, chapter 7 deals with Social Mobilization—A strategy for Poverty Alleviation. Chapter 8 deals with Gender Budgeting—Issues—Priorities—Way forward for the policy matter. Chapter 9 deals with Self-Help Groups and Bank Linkages, Urban Slums and Governance has been presented in chapter 10. Chapter 11 deals with Role of Technology in achieving Slum Free Cities, Role of Training and Researching Institutions in Improving Urban Environment—Regional Centre for Urban Environmental Studies has been presented in chapter 12. Summary and conclusions are presented in chapter 13 and Bibliography has been presented at the end.

Background of the Study: Environment—Meaning, Nature and Ecosystem

> The term environment means surroundings. It refers to conditions in which organisms consisting air, water, food, sunlight etc., live and become living sources for all the living and non-living beings including plant life. Environment too includes temperature, wind and electricity. In nut shell, "Environment is the life support system. It is from the environment that all the essential necessities of life are derived."

According to C.C. Park (1980) the term 'environment' refers to the sum-total of conditions which surround man at a given point of space and time. Goudi (1984) states that, environment is the representative of physical components of the earth wherein man is the important factor influencing his environment. According to K.R. Dikshit (1984) our minimum concern is the quality of space we live in, the purity of air we breathe, the food we eat, the water we drink and the resources we draw from our environment to support our economy.

According to the encyclopaedia of Britannica, the term 'environment' means the entire range of external influence acting on an organism, both the physical and biological, and other organisms (i.e.) forces of nature surrounding an individual.

It is deduced that "the environment supports both the physical and bio having a bearing on human life whether it is external factor or internal factor are both called as exogenic and endogenic environment" and "Pollutants are Polluted." (Quotation Mine please).

Components of Environment: Three components consist of environment. They are:

> (A) A biotic or Non-living component, which further divided into the following three categories, namely: (a) Lithosphere (rock, soil and solid air), (b) Hydrosphere (water component), (c) Atmosphere (gaseous envelope), which is further divided into four zones, namely, (a) troposphere, (b) Stratosphere, (c) Inosphere, and (d) Exosphere.

3. Biotic or living component, consisting of flora and fauna including man; and

4. Energy component includes solar energy geochemical energy, thermal electrical energy, and hydro electrical energy, nuclear (atomic) energy, energy due to radiation etc., helps in maintaining the real life of organisms.

Types of Environment: Two types of environments have been identified, they are:

1. Natural environment with self regulating mechanism and it is called as homeostatic environment mechanism. Under this type, any change in the system caused due to natural processing is counter balanced by the changes in the components of the environment.
2. Man made environment, such as industrial revolution, communication media, such as telephone, telex, fax satellite, agricultural implements, mechanization, energy, sources such as nuclear and atomic energy, hydro and thermal energy.

It is deduced that "human environment creates new human environmental problems such as deficiency of food, clothing and shelter and also in the areas such as sanitation, habitation, (settlement) health education, calories of food infrastructure leads to deficiencies and in terms of poverty and it has an impact on the Quality of life and Quantity of infra" (Quotation Mine Please).

Ecosystem

The U.S. Council on Environment Quality defines ecosystem as the interdependence of living and non-living parts, i.e., man, animals, plants, forests and lakes etc.

Ecology cycles: It means the continuing circle of ecosystem. It is a total functional system based on mutual dependency.

Pollution

The Royal Commission on Environmental Pollution in UK, in its third report and defines, the term pollution,

> "The introduction by man into the environment of substances or energy liable to cause hazards to human health, harm to living resources and ecological systems, damage to structure or amenity or to interference with legitimate uses of the environment".

According to McLaughtin, "Environmental Pollution means the introduction by man into any part of environment, of wastes, water, energy, or surplus energy which so changes the environment directly or indirectly adversely to effect the opportunity of men to use and enjoy it."

It is deduced that "man's entry into any part of Urban Environment leads to dearth of the existing resources such as urban space, urban shelter, urban food through P.D.S. (Public Distribution System), Urban water, Urban health, education, infrastructure and there is every need indeed to provide the aforesaid functions by governance over space, time and tackle it through their urban resource functionary (through their policies and programmes) to urban voter to avoid urban congestion with urban slums and their management" (Quotation Mine Please).

An attempt is made in this chapter to present various factors to understand the urban environment process and problems along with environmental hazards such as urban poverty and urban slums. Sanitation, Urban slums and Quality, Peri-urban areas, Decentralization of powers and functions; are presented Urban Governance, Need based training programmes, and women empowerment and development have been presented as back ground or back drop of the present study on urban and environmental studies in the following paragraphs.

Environmental Protection

Constitution of India and Environmental protection, the following are some of the important Articles of the Constitution of India, which have relevance to the subject of environmental protection, namely

I. Articles 136, 137, 226, 227, 246, 249, 250, 252, 253, 254, 356 (right to write remedy, special leave appeal, power of Parliament to make laws etc.).

II. Fundamental Rights—Articles 14, 19(1)(g), 21, 32, and 226 etc.
III. Directive principles of state policy—Articles 47, 48, & 49
IV. Fundamental Duties: (part IV-A), 51 A(g);
V. Seventh Schedule
List. I—Entries 52 to 55 and 57
List II—Entries 6, 14, 18, 21, 24, 25.
List III—Entries 17-A, 17 B, 20 (c) and (d).

Environment and provisions of Indian penal code—provisions relating to offences affecting the public health, safety, convenience, decency and morals contemplated in chapter XIV of the Indian Penal Code (IPC) have same relevance to the environmental matters of all the offences covered by this chapter of IPC, the offences of "Public Nuisance" is more relevant in the context of the Environmental pollution[1] and powers of the Central Government to ensure protection and improvement of environment—chapter 11 of the Act containing sections 3 to 6, empowers the Central Government to take measures to protect aid improve environment, appointment of officers and their powers and functions, power to give directions to any person, officer or any authority, and to make rules to regulate the environmental pollution respectively.**

***Preservation of the environment and keeping ecological balance unaffected is a task which not only Governments but also every citizen must undertake. It is a social application and laws remind every Indian citizen that it is his fundamental duty as ensured in Article 51 A(g) of the constitution.

(IV) *Ref: Environmental Protection*—Public Interest Litigation (PIL): In India, the law relating to environment has gained significant movement only through the public interest litigation (P.L.).

(V) The Environment (Protection) Act, 1986.

** *Ibid.*, p. 125.

*** p. 134 (IV) Ref: p. 147. (V) p. 1.

Official Estimation of Poverty and Identification of the Poor[2]

Poverty estimates are focused on ten points, a distribution of household expenditure and a poverty line or cutoff that separates the poor from the non-poor households. Preliminary work of Dadabhai Naoroji's paper, "Poverty in India" in 1876 and the estimates of subsistence needs were presented to exhibit that Indians fell far below. Later, work was particularly by the efforts of National Planning Committee (NPC) in 1938, which first referred to a monetary range of between Rs. 15 to Rs. 20 to ensure a basic minimum standard of living. After Indian Independence, the Nation's first attempt at a poverty line was through the efforts of a working group of eminent economists in the year 1962 with three basic recommendations:

- The national minimum for each household consisting of five persons should not be less than Rs. 100 per month at 1960-61 prices or Rs. 20/- per head. For Urban areas, this amount has been raised to Rs. 125/- per household per month.
- Thus excluded expenditure on health and education, both of which were expected to be covered by the state; and
- An element of subsidy for urban housing was to be provided at Rs. 10/- per month or 10 per cent as rent element payable from the proposed National minimum of Rs. 100 per month.

The above norms were adopted by the Planning Commission in its paper entitled,

> "Perspectives of Development, 1961-1976: Implications of planning for a minimum level of living."

The 1979 Task Force on, "Projections of Minimum need and effective consumption demand," grouped data of household consumption expenditure from different rounds of the NSS. This is a significant report, really that the methodology recommended therein has survived to date, with relevant modifications from time to time. The following are the recommendations.

- Average individual calorie requirement would be estimated separately for rural and urban areas with special consideration to age, sex and activity distribution.
- Poverty line estimates would correspond to the calorie requirements using the 28th round (1973-74) of NSS data.
- The commodity wise private consumption is to be estimated using Linear expenditure System (LES).
- For the calorie requirement, the minimum requirement, rather than the average requirement, was measured in consideration of the fact that there is a variation in calorie requirement.

Later, the Expert Group on "estimation of proportion and Number of Poor (EGEP)" Chaired by Prof. D.T. Lakdawala evolved a methodology based on the 1979 Task Force,[3] and recommended the following:

- A calorie norm of 2400 calories per capita, per day for rural areas and 2100 calories per capita, per day for Urban areas was considered.
- The Poverty line for 1973-74 was taken as per capita expenditure level at which the calorie norms have to be met as per the NSS household consumption expenditure survey for the corresponding year.
- This was found to be Rs. 49.09 and Rs. 56.65 per capita per month for rural and urban areas respectively at 1973-74 prices.
- The implicit private consumption deflator from Nation Account Statistics (NAS) was found, at that time to be very close to such an index and hence it was used for adjusting the poverty line for the years 1977-78, 1983-84 and 1987-88.
- The Poverty Population was, thus, estimated by applying the updated poverty line to the corresponding adjusted NSS distribution of households by levels of consumption expenditure. To estimate the incidence of poverty at the state level, all India poverty-lines and the adjustment factors were used on the state of specific NSS distribution of households by levels of consumption expenditure uniformly across the States.

- By this methodology, it was estimated that 54.1 per cent of the rural population (2, 442.2 lakhs) and 41.7 per cent of the urban population (473.3 lakhs) or 51.5 per cent of the total population (2,915.5 lakhs) were living below the poverty-line that the time.

This committee attempted to anchor the poverty-line rigidly to average rural and urban energy norms, as well as to ensure that the poverty baskets would be brought by consumers.[4] In 2009, the Planning Commission has set up a working group chaired by Prof. Suresh Tendulkar to consider the critiques of the official poverty-line and suggest a new poverty-line and estimates. The group suggested a new methodology for 2004-05 based on the 61st round of the N.S.S. survey. The salient features of the poverty line are as follows:[5]

- The estimates of poverty would continue to be based on household consumer expenditure collected by NSSO.
- A conscious decision was made to move away from anchoring the poverty lines to a calorie intake norm as this was not found to be well correlated to the Nutritional outcomes.
- Adoption of the mixed recall period (MRP) based estimates for consumption expenditure as the basis for future poverty lines as against the previous practice of using URP estimates.[6]
- MRP equivalent of Urban Poverty-Line Baskets (PLB) corresponding to 25.7 per cent urban head count ratio as the new reference PLB to be provided to rural as well as Urban Population in all the states after adjusting it for within state Urban relative to rural and rural and urban state relative to all India price differentials.
- The proposed price indices are based on the household level unit values (approximated price date) obtained from the 61st round (July, 2004 to June, 2005) of NSS on household consumer expenditure survey for food, fuel and light, clothing and footwear at the most detailed level of disaggregation, and hence much closer to the actual prices paid by the consumers in rural and urban areas.
- According, the committee calculated a poverty head count

ratio of 41.8 per cent for rural areas and 25.7 per cent for urban areas.

The Ministry of Housing and Urban Poverty Alleviation subsequently critiqued the findings of this committee from the point of view of urban poverty. It was pointed-out that expenditure on account of education, health, housing and transport is proportionately higher for urban as compared to rural areas. Further, for housing, transport conveyance, rent etc. adjustment have been made by taking into account data from NSSO on account data from NSSO on actual expenditure. However, whether those actual expenditures are adequate to meet the minimum basic needs does not seem to have been taken into account. Finally, it was felt that abounding the calorie norm did not appear to be wise.

In addition to the estimates *via.* the committees/task forces stated above, poverty has been nationally surveyed through a "Below the Poverty-Line" (BPL) census conducted once every five years, traditionally by the M/o Rural Development (R.D.) to identify poor households in rural areas to be assisted under various programmes of the M/o R.D. BPL censuses have thus been conducted in 1992 for the Eighth Five Year Plan, in 1997 for the Ninth Five Year Plan and 2002 survey households were ranked according to total scores calculated from 0.4 individual scores on 13 items.[7]

In the absence of national urban BPL surveys, for 2011 Census of India, data on slums plan—India was collected in 640 cities/ towns with a population of 50,000 person or more, which was later extended to 1321 towns having population of over 20,000. In total across both phases, 1961 towns were surveyed and out of these 1743 towns reported the presence of slums. However, while the habitat based approach has been quite useful in meeting the targeting of shelter and services towards people living in slums and slum like conditions, not all those living in slums could be characterized as living below the poverty line. Similarly, a purely habitat based methodology excludes a large number of persons who may not live in slums, but never the less face substantive deprivation or vulnerability that would qualify them as being poor. In the present context, it becomes necessary to identify "People" (and households) falling below the poverty-line for the design and delivery of appropriate interventions aimed) at the wider goals of urban poverty alleviation and inclusive urban development.

In a bid to devise a uniform methodology and/or criteria for the identification of BPL households in urban areas, the Planning Commission constituted an expert Group *vide* Notification no. M-11019/10/2010-PP dated 13th May, 2010 chaired by Prof. S.R. Hashim. In its interim report, the expert group has recommended a vulnerability based identification of the urban poor which has formed the basis of the socio-economic and caste census, 2011.[8]

The background of the present problem deals with the survey such as sanitation, urban slums and quality, peri-urban areas, decentralization urban governance, need based training porgrammes, women empowerments and development mechanism of planning process, methodology, Role of governance, private-public partnership plan wise review of allocation have been presented in the following paragraphs.

1. Sanitation

Awadesh Kumar Singh and Atul Pratap Singh in their chapter entitled Urban Sanitation and Rehabilitation of scavengers in India discussed how sanitation is the basis of a healthy and civilizes living. It highlights low absence of sanitation facilities leads to water borne diseases. It focuses on integrated low cost sanitation programme, a flagship scheme implemented by the Ministry of Housing and Urban Poverty Alleviation in association with HUDCO and urban local bodies to improve urban sanitation.

Narayana, T.D.[9] in his article, "Sanitary Toilet and Open Defecation Scenario in India" looks at the menace of open defecation in context of the urbanization happening at a fast pace and how despite the efforts made by Government of India and State Governments the defecation is still on the rise.

2. Urban Slums and Quality

Arun K. Singh and Karuna Kaj in their articles entitled 'urban slums'. An enquiry into concept characteristics and policy intervention, discussed how into days ward, slums and their existence is a reality in urban areas across the globe. They attempted to examine the concept, characteristics and policy interventions to improve living conditions of slum dwellers.

Nasiruddin and Ishtiaq jointly presented in this articles entitled, "Slums of Delhi: Issues, Planning and Management Analysis" the various schemes launched by the concerned authorities in order to improve the quality of life in the slums and re-housing/resettling those settlements on the outskirts of the city. It also proposes an alternate housing scheme for the slum dwellers on the same site where they live. This scheme may be affordable, accessible, and habitable to their as well manageable by the authorities Generated Global Positioning System (GPS) techniques were also used to collect relevant information.

3. Peri-Urban Areas

Sandeep Kumar and O.P. Singh in their articles, "Rural Urban Continuum and Development of Peri-Urban Areas" in Lucknow focused on the problems of rural areas. Urban fringe which pose a major challenge to urban policy planners. They attempted to highlight the environmental degradation, natural resources, conflicts, health concerns, socio-economic, cultural, psychological factors and social injustice which are particularly acute in the Peri-Urban situation and needs immediate attention of the academicians, planning and administrators.

4. Decentralization

Pavan Kumar Bahta in a article, "74th C.A. and Municipal Corporation," Simple Attempts to compile and evaluate the provisions in the conformity legislations regarding three of the most important aspects of municipal decentralization namely functional decentralization, financial decentralization and popular participation in the provision and monitoring of affairs of Municipal Corporation, Simla.

Urban Governance

Lokendra Malik and Avneet Kaur, "Urban Governance in India: An Analysis" highlighted that the urbanization process, the cutting edge of economic growth and development is not isolated from these crises such as crises of governance manifests itself in multifarious ways, such as civil society movements for more equitable, just and more inclusive systems of governance processes, equitable distribution of natural resources, crises of environmental governance, terrorism and so on. The author has made an attempt to highlight the crises of governance emerging in the contemporary governance process from the point of view of urban governance process from the point of view of urban governance mainly focused on four points. They are: (1) Unravels the meaning of governance and the need of good governance with special reference to urban governance processes; and (2) Articulated some of the emerging issues of urban governance.

Need Based Training Programmes

Devendiran, C. and Muthu Lakshmi, in their articles entitled, "Need Based Training Programmes for Self-Help Groups in Mizoram" presented that "at present SHG's are functioning very effectively in almost all the States of our country". In particular, women are taking an active part in the SHG's. They have realized the importance of SHG's towards their non-economic, political and social empowerment.

Women, Empowerment and Development

"Economic organization and empowerment has helped to build the women member's capacities and skills as also to improve social participation and decision-making powers. It can be stated that micro credit and SHG's have provided a strong basis for economic viability and are helping the women to move on the path of development by enhancing their economic status and overcoming social and cultural barriers of development. SHG is a successful strategy of people's participation and empowerment of women on the path of development. Socio-economic constraints have suppressed women's potential for development by not allowing them to utilize their skills and capacities fully. Today, SHG's are paving the way to liberate women from the clutches of constraints and barriers to development. They are helping the Poor Women to engage in economic activity leading to socio-economic empowerment and building confidence in them to be self reliant"[10].

"There is a need to decentralize the planning process: to stimulate local people's participation in planning, implementation, monitoring and evaluation of development projects and a suitable mechanism should be evolved to involve voluntary agencies and other people's in situations at various stages of development programmes/projects. Voluntary agencies should further ensure the participation of poor women in the development process:

"The dynamic role of women's contribution to the National economy as partners and equal citizens must be reiterated and translated into programmes and projects. The National Resource Centre would be responsible for revamping the existing content/ methodology and monitoring of training at all levels".[11]

It is observed that there has been a haphazard and unplanned growth of urban areas resulting to growth of slum settlement with poor living conditions. It is argued that the Private-Public-Partnership (PPP) in the housing sector must be encouraged to provide low cost housing to the poor[12].

Mechanism—Planning Process

With reference to Poverty Alleviation Schemes (PAS) those sustainable mechanisms needs to be evolved to provide livelihoods to the poor people in cities. The need for comprehensive policy for the people living below poverty line and suggested building up cluster type accommodation facilities in urban centres for the poor people is a necessary prerequisite.

Shelter

Development of orphanages by the housing agencies for providing shelter to thousands of orphans rendered out of the station.

Medical

Insurance to the poor people for various ailments like cancer, heart and AIDS etc.

Methodology

It is the time to examine the concept of poverty-line and is it to be measured. It is felt that a time has possibly come when we should rise above the calorie definition of poverty.

Mechanism

A programme for urban poverty alleviation across the nation has served the purpose or there's a need to have a more innovative and flexible approach according to specific needs and aspirations of the poor people living under different spatial and environmental conditions.

A state specific or even city specific intervention strategies need to be adopted to deal with this multi-faceted problem

Present work: There is every need to review strategies for urban poverty alleviation including issues relating to definition and trends of Urban Poverty, BPL survey and actual identification of BPL families, micro-finance, convergence of other pro-urban poor programmes, basic services to the urban poor, mobilization and empowerment of urban poor women through self-help groups, formation of T & C S and NGO's and C.B.O. in poverty related issues. It should have to focus on various dimensions of urban poverty and interventions for urban poverty alleviation.

Observation II

Increase of urban population is traditionally on two counts—(1) Natural population growth plus, (2) Inward migration from rural areas. The poor people in rural areas who are squeezed out of the economic system due to natural demographic process and reduction in land holding etc. are forced to migrate to the cities in search of employment. Industrialization and construction activities also attract people from rural to cities. Cities could not cater to the poor and do not adequately provide for neither land at affordable costs nor basic services like housing, water and sanitation.

Necessity

There is a need for a sustainable, equitable, humane and socially inclusive plea to cater to the basic requirements of the urban poor for development.

Role of Governance

1. UPA and the present Government should be committed for the eradication of poverty and to the protection of vulnerable groups.
2. Tenth plan target is one, which include the reduction of poverty ratio by 5 percentage points by 2007 and by 15 percentage by 2012 as also providing gainful employment.
3. The living conditions in many slums are sub-human, with no provision of essentials such as water, sanitation, toilets, decent and adequate housing, roads and electricity, health and education. The provision of these services is critical if the lives of slum dwellers are to be improved.
4. Under VAMBAY, the housing and sanitation needs of the slum dwellers are being addressed in a targeted manner by covering at least one lakh slum families annually.

It has been identified that upto 2004-2005, Government has covered 3.56 lakh beneficiaries under VAMBAY by way of subsidized housing and have built over 64,000 community toilets to provide clean community sanitation in the slums-under NSDP, it is cumulatively covered a total slum population of 4.12 crore by an environmental improvement in slums which is more than 50 per cent of India's slum population.

In order to ensure for improving the quality of life of the urban poor, the government is considering and addressing the issue, in a mission mode. It is proposed to put in place a targeted programme to focus on the areas inhabited by the urban poor in the cities.

"A set of basic services for the urban poor, inter area, security of theme: (1) Improved housing, (2) Water Supply and Sanitation, basic education, health cover, social security last but not the least, transparency in the entire process are to be proposed for consideration in the new scheme of things.

Private Public Partnership (PPP) in providing social housing and urban basic service to the poor and seek the considered views of all stakeholders so that the varied experiences in states can lead to a variety of successful models.

Conclusions

1. It is concluded that Environment needs protection. It could be done from the individual/group level/district or state level through administrative reform or so, on the lines of legal terms and conditions. Environmental protection act really protect the nations as well as people from the damaging man-made environment.
2. Further, there is every need to evolve its own policies and programmes besides the implementation of Government of India programmes for the Urban Poverty Alleviation. Administrative reforms may be initiated, introduced and implemented wherever there is a need keeping in view of the necessity to augment the programmes and policies either Central/State government for development of the Urban Poor.
3. Urban Poverty has been mounting up day-by-day or even year by year. To find a solution to the increasing urban poverty, it is apt to introduce new infra in sub-urban regions, which helps to stop migration from rural to urban atleast to some extent.
4. There is every need to study the trend patterns of population at each unit in order to identify the flow of migration and necessary action should be taken to curts it by the governance for the welfare of the people and also not to face the mounting slums in urban areas in future.

NOTES

1. Dr. N. Maheswara Swamy, Law Relating to Environmental Pollution and Protection, 3rd edition, Asian Law House, Hyderabad (2007-08), p. 117.
2. Annexure: Official Estimation of Poverty and Identification of the poor; "Report of the working group on Urban Poverty, Slums and Services Delivery System" Steering Committee on Urbanization, Planning Commission, New Delhi; 3rd October, 2011.
3. Government of India, Planning Commission, 1993.
4. Srinivasan, 2007, *op. cit.*, pp. 41-58.
5. Government of India, Planning Commission, 2009.

6. The reason being that MRP captures household consumption expenditure of poor households on low frequency items of purchase more satisfactorily than the earlier 30 day recall period.
7. These include operational holding of households, type of house possessed, food security, access to sanitation, water and clothing, education and health status of the households, indebtedness, means of livelihood, consumer durables possessed among others (*Source*: Hirway, 2003).
8. Planning Commission, 2011-A.
9. 'Urban Panorama', a Journal of *Urban Governance and Management*, Vol. XIII, January—June, 2014, No.1, Published by Regional Centre for Urban & Environmental Studies, Government of India, Lucknow, June, 2014.
10. Usha Rani, D., P.J. Reddy and M.V.S. Reddy, 'Women in Development': Empowerment through Self-Help Groups in Andhra Pradesh, pp. 623-24.
11. Kiran Prasad (Ed.), "Communication and Empowerment of Women: Strategies and Policy Insights from India", The Women Press, Delhi.
12. Geeta Tiwari, "Empowerment of the Women" Mahaveer & Sons, New Delhi, 2008, pp. 125-161.

3
Urban Poverty Alleviation Programmes

G. Vasant Kumar

SECTION ONE

Urban Poverty Alleviation Programme (UPAP) may be possible only through the Five Year Plans (FYP) in India. Urban Poverty has been linked up with the prospects such as Education, Health, Sanitation, Housing, and Shelter, Livelihoods, Skilled Development Programmes, Social security and infrastructural facilities. Urban Poverty Alleviation Programmes (UPAP) have been designed to cater to the needs of the people who are living under the below poverty-line and these programmes benefited women, children differently abled group and aged people. The above social and economic group people were the direct beneficiaries of the U.P.A. programmes in India.

> "Non-accessibility" to people for any sort of resources to fulfill their material needs with the benefit through interventions viably and also deficiency of that particular function is called as 'Poverty' and it need not be in terms of financial condition to alleviate and in one way people are enriched with poverty. That is to say that from 'Unique' function to multifunctional absence is also called as poverty and it has its impact/imprint on the life of the people (human being) and certainly leads to add to "Urban Poverty" and it needs to be rectified for achieving 'balanced' and 'integrated' development of a region/town/urban centre/city centre should be prone to Urban Poverty Alleviation Prgramme (UPAP) and it is considered as a

progressive step to take necessary action in that direction in deed" (Quotation Mine Please).

The schematic representation of urban poverty in the following figure is presented in order to understand the concept, content and also to find vulnerable and viable solution through the identified intervention.

Urban Poverty Diagram

Government of India has been taking several measures for Urban Poverty Alleviation Programme (UPAP) since independence has identified thrust areas for Housing Planning and Development is possible only through five year plan. So, Government of India has established the planning for development in order to achieve the goals and objectives. The problem of Planning Commission for development in order to achieve the goals, and objectives. The problem of housing was recognized and housing and urbanization was brought into the policy planning frame-work. Further, it has been identified the problem of affordability as the key issue in the housing sector more so for the low income group. During the first five year plan, the social housing schemes (i.e.) Integrated

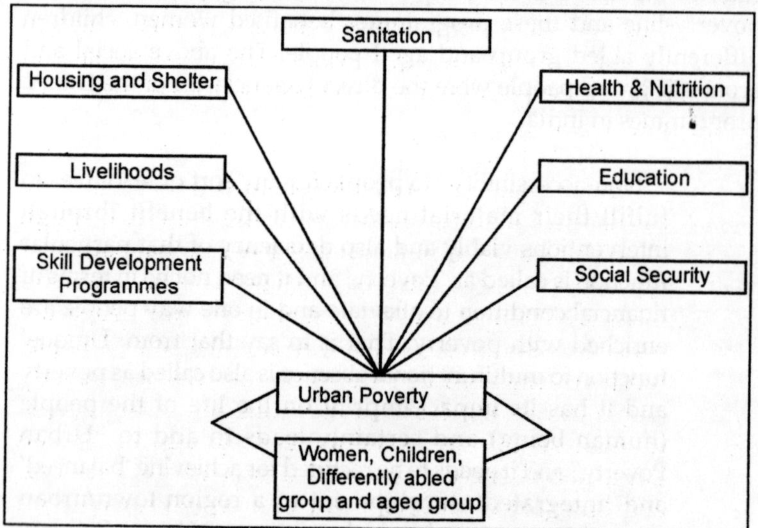

Fig. 3.1: Urban Poverty in Different Areas and Beneficiaries (Urban).

subsidized industrial housing scheme (1952) and low income housing scheme (1954), were launched. As a result, The National Buildings organization was created to formulate low-cost housing designs and building database for the formulation of housing strategies and plans. During the second five year plan, it may be stated that, a statement on the Housing Policy was for the first time made on the 14th August, 1957 in the parliament by the then minister for works, housing and supply along with salient features of the policy. During third five year plan, Government of India thought that the Housing Policies should be linked with economic development and industrialization policies. During the annual plans (1996-1969), Government of India has introduced the concept of Economically Weaker Section (EWS) of society was introduced. EWS housing was integrated with the subsidized in Industrial Housing Scheme in operation since the inception of five year plan. During fourth five year plan, an innovative novel scheme relating to a major issue concerning the government was providing housing and finance to a vast majority of low-income families. Such families require a longer period of repayment and soft terms of loans. HUDCO was established as a sectoral institution for comprehensively dealing with the problem for finding a solution for a growing housing shortage rising development number of slums were identified in this context it is from 1st to Eleventh FYP has been described and presented in a table format. The thrust areas are quite important not only for identification but also to cater to the needs of the people, for policy preparation for implementation by Government of India and also for different States in India.

Thrust Areas for Housing and Urban Poverty Alleviation Through the Five Year Plans[1]

First Five Year Plan (1951-1955)

- The problem of housing was recognized and housing and urbanization was brought into the policy planning framework;
- It identified the problem of affordability as the key issue in the key issue in the housing sector more so for the low-income groups;

- Reduction in the cost of construction through savings on building materials and cutting down of wasteful use of labour were recommended as solution to improve affordability;
- Housing needs of the refugees given priority—A number of new towns were established in different parts of the country for housing refugees from Pakistan;
- Two Social Housing Schemes, Integrated Subsidized Industrial Housing Scheme (1952) and Low Income Housing Scheme (1954), were launched;
- Several institutions were set up and an independent Ministry of Works and Housing was established. The National Buildings Organization was created to formulate low-cost housing designs and build up a database for the formulation of housing strategies and plans.

Second Five Year Plan (1956-1961)

- Schemes for subsidized Industrial Housing and Low Income Group (LIC) were further strengthened;
- LIC got associated with the government and launched a scheme to provide loans to the middle-income groups (MIG);
- New schemes like Plantation Labour Housing Scheme, Village Housing Scheme and Land Acquisition and Development Scheme were launched;
- A scheme for slum clearance was introduced; schemes for Scheduled Caste, other backward classes in rural villages were launched;
- Housing programmes for the employees of Central/State government agencies were undertaken;
- Establishment of Delhi Development Authority (DDA) under an Act of the Parliament for implementing the Master Plan;
- Government shifted its policy of granting direct loans for the development of sites and plots to individuals to giving assistance to State governments and local authorities;
- A statement on the Housing Policy was for the first time made on the 14th August, 1957 in the Parliament by the then Minister for Works, Housing and Supply. Salient

features of the policy are: Subsidy to those who need it the most, set-up housing corporations in the states to provide loan finance with the Central Government providing the necessary subsidy, indigenous building material will be used to the maximum extent, a separate department to expedite the implementation of housing schemes.

Third Five Year Plan (1961-1966)

- Housing policies should be linked with economic development and industrialization policies;
- Efforts to increase housing stock by various agencies—public, private or cooperative;
- Efforts to create conditions in which the entire programme of housing construction, both public and private be oriented to serve the requirement of the LIG category in the community;
- Placed emphasis on land acquisition and development;
- Many of the States during this period established housing boards to eliminate housing shortage with a focus on meeting the housing needs of LIG and slum-dwellers; and
- Level of activity by public agencies was found to be slow and hence financial institutions were established to provide financial and technical assistance to metropolitan authorities, state housing boards and other urban institutions for financing the development of housing and urban development projects.

Annual Plans (1966-1969)

- The concept of Economically Weaker Section (EWS) of society was introduced during this period. EWS housing was integrated with the Subsidized Industrial Housing Scheme (SIHS) in operation since the inception of First Five Year Plan.

Fourth Five Year Plan (1969-1974)

- Emphasis on strengthening and toning up of public agencies for meeting the housing needs and application of planning principles for the orderly development of urban centres;

- The plan laid great emphasis on self-help for improving the housing situation;
- In slum areas the concept of slum clearance was replaced by slum improvement and the urban authorities were asked to take a more positive and realistic view of the people and their problems.
- A distinct change in the policy framework was effected involving a shift from formal housing to sites and services pogrammes and environment improvement of slums;
- A scheme for environment improvement of slums was introduced in 1972 in selected cities to provide the basic services;
- 1950s, 1960s and 1970s can be described as the ones in which institution-building in the field of human settlement financing took place;
- A major issue concerning the government was providing housing finance to a vast majority of low-income families. Such families require a longer period of repayment majority of low-income families. Such families require a longer period of repayment and soft terms of loans. In this context, HUDCO was established as a sectoral institution for comprehensively dealing with the problem of dealing of growing housing shortages, rising number of slums.

Fifth Five-Year Plan (1974-1979)

Addresses to the following limited objective in the housing sector:

- Preservation and improvement of the existing housing stock;
- Provision of house sites to a million landless labourers as a part of the Minimum Needs Programme;
- Continuance of the existing schemes to provide subsidized houses to certain weaker sections of the community;
- Extension of support to institution agencies;
- Intensification of research in and development of cheap building materials;
- In 1977, a draft Fifth Five Year Plan was reformulated with

emphasis on the aspect of self-help housing, provision of house sites and assistance to rural landless labourer;

- Housing Development Finance Corporation (HDFC) was set up in 1977 to provide finance for new residential housing to individuals, association of individuals and co-operative societies and to companies for staff housing.

Sixth Five-Year Plan (1980-1985)

- Emphasis on housing activities in small and medium towns, adoption of cost-cutting technologies, evolving of building bye-laws which are more sensitive to the needs of the people;
- The plan envisaged that instead of providing direct subsidy for EWS, the strategy should be to provide sites and services to this category;
- The planners increasingly recognized the remarkable role played by HUDCO particularly in the field of social housing in urban and rural areas.

Seventh Five Year Plan (1985-1990)

- Promotion and encouragement of self-help housing;
- Provision to identified rural families house-sites and assistance for construction of dwellings for those families already provided with house-sites;
- Cost of housing units under social housing scheme to be kept within the paying capacity of the target group;
- Providing stimulus and support to private housing for MIG and LIG;
- Securing reduction in construction cost by adopting low-cost housing techniques and development of cheap building materials;
- The plan emphasized that HUDCO should play an important role in conjunction with state governments for providing finance to weaker sections for house-building activity;
- Housing authorities and housing boards to concentrate on land acquisition and development in urban areas and on provision of house sites in rural areas instead of going in for direct construction of houses;

- It was proposed to continue various housing schemes initiated earlier under the Minimum Needs Programme and the rural housing and slum improvement efforts;
- The Global Shelter Strategy (GSS) adopted by the United Nations in 1988 called upon government to take steps for the formulation of a National Housing Policy (NHP). Accordingly, a draft NHP was prepared by the Ministry of Urban Development during this period;
- The government has set up Building Materials and Technology Promotion Council (BMTPC) with the objective of bridging the gap between laboratory development and large-scale field application of innovation materials and technologies. Setting up a network of building centres as a centrally sponsored scheme to affect savings in construction cost through promotion of low-cost and innovative building materials and technologies and building of local delivery system.

The Eighth Five Year Plan (1992-97)

A significant aspect with regard to the Eighth plan is that it has been set against a National Housing Policy. The objectives of the Eighth Five Year Plan are to be achieved through the following tasks/instruments:

- Expand the provision of basic infrastructure facilities in rural and urban areas in order improve the overall environment of habitat and provide appropriate conditions for the majority of the households to have access to housing;
- Remove legal constraints to increase supply of serviced land as well as rental housing;
- Extend stimulus and support for private housing on an expanded scale through enhancing the flow of credit to housing sector through housing finance institutions (HFI's) as well as other measures like tax incentives;
- Encourage use of low-cost building materials and cost–effective technologies;
- Promote self-help housing as well as shelter up-gradation by providing better access to finance, land, materials and

technology through appropriate delivery systems to the poorer segment of the rural population;

- Provide financial and institutional support through both formal and informal systems for environmental improvement;
- Establish an effective Management Information System for housing and urban infrastructure accessible to both private and public development agencies;
- Evolve special assistance programmes in the form of subsidy, preferably in kind, differential rate of interest and delivery support for disadvantaged groups.

The social/other schemes initiated in earlier plans are to be continued either in their existing or modified forms. More important amongst these are:

1. The scheme of house sites-cum-construction assistance initiated to give a boost to housing in rural areas during the seventh plan and included in the State Sector within the Minimum Needs Programme;
2. The Indira Awas Yojana (IAY) introduced in the Central Sector in 1985-86 forming part of Rural Landless Employment Generation Programme (RLEGP) for construction of houses for SCs/STs and free bonded labour;
3. The Centrally sponsored scheme for the establishment of building centres initiated in 1988 to promote technology transfer to the grassroots level and to encourage the use of new alternative materials;
4. To tackle the problem of housing in urban areas, including improvement of slums and squatter settlements, the State shall assist in:
   - Increasing the availability of residential land, with particular reference to the needs of poor sections;
   - Support incremental self-building through financial and technical support;
   - Encouragement to up-gradation and progress development of low income settlements; and
   - Promotion of appropriate technologies that maximize the use of locally available and recycled materials.

The Ninth Five Year Plan (1997-2002)

- While the housing needs of all segments of the population will have to be met, the Ninth Plan will focus specially on households at the lower end of the housing market, the priority groups identified for such support are: people below the poverty line, SC/ST, and women-headed households;
- There will be provision for more direct intervention by the government in the case of the lower segments of the housing market and selected disadvantaged groups; Subsidy would continue to be provided for some more time and the flow mechanism will be made more transparent and increasing routed outside the financial system;
- The Plan recognized the need to strengthen the linkages and inter-dependency between shelter and income up-gradation. To promote this, the Ninth Plan will support the use of composite credit instrument, modify land-use patterns, and city master plans, and strengthen the linkages between farm and the non-farm sector in the rural and semi-urban areas. The NGOs and other voluntary organizations will have to play the role of a catalyst.

The Tenth Five Year Plan (2002-2007)

- The Tenth Plan Working Group on Housing has observed that around 90 per cent of housing shortage pertains to **the weaker sections.** There is a need to increase the supply of affordable housing to the economically weaker sections and the low-income category through a proper programme of allocation of land, extension of funding assistance, and provision of support services;
- In order to facilitate larger housing delivery for the weaker sections and low income groups, the on-going programme for providing additional 2-million houses every year needs to be continued;
- The proposed programme of Valmiki Ambedkar Aawas Yojana (VAMBAY) along with the total city sanitation component of Nirmal Bharat Abhiyan (NBA) for meeting the housing and sanitation requirements of the urban poor

need to be taken up in all urban areas, so as to promote 'cities' without 'slums'. Provision needs to be made for a central subsidy of Rs. 1000 crores annually during the tenth period with the matching amount contributed by the State governments/local bodies or as loan from HUDCO;

- In order to increase the proportion of household savings to be invested in the housing sector, as well as to provide houses to those who cannot as yet afford to have their own houses, there is need to encourage **promotion of rental housing by private sector, public sector, as well as cooperatives and individuals:** This requires legislative changes in the existing rent control laws, and has been a matter in which very little progress has been achieved.
- A special emphasis need to be laid on the strengthening of the Building Centre Movement, with particular focus on coverage of uncovered districts in the country numbering about 200. A central grant allocation of Rs. 20 crores during the Tenth Plan period need to be provided for the same;
- HUDCO earmarks 55 per cent of its housing portfolio funds to Weaker Sections and Low Income Groups, with differential interest rates, high loan component for lower cost units, and longer repayment period. Though its releases are somewhat less than sanctions, it is noteworthy that HUDCO has sanctioned 13.61 lakh urban housing units and 20.21 lakh rural housing units in the three years form 1998-99 to 2000.01 under the 2-Million Housing Scheme. The other factor in HUDCO operations for the mass housing programmes is the dependence on State government guarantees, which as noted elsewhere, eliminates parts of the Country form its operations;
- HUDCO has been in the forefront of Government's efforts to come to the aid of disaster affected household, and has provided financial assistance for disaster rehabilitation housing to the tune of Rs. 2360 crores for construction of over 40 lakhs houses for earthquake, cyclone, and flood victims;
- A special programme for Strengthening and Retro-Fitting of Housing Stock in Vulnerable Regions threatened by Natural Hazards needs to be taken up with the participation of the State governments, BMTPC and HUDCO;

The Eleventh Five Year Plan (2007-12)

The housing shortage is most acute for the EWS and LIG, almost 99 per cent of the shortage is for this class. Hence, the emphasis is on providing affordable housing through schemes JNNURM, Affordable Housing in partnership, ISHUP and RAY.

Evaluation of Programmes on Urban Poverty Alleviation through the Plan Period:

Five Year/ Annual Plan	*Year(s)*	*Major Thrust Areas/Programmes*
II	1956-61	Urban Community Development (UDC) project (pilot), started in 1958, and based on an area-oriented approach.
IV	1969-74	Scheme for Environmental Improvement of Urban Slums (EIUS) launched in 1972, to provide basic amenities like safe drinking water supply, sewerage, storm water drainage, pavements, community baths and latrines, street lighting etc. to slum-dwellers. In 1974, it was transferred to State governments for implementation.
V	1974-79	The Urban Land (Ceiling and Regulation) Act (ULCRA), enacted to prevent concentration of land holding in urban areas, and for construction of houses for LIG.
VI	1980-85	Emphasis on integrated provision of services along with shelter, particularly for the poor. Launch of Integrated Development of Small and Medium Towns (IDSMT), and initiation of Urban Basic Services (UBS) programme in 1981, with an aim to cater to the basic physical and social needs of the urban poor with a view to improving their living conditions.
VII	1985-90	Based on the recommendation made by the National Commission on Urbanization (NCU), Government of India adopted a four-pronged strategy for addressing the issues of growing incidence of urban poverty;
	1985-90	(i) Employment creation for low income communities through promotion of micro-enterprises and public works; (ii) Housing and shelter up-gradation; (iii) Social development planning with special focus on development of children and women; and (iv) Environmental up-gradation of slums. Consequently, two schemes were started, namely: (i) The Nehru Rozgar Yojana (NRY), 1989 for employment/ livelihoods promotion ; and (ii) The Urban Basic Services for the poor (UBSP), 1990, which was a modified UBS Programme.

(*Contd.*)

(Contd.)

Five Year/ Annual Plan	*Year(s)*	*Major Thrust Areas/Programmes*
		The UBSP Programme envisaged fostering community structures comprising urban poor for ensuring their effective participation in their developmental activities
Annual	1990-92	The constitution 74th Amendment Act was passed by parliament, which envisaged urban poverty alleviation, slum up-gradation and protection of interests of weaker sections as amongst the functions of Urban Local Bodies.
VIII	1992-97	Prime Minister's Integrated Urban Poverty Eradication Programme (PMIUPEP) was started in 1995, for improving the quality of life of urban poor by creating a facilitating environmental through community-based planning and implementation. The PMIUPEP incorporated within itself all the components of UBSP & NRY. Launch of National Slum Development Programme (NSDP) in 1996, covering physical infrastructure like water supply, storm water drains, sewer, community latrines, widening and paving of existing lanes, street lights etc. and social infrastructure pre-school education, non-formal education, adult education, maternity, child health and primary health care including immunization etc.
IX	1997-2002	Launched of Swarna Jayanti Shahari Rozgar Yojana (SJSRY), in 1997, after subsuming existing schemes like NRY, UBSP and PMIUPEP.
X	2002-2007	Launch of Jawharlal Nehru National Urban Renewal Mission (JNNRUM) a flagship programme of the GoI, in 2005.

Conclusion

1. Planning commission of India has designed the time bound programmes in order to achieve social welfare and development. G.O.I. has taken several steps in order to identify thrust areas for Housing. The problem of housing was recognized and housing and Urbanization was brought into the policy planning framework.
2. Affordability is the key issue in the housing sector particularly related to low income group and Housing policy was spelt out in parliament in year 1957 and thus the housing policies have been linked up with economic development and industrialization policies.

3. Concept of economically weaker section (EWS) of the society has been introduced to plan and develop social groups. Thus provided subsidized houses to certain weaker sections of the community was possible during FFYP.
4. During SFYUP, a draft NHP was prepared by the M/o Urban Development during this period.
5. During EFYP with a task of expanding the overall of basic infra-facilities in rural and urban areas in order to improve the overall environment habitat and provided appropriate conditions for the majority of the households to have access to housing. Particularly, the Indira Awas Yojana (IAY) was introduced in the central sector in 1985-86.
6. Government of India has tackled the problem of housing in urban area, including improvement of slums and squatter settlements particularly encouraged the up-gradation and progressive development of low income settlements.
7. Subsidy has been continued for some more time and the flow mechanism was made more transparent and increasingly routed out-side the financial system.
8. NFYP has recognized the need to strengthen the linkages and inter-dependency between shelter and income up-gradation the efforts in this direction are highly appreciable.

SECTION TWO

Urban Poverty Alleviation Programmes (National and State Level)—Its Status and Structure—Environmental Impact Assessment [EIA]

Urban Poverty Alleviation Programme (UPAP) and Public Distribution Systems (PDS) are important aspects to seek the welfare of the people living under BPL. Poverty reduction is an important goal of the Urban Policy. Urban growth is a result of: (1) Natural increase in population, (2) Net migration from rural areas to urban areas, and (3) Re-classification of towns. The common notion is that migration largely finds a place in urban growth which is partially correct. Therefore, it is necessary to view Urban Poverty as distinct from rural poverty and net increase as mere transfer of rural and population to urban areas.

The present chapter deals with the following programmes relating to Urban Poverty Alleviation Programmes (UPAP). They are:

1. Nehru Rozgar Yojana (NRY),
2. Urban Basic Services for the Poor (UBSP),
3. Prime Ministers Integrated Urban Poverty Eradication Programme (PMIUPEP),
4. The Self employment component of NRY and PMIUPEP have been (combined) jointly formed into a single programme valid for all the urban areas all over the country,
5. The Swarna Jayathi Shahari Rozgar Yojana (SJSRY),
6. The Urban Self Employment Programme (USEP),
   Components: (1) Self-employment through setting up micro-enterprises and skill development.
   Components: (2) Development of Women and Children in Urban Area (DWCUA)
7. The Urban Wage Employment Programme (UWEP)
8. Wider implications for the Twelfth Five Year Plan Beyond the TOR.
9. USEP progress-2009-2010 to 2013-2014.
10. Rajiv YUVA Kiranalu—Placements—Consolidated (01/04/2013-01/04/2014 to 31/03/2015).
11. Livelihood Skill Training Reports.
12. UWSP—Urban Women Self-Help Programme (Progress during 2011, 2012, and 2013)—Evaluation.
13. SHGS, SLFs and TLFs in Andhra Pradesh.

PART B

Part B deals with National Urban Livelihoods Mission (NULM). All the aspects have been presented in the following paragraphs.

Source: National Urban Livelihoods Mission (NULM), Planning Commission, Government of India, New Delhi (website)

Urban poverty leads to:

(a) Proliferation of slum and *bustees*,
(b) Fast growth of the informal sector,

(c) Increasing causalisation of labour,
(d) Increasing pressure on civic services,
(e) Increasing educational deprivation and health contingencies.

The Urban Poverty Alleviation Programmes (UPAPs) which were in operation during eighth plan are as follows:

Nehru Rozgar Yojana (NRY)

In order to alleviate the conditions of urban poor, a centrally sponsored programme—Nehru Rozgar Yojana—was launched at the end of the Seventh Five Year Plan (October,1989) with the objective of providing an employment to the urban unemployed and underemployed poor. The Central government indicated its overall contribution while the essential task of identifying, earmarking and coordination the relevant sectoral inputs was undertaken by the State governments. The NRY consisted of three schemes namely: (i) The schemes of Urban Micro-Enterprises (SUME), (ii) The Scheme of Urban Wage Employment (SUWE); and (iii) The Scheme of Housing and Shelter Up-gradation (SHSAU). The physical and financial details of the implementation of these Schemes are at *Annexure-I* and *Annexure–II* respectively. During the Eighth Plan, 92 per cent of the available funds were utilized and but for the shortfall, the number of dwelling units upgraded/in progress under SHASU, the targets have been achieved under all the other schemes.

Urban Basic Services for the Poor (UBSP)

The UBSP Programme was implemented as a Centrally Sponsored Scheme during the Eighth Five Year Plan with the specific objectives of effective achievement of the social sector goals. Community organization, mobilization and empowerment; and convergence through sustainable support system. The expenditure on the Programme was being shared on a 60:40 basis between the Central and the State governments and UTs (with legislatures). Further, the per capital expenditure on any slum pocket is Rs. 75/- in the first year and Rs. 50/- from the second year onwards after the basic infrastructure is developed. The UBSP was targeted to cover 70 lakh urban poor beneficiaries in 500 town during the Eighth plan period. The Programme has achieved the physical target of 70 lakh beneficiaries during the Eighth Plan period in 350 towns against the release of the Central share of Rs. 8090 lakh, the release of the State share was Rs. 3439.64 lakh. As on 31.03.1997, 353 towns and 4993 slum pockets have been selected for coverage and 75 lakh beneficiaries have been covered.

Prime Minister's Integrated Urban Poverty Eradication Programme (PMIUPEP)

Recognizing the seriousness and complexity of urban poverty problems, especially in the small towns where the situation is graver due to lack of resources for planning their environment and development, the PMIUPEP was launched in November, 1995. The PMIUPEP was a Rs. 800 crore scheme covered for the period up to the year 2000. Programme was applicable to all Class II urban agglomeration with a population ranging between 50,000 and 1 lakh subject to the condition that elections to local bodies have been held. The Programme was being implemented on a whole town/project basis extending the coverage to the entire targeted group for recurring a visible impact. During 1995-96 and 1996-97, Rs. 176.40 crore was released to the States/UTs. Most of the States are in the preparatory stages of the Programme, such as house-to-house survey, spatial mapping, need assessment, developing Iterative project reports, building community structures etc. which take quite some time. The physical achievements as reported by the States are as under:

(a) House-to-House survey has been completed in 213 towns.
(b) Town-wise project reports have been prepared for 229 towns.
(c) Under the self-employment component, 2077 applications have been forwarded to banks/HUDCO, out of which 4743 cases have been approved by HUDCO.
(d) As many as 8382 Neighbourhood Groups, 1200 Neighbourhood Development Committees and 444 Thrift and Credit Societies have been formed.

The Performance of the UPAPs in the Eighth Five Year Plan Reveals

- That although urban poverty is no less severe than rural poverty, the priority accorded to alleviation of urban poverty is low as the common perception is that urban poverty is a transfer of rural poverty into urban areas;
- That UPAPs are highly fragmented and have overlapping objectives and strategies.
- That integration of UPAPs with sectoral development and area development programmes has been overlooked.
- That the role of voluntary organizations and community based organization in planning and implementation of UPAPs is on the periphery.

The Planning Commission's (Modified Expert Group) estimates of urban poverty show a decline in the percentage of urban poor from 38 per cent (1987-88) to 32.36 per cent (1993-94). As per the Modified Expert Group the number of urban poor is 763.37 lakh in 1993-94. The Hashim Committee, which was set up to review and rationalize Centrally Sponsored Schemes for poverty alleviation and employment generation, had gone into the question of rationalization of the existing poverty alleviation programmes and recommended that:

1. The self-employment component of NRY and PMIUPEP be combined into single programme valid for all the urban areas all over the country.
    - The Planning Commission's (Modified Expert Group) estimates of urban poverty show a decline in the percentage of urban poor from 38 per cent (1987-88) to 32.36 per cent (1993-94). As per the Modified Expert Group the number of urban poor is 763.37 lakh in 1993-94.
    - The Hashim Committee, which was set up to review and rationalize Centrally Sponsored Schemes for poverty alleviation and employment generation, had gone into the question of rationalization of the existing poverty alleviation programmes.
    - Based on the recommendation of the Committee the

Swarna Jayanthi Shahari Rozgar Yojana (SJSRY) has been launched with effect from 1.12.97 and NRY, PMIUPEP and UBSP have been phased out.

- The programme has two sub-schemes namely, (a) Urban Self-Employment Programme and components of the NRY and PMIUPEP have been re-organized under this single programme. The shelter up-gradation components of both NRY and PMIUPEP has been merged with the National Slum Development Programme.

2. The urban wage employment component as well as the physical infrastructure development component under the NRY and the PMIUPEP be merged and be made applicable to all the urban areas with a population less than 5 lakhs. This component may be separated from the self-employment component as a separate scheme with a distinct identity; and
3. The shelter up-gradation/housing component under NRY and PMIUPEP be retained either as a separate scheme or merged with the Slum Development/Basic Services Schemes operating at present.

The Swarna Jayanthi Shahari Rozgar Yojana (SJSRY)

In pursuance of the above recommendations, during the Ninth Plan it s proposed to launch the Swarna Jayanthi Rozgar Yojana (SJSRY) and phase out NRY, PMIIUPEP and UBSP. The SJSRY is to be a Centrally Sponsored Scheme applicable to all the urban areas with expenditure to be shared in ratio 75:25 between the Centre and States/UTs. The programme has become operational on December 1, 1997. This programme would have two sub-schemes, namely, (i) Urban Self-Employment Programme and (ii) Urban Wage Employment Programme. The self-employment and wage employment components of the existing NRY and PMIUPEP have been reorganized under this single programme. Further the shelter up-gradation components of both NRY and PMIUPEP will be merged with the National Slum Development Programme.

The Swarna Jayanthi Shahari Rozgar Yojana (SJSRY) seek to provide gainful employment to the urban unemployed or underemployed poor by encouraging the setting up of self-employment ventures or provision of wage employment. This programme will rely on the creating of suitable community structures on the UBSP pattern and delivery of inputs under this programme will be through the medium of urban local bodies and similar community institutional structures.

The Swarna Jayanti Shahari Rozgar Yojana rests on the foundation of community empowerment towards this end, community organizations like Neighbourhood Groups (NHGs), Neighbourhood Committees (NHCs) and Community Development Societies (CDSs) will be set up in the target areas based on the UBSP pattern. The CDSs will be the focal point for purposes of identification of beneficiaries, preparation of applications, monitoring of recovery and generally providing whatever other support is necessary to the programme. The CDSs will also identify viable projects suitable for that particular area.

These CDSs may also set themselves up as Thrift and Credit Societies to encourage community savings, as also other group activities. A maximum expenditure at the rate of Rs.100 per member for the first year and Rs.75 per member for each subsequent year will be allowed for activities connected with the CDSs.

The Urban Self Employment Programme (USEP)

This programme will have three distinct components:

(i) Assistance to individual urban poor beneficiaries for setting up gainful self-employment ventures.

(ii) Assistance to groups of urban poor women for setting up gainful self-employment ventures. This sub-scheme may be called "The Scheme for Development of Women and Children in the Urban Areas (DWCUA)".

(iii) Training of beneficiaries, potential beneficiaries and other persons associated with the urban employment programme for up-gradation and acquisition of vocational and entrepreneurial skills.

Coverage

(i) The programme will be applicable to all urban towns in India.

(ii) The programme will be implemented on a whole basis with special emphasis on urban poor clusters.

Target Groups

(i) The programme will target the urban poor, i.e. those living below the urban poverty line, as defined form time to time.
(ii) Special attention will be given to women, persons belonging to Scheduled Castes/Tribes, Disabled persons and other such categories as may be indicated by the Government from time to time. The percentage of women beneficiaries under this programme will not be less than 30 per cent. The SCs and STs must be benefited at least to the extent of their proportion in the local population. A special provision of 3 per cent will be reserved for the disabled under this programme.
(iii) There will not be any minimum educational qualification set for beneficiaries under this programme. However, to avoid an overlap with the PMRY scheme, for self-employment component, this scheme will not apply to beneficiaries educated beyond the IX standard. As regards the wage employment component, there will be no restrictions of educational qualifications whatsoever.
(iv) A house-to-house survey for identification of genuine beneficiaries will be undertaken. Non-economic parameters will also be applied to identify the urban poor in addition to the economic criteria of the urban poverty line.
All other conditions being equal, women beneficiaries belonging to women-headed households will be ranked higher in priority than other beneficiaries.

Components

Self-employment through Setting up Micro-enterprises and Skill Development

To avoid duplication with the ongoing Prime Minister's Rozgar Yojana (PMRY), this component of SJSRY is confined to the below poverty line beneficiaries who have no education up to ninth standard, with emphasis on those accorded a higher priority on the basis of the non-economic criteria. The maximum unit cost will be Rs.50,000 and the maximum allowable subsidy will be 15 per cent of the project cost, subject to a limit of Rs.7,500. The beneficiary is required to contribute 5 per cent of the project cost as margin money. In case a number of beneficiaries decide to jointly set up a project, such project will be eligible for a subsidy which will be equal to the total of the permitted subsidy per person as per the above criteria. In this case to the provision relating to 5 per cent margin money per beneficiary will apply. The overall project cost, which can be permitted, will be the total of the individual project cost allowable per beneficiary.

Skill development through appropriate training is another element of this programme. The unit cost allowed for training will be Rs. 2000 per trainee, including material cost, trainer's fees, other miscellaneous expenses to be incurred by the training institution and the monthly stipend to be paid to the trainee. The total training period for skill up-gradation may vary from two to six months, subject to a minimum of 300 hours. Infrastructural support may also be provided to the beneficiaries setting up micro-enterprises in relation to marketing of their products etc.

Development of Women and Children in Urban Areas (DWCUA)

This scheme is distinguished by the special incentive extended to urban poor women who decide to set up self-employment ventures as a group as opposed to individual effort. Groups of urban poor women will take up an economic activity suited to their skill, training, aptitude and local conditions. Besides generation of income, this group strategy will strive to empower the urban poor women by making them independent as also providing a facilitating atmosphere for self-employment. To be eligible for subsidy under this scheme, the DWCUA group should consist of at least 10 urban poor women.

Financial Pattern

The DWCUA group society will be entitled to a subsidy of Rs. 1,25,000 or 50 per cent of the cost of project whichever is less.

Where the DWCUA group sets itself up as a Thrift and Credit Society, in addition to its other entrepreneurial activity, the group/ Thrift and Credit society will also be entitled to a lump-sum grant of Rs. 25000 as a revolving fund at the rate of Rs. 1000 maximum per member. This revolving fund will be available to a simple Thrift and Credit Society also even if the society is not engaged in any project activity under DWCUA.

The Urban Wage Employment Programme (UWEP)

This programme seeks to provide wage employment to beneficiaries living below the poverty line within the jurisdiction of urban local bodies by utilizing their labour for construction of socially and economically useful public assets. This programme will apply to urban local bodies, the population of which is less than 5 lakhs as per the 1991 Census.

The material-labour ratio for works under this programme will be maintained at 60:40. The prevailing minimum wage rate, as notified from time to time for each area, will be paid to the beneficiaries under this programme. This programme will be dovetailed with the State sector EIUS scheme as well as the National Slum Development Programme (NSDP). This programme is not designed to either replace or substitute the Environmental Improvement of Urban Slums (EIUS), the NSDP, or any other State sector schemes.

Project Administration

At the community level, a Community Organizer (CO) will be appointed for about 2000 identified families. The Community Organizer should, as far as practicable, be a woman. At the town level, there will be an Urban Poverty Eradication Cell under the charge of a Project Officer. The Project Officer will be responsible for coordinating the activities of all the CDSs and COs. At the district level, the State Government will constitute a District Urban Development Agency (DUDA) with an officer designated as the District Project Officer. At the State level, there will be a State Urban Development Authority (SUDA), which will be headed by a full-time senior officer of the State Government. The SUDA will be designated as the State Nodal Agency for urban anti poverty programmes. At the national level, the Department of Urban Employment and Poverty Alleviation will be the nodal department. The programme will be monitored and overseen by the UPA Division. The Ninth Plan, in particular, needs to focus on the effective implementation and management of urban poverty alleviation programmes (UPAPs). Targeting of urban poor is essential for the success of any anti-poverty programme. Therefore, the UPAPs should be designed to accommodate flexibility in operation. The key components of the Ninth Plan strategy would be:

- Effective targeting using either a self-identification system or a selection process by institutions responsible for financing and managing UPAPs s faulty targeting will enhance income inequalities.
- A "bottom up" approach should be adopted for UPAPs which should be routed through community based organizations. There should be effective participation of community institutions for extending loans and for aiding loan recoveries made under UPAPs.
- Since the problem of urban poverty is a manifestation of the higher incidence of marginal and low income employment in the informal sector, it is essential to upgrade informal sector occupations. Hence there is a need for emphasis on generation of self-employment in processing and services sector, improving the access to technology and credit and above all improving the general legal and physical environment which governs the working of the informal sector.

The policy framework adopted by the Government of India also mentions that "a frontal attack on poverty is an important element in development policy. This is the main rationale for anti-poverty programmes".

Urban Challenges

"Wider Implications for the Twelfth Five Year Plan Beyond the TOR."

1.1 Water, sanitation and solid waste management and urban poverty linkages between the lives and livelihoods of the urban poor to water, sanitation and solid waste management were acknowledged. In particular, issues of livelihood of waste pickers and their contribution to city solid waste management were considered important. It was felt that any debate regarding water, sanitation and solid waste management under the Twelfth Five Year Plan should consider linkages of these sectors with urban poverty.

1.2 Transport Implications: The Working Group was cognizant of the fact that for the provision affordable housing and urban informal sector livelihoods, transport linkages should be important considerations. For example, resettlement of slum dwellers must allow for adequate transport linkages and where ever possible, the relocation of the poor must occur on inter-city and inter-city transport corridors. Also informal sector livelihoods depend on non-motorized transport and small vehicles including cycles, cycle rickshaws, auto-rickshaws etc. The Twelfth plan document should consider the implications of transport planning on the urban poor.

1.3 The working group took a strong view regarding the measurement of urban poverty as being either above or below a 'line'/cut off' representing consumption expenditure. It was felt that the way in which Urban Poverty Alleviation is tackled at the programmatic level requires a measurement of vulnerabilities and not consumption/income poverty. The recommendation is for data on the various vulnerabilities to be collected (gathered) and eligibility for coverage under a scheme to be dependent on vulnerability rather their possession of a BPL card.

1.4 Another Concern related to the issue of informal livelihood and urban poverty is the concern regarding urban cultural heritage conservation. *The incidence of slums around* Urban heritage structure is generally viewed negatively instead of a focus on the livelihood opportunities for the urban poor related to tourism and conservation. Additionally the documentation and preservation of urban cultures is not seen as a priority as cities are conceived of and planned as a built environment as opposed to also being sites of culture. An exploration of the ways in which urban poverty alleviation and urban cultural heritage interact positively needs to be undertaken. This includes movable or immovable objects, sites, and structures, groups of structures and natural features and landscapes that have archaeological, paleontological, historical, architectural, religious, aesthetic or other cultural significance.[2]

Rajiv Yuva Kiranalu

***Southern Regional Conference on Skill Development* (3/3/2012)**

- >1 ct. Youth of < 35 yrs age are expected to enter the Indian Job Market every year for the next 15 yrs.
- CII estimated that 56 lakh workers will be required in AP alone by 2015. Unskilled: 20-30 lakh.
- Major potential in—Textiles, Construction, Tourism, Hospitality, Retail Management, Pharmaceuticals, Biotech, IT, ITES etc.

  Young people need jobs ↔ industry needs workers can we harness he demographic dividend and create.

Sector-wise human resources required in Andhra Pradesh is presented in Table 3.1. It is seen from Table 3.1 that 13 items in which the current employment (in lakhs) and incremental demand by 2015 (in lakhs), and the total demand (in lakhs) out of which the construction activity exhausts more population 42.10 lakhs, as total demand, wherein 22.00 for current employment and 20.10 lakhs as incremental demand by 2015. Tourism occupies 2nd position among the other items as it is seen from Table 3.1.

A.P. Scenario

Rajiv Yuva Kiranalu

Vision

To convert non-literate, school drop-out unskilled unemployed

Table 3.1: Sector-wise Human Resources Requirement—AP

Sl. No.	*Industry*	*Total Demand (In Lakhs)*	*Current Employment (In Lakhs)*	*Incremental Demand by 2015 (In Lakhs)*
1.	Construction	42.10	22.00	20.10
2.	Textiles	18.26	7.45	10.81
3.	IT & ITES	8.93	1.52	7.41
4.	Healthcare	8.50	2.90	5.59
5.	Tourism	13.66	8.51	5.15
6.	Drugs and Pharma	4.78	2.30	2.48
7.	Banking and Insurance	2.68	1.35	1.32
8.	Engineering	2.15	0.99	1.16
9.	Mines and Minerals	2.25	1.14	1.11
10.	Agri. & Food Processing	2.80	1.98	0.83
11.	Chemicals and Fertilizers	1.31	0.87	0.44
12.	Biotech	0.24	0.05	0.19
13.	Paper	0.33	0.21	0.11
	Total	**107.99**	**51.27**	**56.70**

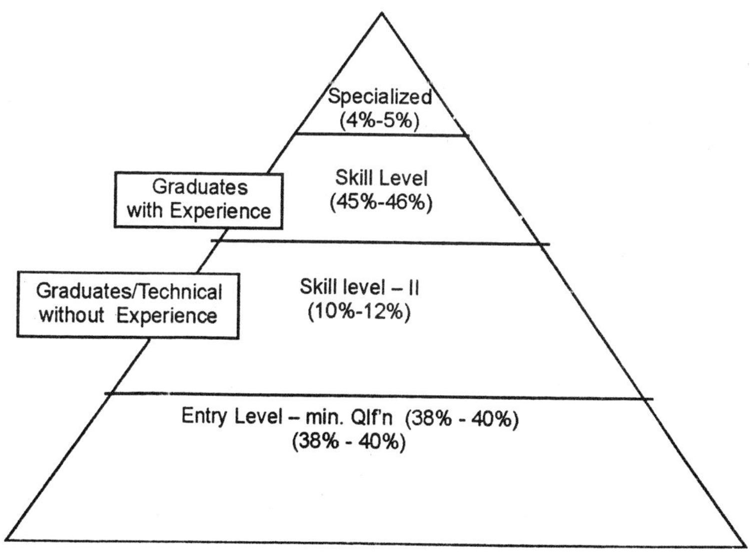

Fig. 3.2: Manpower Requirement

youth into productive workforce by building their skills; thereby promoting inclusive growth.

Goal

15 lakhs jobs to youth by 2014-15.

Institutional Arrangements—State Level

REECAP

- Chairman—Hon'ble CM
- 9 Cabinet Ministers, 9 Prl. Secretaries, 10 Eminent industrialists and academia as members.

To lay down macro policy environment and provide guidance.

REEMAP

- A Registered society to act as an umbrella for skill development efforts taken up by key departments.

To ensure implementation on Mission mode.

Institutional Arrangements—State Level

REEMAP will function through 7 Sub-Missions:

1. Sub-Mission for Rural Employment—for rural youth from SHG HH
2. Sub-Mission for Urban Slums-for youth of Urban slum based SHGs
3. Sub-Mission for Urban area—for youth of urban areas and ITI (pass/fail) and unemployed
4. Sub-Mission for placements for polytechnic (pass/fail)
5. Sub-Mission for Differently—Abled
6. Sub-Mission for Minorities
7. Sub-Mission for Hyderabad city

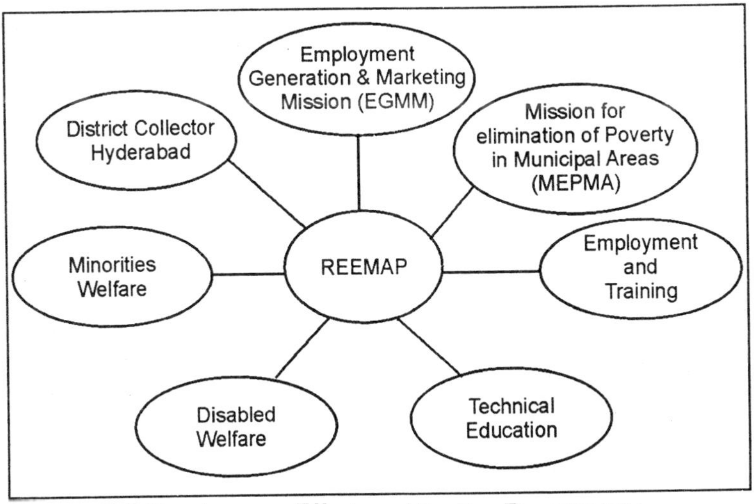

Fig. 3.3: Skill Development Efforts and the Key Departments

Strategy for Implementation

- Targets bottom most of the pyramid
- Eectronic Registry of unemployed youth
- Mapping of job opportunities industry-wise
- Industry focused skill development to youth which is logically linked to jobs in the industry
- Identification of jobs → job specific trainings → placements in industry
- Post-placement follow-up
- GoI collaboration

Close coordination with industry, professional Trg. partners and skill development agencies.

Table 3.2: Rajiv Yuva Kiranalu-Road Map

Sl. No.	Year	Placements to be achieved (in lakhs)
1.	2011-2012	2.466
2.	2012-2013	4.994
3.	2013-2014	6.142
4.	2014-2015	1.754
	Total	**15.356**

Step-by-Step Implementation Process

Assessment of Demand

- Identify Growth/Potential sectors in the district.
- Hold meeting with Industry representatives.
- Identify specific jobs/placements industry-wise.
- Identify the skill sets required.

Establishing Relevant Infrastructure

- Locate standardized course syllabus
- Set-up training centres

Mobilizing Candidates and Training

- Identify the Trainees/Candidates
- Train the Candidates

Placement

- Placement of the Trainees.
- Post placement follow up.

Pre-Placement Services

Mobilization of Candidates

- On-line Registration
- House to House Survey
- Fixed day interaction with SHG Federations.
- Word of Mouth
- Local advertising

Capture Course Preference of Candidates

The following paragraphs the impact of USEP progress for the year 2009-2010 is presented in Table 3.3. Likewise for the remaining years Table 3.4 for 2010-11, Table 3.5 for the year 2011-2012, Table 3.6 for the year 2012-13, for Table 3.7 explains for the

Table 3.3: Financial year 2009-2010 U.S.E.P. Progress

USEP Progress for the year All amounts in Rs. lakhs										
Sl. No.	District	Target	No. of Applications	Sanctioned	Grounded	Not Grounded	Unit Cost	Bank Loan Amount	Subsidy Amount	Beneficiary Contribution
1.	Anantapur	0	611	552	550	2	270.63	189.44	67.66	13.53
2.	Chittoor	0	436	382	382	0	185.52	129.87	46.38	9.28
3.	Cuddapah	0	249	247	247	0	101.97	71.38	25.49	5.10
4.	East Godavari	0	425	422	422	0	209.55	146.69	52.39	10.48
5.	Guntur	0	1080	1044	1044	0	373.89	261.72	93.47	18.69
6.	GVMC	0	72	72	72	0	32.65	22.86	8.16	1.63
7.	Krishna	0	458	443	443	0	185.10	129.57	46.28	9.26
8.	Kurnool	0	485	478	478	0	351.52	246.06	87.88	17.58
9.	Nellore	0	348	345	337	8	178.55	124.99	44.64	8.93
10.	Prakasam	0	484	478	478	0	246.63	172.64	61.66	12.33
11.	Srikakulam	0	173	173	173	0	73.85	51.70	18.46	3.69
12.	Visakhapatnam	0	51	51	51	0	19.25	13.48	4.81	0.96
13.	Vizianagaram	0	114	111	111	0	52.09	36.46	13.02	2.60
14.	VMC	0	496	494	494	0	122.85	86.00	30.71	6.14
15.	West Godavari	0	534	472	472	0	228.93	160.25	57.23	11.45
	Total	0	6016	5764	5754	10	2632.98	1843.11	658.24	131.65

Source: MEPMA, Hyderabad, Andhra Pradesh.

Table 3.4: Financial Year: 2010-2011 U.S.E.P. Progress

USEP Progress for the year All amounts in Rs. lakhs

Sl. No.	District	Target	No. of Applications	Sanctioned	Grounded	Not Grounded	Unit Cost	Bank Loan Amount	Subsidy Amount	Beneficiary Contribution
1.	Anantapur	0	525	397	397	0	201.60	141.12	50.40	10.08
2.	Chittoor	0	465	387	387	0	308.70	216.09	77.18	15.44
3.	Cuddapah	0	396	347	347	0	162.55	113.79	40.64	8.13
4.	East Godavari	0	533	505	505	0	388.48	271.94	97.12	19.42
5..	Guntur	0	909	779	779	0	327.53	229.27	81.88	16.38
6.	GVMC	0	61	57	57	0	70.90	49.63	17.73	3.55
7.	Krishna	0	674	640	640	0	385.60	269.92	96.40	19.28
8.	Kurnool	0	476	418	418	0	336.10	235.27	84.03	16.81
9..	Nellore	0	321	308	308	0	180.75	126.53	45.19	9.04
10.	Prakasam	0	417	387	387	0	281.49	197.04	70.37	14.07
11.	Srikakulam	0	252	236	236	0	148.95	104.27	37.24	7.45
12.	Visakhapatnam	0	172	105	105	0	102.61	71.83	25.65	5.13
13.	Vizianagaram	0	252	241	241	0	165.72	116.00	41.43	8.29
14.	VMC	0	714	35	35	0	6.85	4.80	1.71	0.34
15.	West Godavari	0	541	493	493	0	349.12	244.38	87.28	17.46
	Total	0	6708	5335	5335	0	3416.95	2391.88	854.25	170.87

Source: MEPMA, Hyderabad, Andhra Pradesh.

Table 3.5: Financial Year: 2011-2012 US.E.P. Progress

USEP Progress for the year – All amounts in Rs. Lakhs										
Sl. No.	District	Target	No. of Applications	Sanctioned	Grounded	Not Grounded	Unit Cost	Bank Loan Amount	Subsidy Amount	Beneficiary Contribution
1.	Anantapur	400	552	246	246	0	172.00	120.40	43.00	8.60
2.	Chittoor	500	696	560	560	0	548.02	383.61	137.01	27.40
3.	Cuddapah	450	616	441	441	0	406.55	284.59	101.64	20.33
4.	East Godavari	400	543	200	200	0	261.25	182.88	65.31	13.06
5.	Guntur	800	852	652	652	0	417.46	292.22	104.37	20.87
6.	GVMC	800	164	78	78	0	93.04	65.13	23.26	4.65
7.	Krishna	400	686	422	422	0	337.05	235.94	84.26	16.85
8.	Kurnool	500	573	352	352	0	395.99	277.19	99.00	19.80
9.	Nellore	450	477	313	313	0	287.40	201.18	71.85	14.37
10.	Prakasam	300	440	142	142	0	50.70	35.49	12.68	2.54
11.	Srikakulam	280	208	177	177	0	117.75	82.43	29.44	5.89
12.	Visakhapatnam	150	134	80	80	0	93.79	65.65	23.45	4.69
13.	Vizianagaram	250	180	135	135	0	126.35	88.45	31.59	6.32
14.	VMC	700	194	165	165	0	129.26	90.48	32.32	6.46
15.	West Godavari	300	383	198	198	0	200.10	140.07	50.03	10.01
	Total	**6680**	**6698**	**4161**	**4161**	**0**	**3636.71**	**2545.71**	**909.21**	**181.84**

Source: *Source*: MEPMA, Hyderabad, Andhra Pradesh.

Table 3.6: Financial Year: 2012-2013, U.S.E.P. Progress

USEP Progress for the year – All amounts in Rs. Lakhs										
Sl. No.	*District*	*Target*	*No. of Applications*	*Sanctioned*	*Grounded*	*Not Grounded*	*Unit Cost*	*Bank Loan Amount*	*Subsidy Amount*	*Beneficiary Contribution*
1.	Anantapur	551	587	557	300	257	490.49	343.34	122.62	24.52
2.	Chittoor	648	804	769	528	241	834.99	584.49	208.75	41.75
3.	Cuddapah	500	554	496	322	174	482.65	337.86	120.66	24.13
4.	East Godavari	681	610	580	340	240	1022.65	715.86	255.66	51.13
5.	Guntur	603	695	645	451	194	655.82	459.07	163.96	32.79
6.	GVMC	804	365	322	129	193	308.84	216.19	77.21	15.44
7.	Krishna	509	562	496	317	179	502.35	351.65	125.59	25.12
8.	Kurnool	614	620	565	213	352	768.57	538.00	192.14	38.43
9.	Nellore	376	435	405	278	127	297.22	208.06	74.31	14.86
10.	Prakasam	332	355	303	174	129	279.05	195.34	69.76	13.95
11.	Srikakulam	200	122	122	121	1	109.85	76.90	27.46	5.49
12.	Visakhapatnam	121	106	104	44	60	118.85	83.20	29.71	5.94
13.	Vizianagaram	208	212	211	140	71	216.61	151.63	54.15	10.83
14.	VMC	157	354	354	195	159	256.42	179.50	64.11	12.82
15.	West Godavari	421	423	417	297	120	445.21	311.65	111.30	22.26
	Total	6725	6804	6346	3849	2497	6789.57	4752.74	1697.39	339.46

Source: MEPMA, Hyderabad, Andhra Pradesh.

Table 3.7: Financial Year: 2013-2014 U.S.E.P. Progress

Sl. No.	District	Target	No. of Applications	Sanctioned	Grounded	Not Grounded	Unit Cost	Bank Loan Amount	Subsidy Amount	Beneficiary Contribution
1.	Anantapur	550	671	413	116	297	379.80	265.86	94.95	18.99
2.	Chittoor	600	664	607	366	241	698.80	489.86	174.95	34.99
3.	Cuddapah	500	663	436	243	193	403.55	282.49	100.89	20.18
4.	East Godavari	600	894	468	311	157	567.05	396.94	141.76	28.35
5.	Guntur	600	587	504	248	256	464.82	325.37	116.21	23.24
6.	GVMC	800	538	536	395	141	717.15	502.01	179.29	35.86
7.	Krishna	500	592	541	352	189	549.15	384.41	137.29	27.46
8.	Kurnool	600	591	488	130	358	664.95	465.47	166.24	33.25
9.	Nellore	400	500	435	337	48	293.55	205.49	73.39	14.68
10.	Prakasam	300	560	316	225	91	284.10	198.87	71.03	14.21
11.	Srikakulam	200	175	155	121	34	162.30	113.61	40.58	8.12
12	Visakhapatnam	125	160	132	117	15	118.12	82.68	29.53	5.91
13.	Vizianagaram	200	263	159	41	118	161.15	112.81	40.29	8.06
14.	VMC	250	110	110	14	96	182.50	127.75	45.63	9.13
15.	West Godavari	400	486	328	191	137	387.48	271.24	96.87	19.37
	Total	6625	7454	5628	3257	2371	6034.47	4224.86	1508.9	301.8

Source: MEPMA, Hyderabad, Andhra Pradesh.

financial year 2013-14. These tables in nutshell explains the financial variations over a period of time and the districts performance could be identified in Andhra Pradesh.

National Urban Livelihoods Mission

Economic development and urbanization are closely linked. Cities in India are emerging as the country's engines of economic growth, with a contribution of more than 60 per cent to GDP. As per Census of India, 2011, India's urban population is now 377 million which shows a 31 per cent increase from 2001. The Report on Conditions of Work and Promotion of Livelihoods in the Unorganized sector by the National Commission on Enterprises in the Unorganized Sector brought out in August 2007 (NCEUS, 2007) reveals that in 2004-05, out of India's total workforce, 92 per cent are working in the informal economy. The urban informal sector comprises a large part of the unorganized non-agriculture sector. Low levels of education and skill in the unorganized sector workers have resulted in their inability to access the opportunities offered by emerging markets. This underscores the critically of skill up gradation for better livelihoods opportunities in urban areas.

Most of the poor are involved in informal sector activities where there is a constant threat of eviction, removal, confiscation of goods and almost non-existent social security cover. Even when segments of the urban population are not income-poor, they face deprivation in terms of lack of access to sanitary living conditions and their well-being is hampered by discrimination, social exclusion, crime, and violence, insecurity of tenure, hazardous environmental conditions and lack of voice in governance.

The dimensions of urban poverty can be broadly divided into three categories: (i) residential vulnerability (access to land, shelter, basic services, etc.); (ii) social vulnerability (deprivations related to factors like gender, age and social stratification, lack of social protection, inadequate voice and participation in governance structures, etc.); and (iii) occupational vulnerability (precarious livelihoods, dependence on informal sector for employment and earnings, lack of job security, poor working conditions, etc.). These vulnerabilities are inter-related. Amongst the urban poor, there are sections subject to greater vulnerability in terms of the above classification; these include women, children, and the aged, SCs,

STs, minorities and differently-abled persons who deserve attention on a priority basis.

The National Urban Housing and Habitat Policy (NUHHP), 2007 aims to promote sustainable development of habitat in the country with a view to ensure equitable supply of land, shelter and services at affordable prices to all sections of the society. The most vulnerable of these are the urban homeless who live with no shelter or social security/protection. Recent pronouncements of the Supreme Court of India have brought into focus the plight of the urban homeless by holding that the right to dignified shelters is a necessary component of the right to life under Article 21 of the Constitution of India. There is therefore a need to develop a policy and programme for the urban homeless.

Urban poverty being multi-dimensional, various vulnerabilities faced by the poor in cities and towns: occupational, residential and social need to be addressed simultaneously in a comprehensive and integrated manner with a targeted focus on the vulnerable groups so that a definitive impact can be made on ground. Residential vulnerability issues are being addressed through programmes like JNNURM and RAY. The other two vulnerabilities: occupational and social can be best addressed by creating opportunities for skill development leading to market-based employment and helping them to setup self-employment ventures. Urban poverty alleviation programmes need to be based on skill development and easy access to credit. It is in this context that a mission-mode approach to urban livelihoods is considered necessary in the form of the National Urban Livelihoods Mission (NULM).

Mission, Principles, Values, Strategy

NULM Mission

To reduce poverty and vulnerability of the urban poor households by enabling them to access gainful self-employment and skilled wage employment opportunities, resulting in an appreciable improvement in their livelihoods on a sustainable basis, through building strong grassroots level institutions of the poor. The mission would aim at providing shelter equipped with essential services to the urban homeless in a phased manner. In addition, the Mission would also address livelihood concerns of the urban street vendors by facilitating access spaces, institutional credit, social security and skills to the urban street vendors for accessing emerging market opportunities.

Guiding Principles

The core belief of National Urban Livelihoods Mission (NULM) is that the poor are entrepreneurial and have innate desire to come out of poverty. The challenge is to unleash their capabilities to generate meaningful and sustainable livelihoods. The first step in this process is motivating the urban poor to form their own institutions. They and their institutions need to be provided sufficient capacity so that they can manage the external environment, access finance, expand their skills, enterprises and assets. This requires continuous and carefully designed handholding support. An external, dedicated and sensitive support structure, from the national level to the city and community levels, is required to induce social mobilization, institutional building and livelihood promotion.

NULM believes that any livelihood promotion programme can be scaled up in a time-bound manner only if driven by the poor and their institutions. Such strong institutional platforms support the poor in building up their own human, social, financial, and other assets. This in turn, enables them access to rights entitlements, opportunities and services from the public and private sectors, while enhancing their solidarity, voice and bargaining power.

As per the Constitution (74th Amendment) Act 1992, urban poverty alleviation is a legitimate function of the Urban Local Bodies (ULB). Therefore, ULBs would need to undertake a lead role for all issues and programmes concerning the urban poor in cities/towns, including skills and livelihoods.

NULM would aim at universal coverage of the urban poor for skill development and credit facilities. It will strive for skills training of the urban poor for market-based jobs and self-employment, facilitating easy access to credit.

Street vendors constitute an important segment of the urban population at the bottom of the pyramid. Street vending provides a source of self-employment, and thus acts as a measure of urban poverty alleviation without major Government intervention. They have a prominent place in the urban supply chain and are an integral part of the economic growth process within urban areas. NULM would aim at facilitating access to suitable spaces, institutional credit, social security and skills to the urban street vendors for accessing emerging market opportunities.

Urban homeless persons who live without shelter or social security/protection are the most vulnerable class, even while they contribute towards sustaining cities with their cheap labour. Life on the streets involves surviving continuously at the edge, in a physically brutalized and challenging environment. There is a need for appropriate policy intervention to address the challenges faced by homeless people, with regard to shelter, social housing and social protection. Accordingly, NULM would aim at providing shelter equipped with essential services to the urban homeless in a phased manner.

NULM would place a very high emphasis on convergence with schemes/programmes of the relevant line Ministries/Departments and programmes of state governments dealing with skills, livelihoods, entrepreneurship development, health, education, social assistance, etc. An alliance strategy will be sought with all concerned departments to promote skills training of rural-urban migrants as a bridge between the livelihoods of the rural and urban poor.

NULM would aim at partnership with the private sector in providing skill training, employment and operation of shelter for homeless. It will strive for active participation of private and civil society sectors in providing shelter to the urban homeless, skill training and placement of the urban poor and also in facilitating technological, marketing and handholding support for the urban poor entrepreneurs who want to be self-employed and set up their own small businesses or manufacturing units.

Values

The mission will espouse the following values:

(i) Ownership and productive involvement of the urban poor and their institutions in all processes;
(ii) Transparency in programme design and implementation, including institution—building and capacity strengthening;
(iii) Accountability of government functionaries and the community;
(iv) Partnerships with industry and other stakeholders; and

(v) Community self-reliance, self-dependence, self-help and mutual-help.

Strategy

NULM will adopt the following strategy:

(i) Building capacity of the urban poor, their institutions and the machinery involved in the implementation of livelihoods development and poverty alleviation programmes through handholding support;

(ii) Enhancing and expanding existing livelihoods options of the urban poor;

(iii) Building skills to enable access to growing market-based job opportunities offered by emerging urban economies;

(iv) Training for and support to the establishment of micro-enterprises by the urban poor-self and group;

(v) Ensure availability and access for the urban homeless population to permanent 24-hours shelters including the basic infrastructure facilities like water supply, sanitation, safety and security;

(vi) Cater to the needs of especially vulnerable segments of the urban homeless like the dependent children, aged, disabled, mentally ill, and recovering patients etc., by creating special sections within homeless shelters and provisioning special service linkages for the them;

(vii) To establish strong rights-based, linkages with other programmes which cover the right of the urban homeless to food, healthcare, education, etc. and ensure access for homeless populations to various entitlements, including to social security pensions, PDS, ICDS, feeding programmes, drinking water, sanitation, identity, financial inclusion, school admission etc., and to affordable housing;

(viii) To address livelihood concerns of the uıban street vendors by facilitating access suitable spaces, institutional credit, social security and skills to the urban street vendors for accessing emerging market opportunities.

NULM Mission Cities and Target Population

In Twelfth Five Year Plan, NULM will be implemented in all District Headquarter Towns and all other cities with a population of 100,000 or more as per 2011 Census. However, other towns may be allowed in exceptional cases on request of the States.

The primary target of NULM is the urban poor, including the urban homeless. The Socio-economic and Caste Census (SECC), 2011 for identification of urban poor is currently under progress. Accordingly, as an interim measure, the target of NULM will be the urban population identified presently as below poverty line population in urban areas by the States/UTs. The coverage may be broadened to include families of disadvantaged groups like SCs, STs, women, minorities, disabled etc. subject to a maximum of 25 per cent of the above urban poor population.

National Urban Livelihoods Mission has the following components. They are:

- I. Social Mobilization and Institutional Development (SM&ID)
    1. Sub-Component—Building Community Institutions: SHGs and their Federations
    2. Sub-Component—Universal Financial Inclusion
    3. Sub-Component—Revolving Fund Support to SHGs and their Federation
    4. Sub-Component—City livelihood centres (CLCs)
    5. Sub-Component—Training and Other Capacity Building Programmes for SHGs and their Federations.
- II. Capacity Building and Training (CB & T)
    1. Sub-Component—Technical Support at National, State and City Levels.
    2. Sub-Component—Training and Other Capacity Building Programmes for MMUS
- III. Employment through Skills Training and Placement (EST & P)
- IV. Self-Employment Programme (SEP)
    1. Sub-Component—SHG-Bank Linkage
    2. Sub-Component—Credit Card for enterprise development
    3. Sub-Component—Technology, Marketing and Other support.

V. Support to Urban Street Vendors (SUSV)
   1. Sub-Component—Pro-Vending Urban Planning
   2. Sub-Component—Skill Development and Micro-enterprise Development-Support for Street Vendors.
   3. Sub-Component—Credit—enablement of street vendors.
   4. Sub-Component—Development of Vendor's Markets.
   5. Sub-Component—Social Security Convergence.

VI. Scheme of Shelter for Urban Homeless (SUH)

VII. Innovative and Special Projects (I & SP)

NULM Administration and Mission Structure

The National Urban Livelihoods Mission will have a three-tier interdependent structure. At the apex of the structure will be the National Mission Management Unit (NMMU), under the Ministry of Housing and Urban Poverty Alleviation, Government of India as an independent society under the charge of a Mission Director reporting to Secretary, Housing and Urban Poverty Alleviation. Till such time an independent society is set up, NULM will operate as a programme of Ministry of Housing and Urban Poverty Alleviation with a dedicated staffing structure. At the State level, there will be State Mission Management Unit (SMMU) under an independent society headed by a Mission Director reporting to the Secretariat Department dealing with Municipalities, which is responsible for implementing skill development/employment/livelihoods promotion programmes. At the city level, a City Mission Management Unit (CMMU) will be established in all NULM Cities to work under the overall guidance of the SMMU.

Technical Advisory Groups (TAGs) at the national, State, and city levels will be established which will consist of experts in skills and livelihoods, financial inclusion, social mobilization, capacity building, representatives from industry associates, etc. The members of National TAG for NULM and Chairperson will be nominated by Minister (HUPA); members and Chairperson of the State TAG will be decided by the Chief Minister of the State/Administrator of the UT concerned and will include two nominations from Ministry of Housing and Urban Poverty Alleviation. Suitable guidelines will be issued by the State/UT concerned for the formulation of City TAGs for NULM.

National Mission Management Unit (NMMU)

NULM will have a Governing Council (GC) chaired by the Minister for Housing and Urban Poverty Alleviation and an Executive Committee (EC) chaired by the Secretary, Housing and Urban Poverty Alleviation. The GC will be the policy-making body setting overall vision and direction to the Mission, consistent with the national objectives. It will lay down priorities and review overall progress and development of the Mission. The composition of the GC will be as follows:

Table 3.8: UPA Administrative Structure

Sl. No.	*Designation*	*Membership*
1.	Minister, Housing and Urban Poverty Alleviation	Chairperson
2-4.	State Ministers of UD/LSG/MA on a rotation basis (x^3) nominated by Chairperson	Member
5.	Member (Urban Development), Planning Commission	Member
6.	Member (Labour and Employment), Planning Commission	Member
7.	Secretary, Urban Development	Member
8.	Secretary, Rural Development	Member
9.	Secretary, Human Resource Development	Member
10.	Secretary, Labour and Employment	Member
11.	Secretary, Micro, Small and Medium Enterprises	Member
12.	Secretary, Women and Child Development	Member
13.	Secretary, Social Justice and Empowerment	Member
14.	Adviser to Prime Minister in charge of Skill Development	Member
15.	Deputy Governor, Reserve Bank of India in charge of Banking Affairs	Member
16.	Chairperson of the Board, National Skills Development Corporation	Member
17-19	Eminent Livelihood Expert/Civil Society/Industry Representative (x^3) nominated by the Chairperson	Members
20.	Secretary (HUPA)	Member-Convenor
21.	Any other member(s) co-opted by the Chairperson	Member(s)

The Executive Committee (EC) will be constituted under the chairperson of Secretary, Ministry of Housing and Urban Poverty Alleviation, GoI, to oversee the activities of the Mission. The EC

Table 3.9: UPA Administrative Structure

Sl. No.	*Designation*	*Membership*
1.	Secretary, Housing and Urban Poverty Alleviation	Chairperson
2.	Secretary, Urban Development or his nominee	Member
3.	Secretary, Financial Services, M/o Finance or his nominee	Member
4.	Deputy Governor, RBI or his nominee	Member
5.	Chairman, Indian Banks Association	Member
6.	Secretary, Rural Development or nominee	Member
7.	Secretary, Labour and Employment or nominee	Member
8.	Secretary, Micro, Small and Medium Enterprises or nominee	Member
9.	Secretary, Department of School Education or nominee	Member
10.	Secretary, Women and Child Development or nominee	Member
11.	Secretary, Social Justice and Empowerment or nominee	Member
12-13.	Senior Advisors (UD) and (LEM), Planning Commission	Members
14.	Mission Director (JNNURM), Ministry of Housing and Urban Poverty Alleviation	Member
15.	Joint Secretary and Financial Adviser, Ministry of Housing and Urban Poverty Alleviation	Member
16-17.	State Secretaries of UD/LSG/ MA on a rotation basis (x^3)	Members
18.	CEO, National Skills Development Corporation	Member
19-20.	Eminent Livelihood Experts/Civil Society Representatives (x^2) as nominated by Minister, Housing and Urban Poverty Alleviation	Members
21-23.	Municipal Commissioners (x^3) on a rotation basis nominated by the Chairperson	Members
24.	Mission Director (NULM, Ministry of Housing and Urban Poverty Alleviation)	Member-Convenor
25.	Any other member(s) co-opted by the Chairperson	Member(s)

will ensure smooth functional linkages between different missions, departments and institutions through its constitution. The Chairperson of the EC may nominate additional members to the Committee as per requirement. The composition of the EC will be as follows:

NULM will be set up as an independent society supported by a 'National Mission Management Unit (NMMU)'. This unit will function under the overall supervision of the Mission Director. The NMMU will support implementation of the National Urban Livelihoods Mission. The Mission Director will be supported by two Directors, 4 Under Secretaries, 5 Section Officers and 6 Assistants, other subordinate staff and a technical support team with at least 10 technical experts.

The NMMU's tasks will be to facilitate the setting up of SMMUs and CMMUs with adequate staffing, provide support in preparing the Perspective Plans (State Urban Poverty Reduction Strategy) and City Livelihood Development Plans, preparation of guidelines under NULM, oversee the implementation of NULM, facilitation of the creating of shelters for urban homeless and liaise with other Missions/Ministries/Departments/Industry associated to explore areas for convergent action at the national, state and city levels.

State Missions Management Unit (SMMU)

The implementation of National Urban Livelihoods Mission at the State level will be managed by a two-tier structure—A Governing Council and an Executive Committee. At the state-level, NULM will also have a Governing Council chaired by the Chief Minister of the State and an Executive Committee chaired by the Chief Secretary of the State.

The composition of the GC will be as follows:

Table 3.10: UPA Administrative Structure

Sl. No.	*Designation*	*Membership*
1.	Chief Minister	Chairperson
2.	Finance Minister	Vice-Chairperson
3.	Minister, Urban Development/LSG/Municipal Affairs/ Administration – in charge of Urban Local Bodies	Member
4.	Minister, Rural Development	Member
5.	Minister, Labour and Employment	Member
6.	Minister, Industry	Member
7.	Minister, Health	Member
8.	Minister, Technical Education	Member
9.	Chief Secretary	Member
10.	State Lead Bank Officer	Member
11.	Representative of Ministry of Housing and Urban Poverty Alleviation, GoI	Member
12-13.	Representative of Urban Local Bodies – Mayors/ Chairpersons (2)	Members
14-16.	Livelihood Experts/Civil Society/Industry Representative (3)	Members
17.	Secretary/Principal Secretary in charge of NULM	Member-Convenor
18.	Any other member(s) co-opted by the Chairperson	Member(s)

Table 3.11: The Composition of the EC will be as follows

Sl. No.	*Designation*	*Membership*
1.	Chief Secretary	Chairperson
2.	Secretary/Principal Secretary i/c of Urban Local Bodies	Member
3.	Secretary/Principal Secretary i/c of Urban Development/Housing	Member
4.	Secretary, Finance	Member
5.	Secretary, Rural Development	Member
6.	Secretary, Labour and Employment	Member
7.	Secretary, Social Welfare	Member
8.	Secretary, Health and Family Welfare	Member
9.	Secretary, Public Works Department	Member
10.	Secretary, Food and Civil Supplies	Member
11.	Secretary Social Justice and Empowerment	Member
12.	Secretary in charge of Primary Education	Member
13-14.	State Lead Bank Officer and Head of another Nationalized Bank	Member
15.	State Representative of RBI	Member
16.	Industry Representative	Member
17-19.	Representative of SHGs/Federations (3)	Members
20.	State Mission Director, NRLM	Member
21.	State Officer in charge of Technical Education/Labour/ Industry	Member
22.	Representative of Ministry of Housing and Urban Poverty Alleviation	Member
23.	State Mission Director, NULM	Member-Convenor
24.	Any other member(s) co-opted by the Chairperson	Member(s)

The projects under SUH would be formulated, constructed and operated by the municipal bodies or other agencies including the private organization identified by the State government or local bodies. Sanction of suitable and viable projects under SUH after appraisal of each project will be done at the level of State EC.

The State Urban Livelihoods Mission (SULM) will be set up as a society and will be supported by a State Mission Management Unit (SMMU) to oversee the implementation of the Mission and other poverty alleviation programmes in the State. The National and the State Missions will have a symbiotic relationship. They will have mutual access to the knowledge and services in the area of urban livelihoods and poverty alleviation.

The SMMU will be headed by a State Mission Director (SMD) who will be assisted by at least 4 Project Officers in charge of skills and livelihood, micro-enterprises, capacity building and finance and administration. The State Mission will have functional autonomy under the overall charge of the Secretary/Principal Secretary concerned for implementing the Mission in the State.

As per the requirements, the State Unit would include expert in the areas of social mobilization, institution development, capacity building and training, microfinance development, livelihoods promotion, skill training and placement in remunerative jobs, gender, communication, MIS monitoring and evaluation, human resource, finance, administration, etc.

The SMMU will have a dedicated MIS Cell to undertake online monitoring. The SMMU will coordinate with programme management units for JNNURM and RAY to ensure convergence of programmes.

The SMMU will have the responsibility to ensure collaboration among various line Departments of the State government to facilitate convergence of activities to derive optimal benefits from NULM and other programmes. It will use the services of national, regional and state resource institutions for the effective implementation of different components of the Mission's programme and will also ensure proper coordination with the city level units of NULM.

Table 3.12: City Mission Management Administrative Structure

Sl. No.	*Designation*	*Membership*
1.	Municipal Commissioner	Chairperson
2.	Officer in charge of NRLM	Member
3.	Officer in charge of Industry	Member
4.	Officer in charge of Modular Employable skills	Member
5.	Chief Medical Officer	Member
6.	District Social Welfare Officer	Member
7.	Senior-most CE/SE/EE of PWD posted at the district	Member
8.	Senior-most district—level officer responsible for primary/secondary education	Member
9.	District Supply Officer	Members
10-11.	Representative of Banks (2)	Members
12-13.	Representative of SHGs/Federations (2)	Members
14.	City Project Officer, NULM	Member-Convenor
15.	Any other member(s) co-opted by the chairperson	Member(s)

City Mission Management Unit (CMMU)

At the city level, NULM will be managed by an Executive Committee chaired by the Municipal Commissioner. The composition of the EC will be as follows:

In addition to livelihood components under NULM, the EC at the city level will be responsible for the planning, implementation and management of facilities created under SUH with the participation of municipal authorities, community representatives, civil society organizations, line departments and elected representatives.

A dedicated unit City Mission Management Unit (CMMU) will be managed by a City Project Officer (CPO). The CPO will be of the rank of a Deputy Municipal Commissioner/Executive Officer specialists in the fields of social mobilization, institution and capacity building, micro-finance, livelihoods/micro-enterprises. In metropolitan cities, the CPO will be assisted by at least two Assistant Project Officers (APO). The functional specialists will be appointed on contractual basis and will undertake activities in the respective fields under the leadership of City Project officer. The CMMU will be linked to the community structures in the cities. The Community Organizers (COs) will be hired by the CMMU to facilitate this linkage. Each CO will cover at least 3,000 urban poor families.

CMMU will be responsible for implementing the Mission's programmes in the city following the NULM guidelines, developing and implementing City/Town Livelihood Development Plan and the administration and finance of NULM in the city.

The MMUs at the State and city levels are envisaged as long-term structures for livelihood and skill development of the urban poor on a continuous basis. Therefore, States will be expected to source human resources for the state and city-level MMIs through dedicated State/Municipal Cadres for Urban Community Development/Poverty Alleviation (created where the same do not exist) who will be supported by experts/professionals on contract basis. Until the formulation and operationalisation of the cadres, funds will be available for various positions for managing NULM on contract basis for a period of five years.

Monitoring and Evaluation

States/UTs will be required to send in Monthly Progress Reports (MPRs)/Quarterly Progress Reports (QPRs) in prescribed formats with regard to targets and achievements. A part from MPRs/QPRs, the Mission Directorate, NULM may prescribe other progress reports as may be considered appropriate from time to time. The States/UTs will establish suitable monitoring mechanisms and monthly reporting from the CMMUs regarding the progress of various components of NULM.

Given the geographic scale and magnitude of the resources and activities to be supported by NULM, a comprehensive and robust IT enabled NULM MIS would be established for tracking of targets and achievements. States/UTs will be required to submit progress reports online.

The monitoring activities will include, but not be limited to, third party evaluation, impact evaluation studies and social audit, etc. The evaluation of the mission will be undertaken during the course of its implementation to effect mid-term correction and align the scheme on the achievement of its key objectives. The cost for these activities will be met under the A & OE component of NULM.

Guidelines for Implementation

The Mission Directorate in the Ministry of Housing and Urban Poverty Alleviation, Government of India will issue a set of detailed operational guidelines from time to time for each component and sub-component of NULM, for effective operationalisation, implementation and monitoring of the Mission.

Conclusion

It is concluded that the Mission Mode approach for the eradication urban poverty may be possible and it is structured in a bottom in processes i.e. Micro-level, meso-level and macro-level and administering them to achieve the objectives through plan development. However, many national level natural hazards may hamper the planning process and development. A strategy of anti-poverty programmes could be implemented, if the people accept them in a right perspective to achieve development.

NOTES

1. Material form the paper prepared by the SNPUPR project for the M/o HUPA in August 2011 to support the Working Groups (PPSU, SNPUPR, 2011).
2. Report of the working group on Urban Poverty, Slums and Service Delivery System, Steering Committee on Urbanization, Planning Commission, New Delhi, 3rd October, 2011, pp. 50 and 51.

4

Environment and Population

A Case Study from India, Andhra Pradesh and Telangana

Smt. Y. Pentamma

Introduction

Environment deals with living organism and essentially has a multidisciplinary approach that presents about an appreciation of global phenomenon and human impact on its integrity. Environmental studies have components that include anthropology, biology (botany and zoology), geography, geology, chemistry, physics, engineering, sociology, health, economics, statistics, computers and philosophy. Rapid economic growth is possible if the resources are utilised optimally. It has been identified that environment is a source and population is a resource to achieve integrated development at various area levels such as world/nation/state or even the district as a micro-level unit below the state level. If planners ignore the optimum utilisation of resource use, sometimes it inevitably leads to environmental degradation which is harmful to human society and qualitative living. In order not to face this situation, planners should plan for sustainable utilization or development, keeping in view the availability of resources on hand.

The 'environment' could be categorized into four types. They are: (i) physical environment, (ii) economic environment, (iii) social environment and (iv) cultural environment.

1. Physical environment essentially has been considered with the existing phenomena of land form structure (e.g. Mountain/plateaus/plain) and its climatic variables such as high, medium and low temperatures, rainfall and cloudiness besides water phenomena leads to total variations within the identified environment and the population.
2. Economic environment deals with economic resources or goods which generate economic development through planning. This essentially deals with agricultural resources and industrial resources which lead to agro-based industrial development.
3. Social environment which is inclusive and deals with social resources or the resources that are used for the development of society over a period of time relating to rural development/urban development/metropolitan development. Here, we consider the resource functioning to different sizes of population and settlements, certainly caters to the needs of the people and the society at large in the name of social advantage by using "social spaces" for social activity.
4. Cultural environment—cultural sites in different geographical regions over a period of time are quite important for development. Heritage is considerably an important factor for development. Spatio-temporal development should be identified within a specified point of time in different geographic regions. Cultural resources are essentially brings glory to the nation if the government will protect them in time for the next generations in the name of "environmental tourism".

Keeping in view of the above situations, it is planned to identify environment and population as a source and resource at different area levels, but it has its positive effects on population (human resource). Sometimes many investigate the hardships and eventually prone to migration of people in new occupations for better livelihoods.

Environment has a multidimensional role to play and population too has a key role to play within the overall environment and population. The incremental role of population has its impact on the socio-economic life of urban population. The increase in population to the total population in between the two census years is dependent on three factors. They are: (1) net increase, (2) internal increase and (3) external increase.

1. Net increase is an increase to the total population of the previous (PO) census year and (PI) within present census years total population (TP).
2. Internal increase is considered as internal growth; and
3. External increase is a factor which is often considered as a migration pull. The increase of population may vary from region to region, state to state or even from nation to nation. The migrants are added up to the total population even it may be during the census year or it may spread over from census to another census year(s). Ultimately, the existing population may need to provide a facility to the existing population. Otherwise, it leads to state of disequilibrium or deficiency and it further leaves an indelible mark on the quality of life, particularly to nation, state or region. United Nations estimates and medium population (United Nations 2001a) shows a world population numbering 2.5 billion in 1950, 6.1 billion in 2000 and 9.3 billion in 2050. It is an important aspect to be considered for the increasing trend of the population and further to identify the resources for future generation at least at the national as well as State level population.

Literature Review

The population in developing countries who live in cities have almost doubled since 1960 (from less than 2.2% to more than 61% to 76%). Urbanization is projected to continue to the next century, by 2030, it is expected that nearly 5 billion (61%) of the world population, 8.1 billion people live in cities. India shares this global trend towards urbanization. India's urban population has doubled from 109 million to 218 million during the last two decades and it is estimated to reach 300 million by 2000 AD. As a consequence, cities are facing the problem of expanding urban slums.

The next half century will be almost as many people added to the world population as the last half century and thereafter, there may be one or two billion more people before growth ceases to halt. Bharat Singh[1] opined that "already densely populated developing countries contribute to over 95 per cent of the population growth and this could lead to environmental deterioration. Developed countries are less densely populated and contribute very little to population growth, however, they cause massive ecological damage by the wasteful, unnecessary and unbalanced consumption and consequences of which could adversely affect both the developed and developing countries". He further opined that "if the current growth rate continues for a few generations more, the carrying capacity of the earth will be greatly exceeded".[2]

N.K. Varma[3] opined that "this urbanization perspective represents a shift in the way population growth has been regarded. During the 1930s and 1940s, a huge widespread fear was that the slow population growth foreseen for the postwar period would not provide sufficient stimulus to the industrial world economy which would lapse back into depression and economic stagnation. Antibiotics, DDT and immunizations, combined with improvements in transportations, communications and food supplies have increased life expectancy by five years each decade and population by more than two per cent per year in the developing world. It is further observed that "population pressure on resources is often the result of restricted access to resources, not of an overall imbalance. Most of the rural population is crowded onto small holdings (less than two hectares) that occupy a small fraction of total agricultural land, often less than 5 per cent. Often times, these small holdings are on erosion prone hillsides with relatively infertile soils or in areas where rainfall is uncertain.[4] It is misleading to describe the resource degradation that results when marginal farmers misuse marginal lands as a consequence of population pressure when in reality it is a consequence of gross inequality in access to resources between the rich and the poor. The influx of sequential and ancillary migrants in urban areas is also a direct repercussion of migration, whether the sex (M/F) adults from rural to urban areas".[5]

Hypothesis: To identify the increase of population, which is described from macro- to micro-data analysis and its impact.

HO

1. The global population has been on an increasing scale.
2. At the macro-level, the population of India too has been on an increasing scale.
3. At the lowest level (state level), the population has also been on an increasing scale.

The above two points (2 and 3) may be examined in the Indian context, including Andhra Pradesh's population from 1971 to to-date besides the projected population for the year 2021.

Problem: The above three points are kept in mind and it is attempted to study and examine the population growth of India in general and Andhra Pradesh State in particular.

Data Analysis

It is seen from Table 4.1 that at the national level, during 1971, the urban population was recorded to a tune of 109.11 million whereas in the respective census years, it has been registered in the following manner. The year 1981 has registered an urban population of 159.46 million and in 1991, it is 217.57 million. It is further observed and examined that the phenomenal increase during 2001 was to a tune of 286.12 million, whereas in 2011, the population in urban areas has increased to 377.11 million. By applying the formula $Dp = (P_1 - P_0)$, wherein P_1 is the present population and P_0 is the past census year population. Stages of increase in population are estimated as DP_1, DP_2, DP_3 and DP_4.

Table 4.1: Urban population in India and Andhra Pradesh—Different census trends

	1971	*1981*	*1991*	*2001*	*2011*	*Estimated population of 2021*
India	109.11	159.46	217.57	286.12	377.11	450.0
Population Mean 1149.37/5	(-) 20.76	(-) 70.41	(-) 12.30	(+) 56.25	(+) 47.24	229.87
Andhra Pradesh	8.40	12.49	17.89	20.81	28.22	40.0
Population Mean 87.81/5	-9.16	-5.07	+0.33	+3.25	+10.66	+17.56

Source: Census of India 2011. Primary census abstract.

Table 4.2 Increase a Decrease of Population

Stage	Year	Population
Stage 1	= 2011	−377.11
	= 2001	(–) 286.12
		DP_1 (+) 90.99
Stage 2	= 2001	286.12
	= 1991	(–) 217.57
		DP_2 (+) 68.55
Stage 3	= 1991	217.57
	= 1981	(–) 159.46
		DP_3 (+) 58.11
Stage 4	= 1981	159.46
	= 1971	(–) 109.11
		DP_4 (+) 50.35

At the national level, four stages of increase of population have been registered. They are presented in Table 4.3 and classified as follows:

Table 4.3: Classification of Increase of Population according to range

1.	Very High	(100-90)
2.	High	(90-70)
3.	Medium	(70-60)
4.	Low	Less than 60

It is observed that five census years were crept into four categories of population sizes, i.e. very high between 100 and 90 million, high between 90 and 70 million. The third and fourth categories follow this order, i.e. medium class spread over 70 to 60 million and above as the low category falls less than 60 million populations.

Gross Observations

1. It is observed that the absolute increase of population dates back from 1971 to 1981 was 50.35 million (stage 4) whereas

the increase has been registered over 1981 was to a tune of 58.11 (stage 3).

2. It is further observed that an increase of 68.55 million from 1991 to 2001 (stage 2). The urban population of India during 2011 was to a tune of 377.11 and the net increase over 2001 is to a tune of 90.39 million populations (stage 1).

It is gratifying to note that the increase of urban population in India is almost swollen to threshold over 1971 and a continuous increase has been registered for a period of 40 years. This macro-level data has been helping us to note and spell out that Malthusian theory of population is almost operational in the Indian environment, particularly the urban population of India.

If we turn to the State level data relating to urban population, it reveals the following facts and facets. By applying the formula, i.e. $DP = (P_1 - P_0)$, wherein P_1 is the present population and P_0 is the past census year population. Stages of increase (DP) in population have been stated as hereunder:

Table 4.4: Net Increase or Net Decrease of Population

Stage 1 = 2011	28.22
= 2001	(–) 20.81
	DP_1 Net increase (+) 7.41
Stage 2 = 2001	20.81
= 1991	(-) 17.89
	DP_2 Net increase (+) 2.92
Stage 3 = 1991	17.89
= 1981	(-) 12.49
	DP_3 Net increase (+) 5.40
Stage 4 = 1981	12.49
= 1971	(–) 8.40
	DP_4 Net increase (+) 4.09

The estimated urban population for 2021 is 40.0 million (Table 4.4) at the State level, also, three stages of the net increase of population has been registered. They are classified and presented in Table 4.5.

Table 4.5: Four stages of Population according to Range

Stage 1	Very High	(10.0-7.0) million	7.41
Stage 2	High	(7.0-4.0) million	5.40
Stage 3	Medium	(4.0-1.0) million	4.09
Stage 4	Low	Less than 1.0 million	

From 1971 to 2011, at the micro-level, it is observed that the urban population has crept into three stages, i.e. very high, high and medium and low stages has not been registered.

Special Observations and Important Points—Andhra Pradesh

If we examine the urban population of Andhra Pradesh during the above census years, the following are the gross observations:

1. It is seen from table 1.1, that the urban population of Andhra Pradesh was to a tune of 8.40 million during 1971 whereas 12.41 million (1981), 17.89 million (1991) and 20.81 (2001) and 28.72 (2011). It can be deduced that the gradual increase of urban population leads to the gradual decrease of comfort due to the non-proliferation (creation) of infrastructural facilities which reflects the quality of life of people at the micro-level.
2. It is further observed that the 1971 urban population of Andhra Pradesh was to a tune of 8.40 million (1971), and it is understood that 'threshold increase' of the urban population that is from 8.40 million to 28.22 million population over a period of 40 years. The influx of sequential and ancillary migrants in urban areas is also the direct repercussions of migration, whether the sex (M/F) adults from rural to urban areas and is considered as a migration for occupation.

Important Points

1. At the micro-level, the population increase has been on a galloping speed (i.e.) from 8.40 million (1971) to 28.22 million in Andhra Pradesh's urban population leaves an indelible mark on social environment i.e. adding to the problem of insufficient infrastructural facilities which reflects on the quality of life.

2. At the national level, the population increase has been on a path of increase or on an increasing trend, i.e. from 109.11 million (1971) and it has been stepped up to a steady increase in urban population growth to a tune of 377.11 million.
3. It is estimated that at the micro-level, the urban population of 2021 would be 40 million and the macro level, it would be @ 450 million.

   "The current population of India is 1.21 billion. The population is expected to grow at the rate of 1.8 to 1.5 per cent per annum by 2030. Therefore, the estimated population of India by 2040 will be in the range of 1.5 to 1.7 billion."

   "The process of urbanization has also become exclusionary in nature as only a few large cities with a strong economic base are also able to raise resources for development, leaving out small and medium towns (Kundu, 2003). India is a 30 per cent urbanised and is expected to reach 40 per cent by 2040."

Urbanisation in Indian cities: As per provisional population of Census 2011, there are 468 cities having population more than 0.1 million.

Keeping in view the above scenario, it is assessed that the increasing population in Indian situation is partly responsible as a causative factor which is termed as 'urban growth' is also equally responsible due to migration or mobility of population and is considered to be almost 'fourfold' as a result of increase of urban population of 1971 urban population to total population.

1. The analysis relating to urban population may reveal further interesting aspects such as decreasing quality of life due to increasing population. It is assessed that the further researches should be useful to the nation/state to take a policy decision by urban governance, for that there is a growing need to undertake further research studies in this direction covering urbanization, migration and slum population and livelihoods for the urban poor.
2. Micro-level surveys have to be conducted in order to identify the reasons for its growth and functioning.

Population and environment have a bearing on macro level structures, and the micro-level study is encouraged at various levels and also to suggest a revised migration policy for the nation as well as for the state, keeping in view of the population growth trend, in-migration and out-migration and so on. It is observed that the impacting parameters for mobility of the population and its focus on the gap and the same may be studied through remote sensing (RS) and GIS methodologies.

Table 4.6: Different administrative units in India—Change of per cent of change over years 2001

Sl. No.	Areas	2001	2011	2001	
1.	Districts	593	640	+47	+7.92
2.	Sub Districts	5463	5924	+461	+8.43
3.	Statutory towns	3799	4041	+242	+6.37
4.	Census towns	1362	3894	+2532	+185.90
5.	No. of Villages	6,38,588	6,40,867	+2279	+0.356

Source: Paper-2 Volume 1 of 2011, Andhra Pradesh.

Table 4.7: Andhra Pradesh: Different administrative units

Sl. No.	Areas	2001	2011	Change in 2001	% of change over 2001
1.	No. of districts	23	23	0	0.0
2.	No. of Sub Districts	1125	1128	+3	0.26
3.	No. of towns	210	353	+143	68.09
4.	No. of Statutory Towns	117	125	+8	6.83
5.	No. of Census towns	93	228	+135	145.16
6.	No. of Villages	28,123	27,800	–323	–1.14

In Table 4.6 different administrative units in India such as no. of districts, sub districts, statutory towns, census towns and no. of villages are presented for two points of time i.e. 2001 and 2011 in order to identify the per cent of change over two periods. It is seen from the table 4.6, that no of districts have been increased to a tune of 47 and their per cent growth is to a tune of 7.92 per cent.

It is observed that no. of sub districts have been on an increasing scale which accounts to a tune of 461 and it works out to 8.43 per cent. The numbers of statutory towns have increased by 242 and the per cent is by 6.37 per cent. Besides the above, census towns have also been increased by 2532 and this increase works out to be 185.90 per cent. It is finally noted that no. of villages have been increased by 2279 and its per cent is to a tune of +0.356. It appears to be insignificant because it is less than one.

In table 4.7, different administrative units have been presented for the years 2001 and 2011, in order to assess the change as well as per cent of change over 2001.

1. It is seen that the total number of districts are 23 and there is no physical change in its structure. Status quo is being maintained
2. No. of sub districts have been on an increase which is grown to a tune of 3 and its per cent is 0.26. It is also insignificant because it is less than one.
3. No. of towns have been increased by 143 and it works out to be 68.09 per cent and no of statutory towns also increased by 8 which works out to 6.83 per cent.
4. No. of census towns are also subjected to change from 93 to 228 and thus the increase is to a tune of 135 and ultimately the per cent works out to 145.16.
5. It is seen that the number of villages were reduced by 323 and it works out to (–) 11.14 per cent. It is further observed that no. of villages might have been clubbed with urban settlements and gained urban status.

Table 4.8: A.P. decadal population growth 2001-2011

Sl. No.	*Persons*	*Rural*	*Urban*	*Total*	*Rural*	*Urban*
1.	8455526	910721	7544805	11.10	1.64	36.26
2.	3982468	282556	3699912	10.34	1.01	34.74
3.	4473058	628165	3544893	11.87	2.29	37.63

Source: Ibid.

A.P. decadal growth in the year 2011 is presented in Table 4.8. Total number of persons, male and female, both for rural and urban have been presented in Table 4.8. The gross observations are as follows:

1. Total urban population is on an increasing scale by 36.26 per cent, where as rural works out to a tune of 1.64 per

cent and the combined per cent to total population is to a tune of 11.10 per cent.

2. It is seen from the table that male urban population is grown to a tune of 34.74 per cent where as female urban population has surpassed even the total urban share by 37.63 per cent. It is highest in its structural composition in the total urban share of population. Decadal growth rate over 2001 and the present census year is presented in Table 4.9.

Table 4.9: Decadal growth rate 2001-2011—Urban persons in Andhra Pradesh

Sl. No.	Name of the District	Per cent	Category
	Telangana		
1.	Rangareddy	92.19	A – High
2.	Medak	89.85	
3.	YSR Kadapa	67.37	
4.	Mahabubnagar	63.30	
5.	Warangal	60.16	B – Medium
6.	Srikakulam	56.59	
7.	Nalagonda	52.94	
8.	Chittoor	51.52	
9.	Karimnagar	46.47	
10.	SPSR Nellore	43.95	
11.	Prakasam	41.67	
12.	Kurnool	39.91	
13.	Nizamabad	38.89	
14.	Krishna	38.25	C – Low
	Andhra Pradesh	36.26	
15.	Visakhapatnam	33.09	
16.	Guntur	28.85	
17.	Khammam	28.35	
18.	Anantapur	24.73	
19.	Vizianagaram	18.92	
20.	Adilabad	14.82	
21.	East Godavari	14.13	D – Very low
22.	West Godavari	7.68	
23.	Hyderabad	4.71	

A comparative status of Decadal growth rate over 2001 and the present census year has been presented in Table 4.9. The observations are as follows:

1. It is noticed that Rangareddy district has gained by 92.19 per cent and the lowest also has been recorded to a tune of 4.71 per cent. These two are located in Telangana region of former Andhra Pradesh.
2. It is observed that Medak district has gained 89.85 per cent whereas YSR Kadapa district has registered a change to a tune of 67.37 per cent and it is located in Rayalaseema region of Andhra Pradesh followed by two Telangana districts, Mahabubnagar and Warangal, have registered with 63.30 and 60.16 per cent of decadal growth.
3. By applying this formula in order to identify the maximum and minimum decadal growth in Andhra Pradesh, the following formula has been adopted. $\left\{\frac{p+q}{p-q}\right\}$ whereas 'p' is the decadal growth rate (highest percentage figure) and 'q' is the lowest decadal growth rate (by district) have been worked out. They are:
   (i) Rangareddy with 92.19 per cent and the lowest being Hyderabad 4.71 per cent.
   By applying this formula, the equation may be written as:
   $$\left(\frac{p+q}{p-q}\right)$$
   Here the p is 92.19 per cent and q is 4.71 per cent
   $$\frac{92.19+4.71}{92.19-4.71}=\frac{96}{87.48} = 1.107699.$$
   It is observed that the maximum and minimum variability has been worked out and it is 1.107699 and almost it falls within (+1.1 to –1.1) range.
   (ii) It is further observed that all the districts have fallen in 4 different groups with A, B, C, and D, grade, Rangareddy and Medak have fallen in A grade with the above 100-75 per cent, whereas 6 districts have fallen between 75-50 per cent. They are YSR Kadapa, Mahabubnagar, Warangal, Srikakulam, Nalgonda and Chittoor. Their decadal percentage growth could be seen from Table 4.9.

(iii) It is observed that from 50-25 per cent range, almost 10 districts have fallen, it is attributed that almost 45 per cent of the total districts have fallen in category 'C'.

(iv) It is finally noted that 'D' grade category gains 6 districts. They are: (1) Anantapur, (2) Vizianagaram, (3) Adilabad, (4) East Godavari, (5) West Godavari, and (6) Hyderabad. This study fills the gap by identifying and recognizing the need to undertake a study on spatial distribution of population growth in Andhra Pradesh, further to identify the indepth causes for its variations and find solutions for the typical problems which they have been facing.

Table 4.10: Micro-population Growth: Quick estimates of population of Telangana State

Sl. No.	*Name of the district*	*Quick Estimates*	*2011 population*	*increase (+) (-) Decrease*
		40,11,997	39,20,750	
1.	Adilabad	27,92,242	27,37,738	+54,504
2.	Nizamabad	24,45,727	28,52,073	-1,06,346
3.	Karimnagar	38,05,177	38,11,738	-6,561
4.	Medak	29,56,309	30,31,877	-75,568
5.	Mahabubnagar	42,14,484	40,42,191	+1,72,293
6.	Nalgonda	35,55,452	24,83,648	+71,804
7.	Warangal	36,19,768	35,22,644	+97,064
8.	Khammam	26,08,188	27,98,214	-1,90,026
9.	Hyderabad & Rangareddy	1,01,10,689	93,06,634	+8,04,055
	Total	3,61,07,976	3,52,86,757	+8,21,219

Source: Eenadu, Monday, September 22, 2014.

Observations

1. It is seen from Table 4.10, quick estimates of population of Telangana region and if we compare the quick estimates with 2011 population, it is observed that there is a total increase of 8,21,219 over 2011 population for the entire former Telangana region of Andhra Pradesh.
2. It is observed that six districts of Telangana State are on an increasing trend in population. They are: (1) Adilabad,

(2) Mahabubnagar, (3) Nalgonda, (4) Warangal, (5) Hyderabad and (6) Rangareddy.

3. It is further observed that the remaining districts of Telangana region are on a decreasing state of population. They are: (1) Nizamabad, (2) Karimnagar, (3) Medak and Khammam, By applying this formula, $\frac{p \times t}{t}$ where p is population and t is time to identify and estimate population for 2021. It is presented in the column of table 4.10.
4. It is important to note that political factor is also responsible for its decrease of population, i.e. districts of Telangana formed separately as statehood from Andhra Pradesh is one of the factor and also it is attributed that the inundated 7 mandals of Khammam district were added with a total of 211 to Andhra Pradesh State. A total of 1,16,796 persons were in former Telangna region are now added to Andhra Pradesh State.
5. Due to administrative constraints, Hyderabad and Rangareddy districts were shown in the metropolitan region GHMC (Greater Hyderabad Metropolitan Corporation) i.e. extension of Urban Areas.
6. It is further observed that Patancheru division has shown in GHMC.

Estimates of Population for 2021

The increase of population of three years has been multiplied by ten then it is divided by 3, gives cumulative increase or decrease for ten years i.e. $\frac{p \times t}{t}$. Here if we examine four district total comes to a total of 34,24,755 person whereas in other districts, the total comes to a tune of 47,99,314, the net population comes to a figure i.e. (+) 13,74,559 persons. Finally, it has been identified through migration, the population is on an increasing scale and it is added to future population.

Observations

1. It is understood from the above Table 4.11 the integrated

Table 4.11: Integrated survey on family size-distribution—Telangana region

Sl. No.	*Name of the district*	*Quick survey estimates*	*2011 population*	*increase (+)*
1.	Adilabad	8,28,795	6,51,770	1,77,025
2.	Nizamabad	7,12,160	5,90,733	1,21,427
3.	Karimnagar	12,35,853	9,80,739	2,55,114
4.	Medak	8,50,860	6,66,764	1,84,096
5.	Mahabubnagar	9,85,557	8,73,859	1,11,698
6.	Nalgonda	11,33,717	8,75,432	2,58,285
7.	Warangal	11,28,407	8,88,553	2,39,854
8.	Khammam	8,56,586	7,47,586	1,09,000
9.	Hyderabad & Rangareddy	28,50,268	21,45,226	7,05,042
	Total	1,05,82,203	84,20,662	21,61,541

Source: Eenadu, 22nd September, 2014, Eenadu.

survey of family size distribution in Telangana State that number of families have increased over 2011 population.

2. The increase in total population is slightly higher.
3. Over a period of three years, an increase has been registered which is to a tune of 8.2 lakh families.
4. A rapid decrease of population in 4 districts of the entire region of Telangana is observed and there is every need to identify the reasons for the same.
5. It is finally identified that the increase of population is attributed that it is due to migration particularly from Seema Andhra as well from other states of India is the cumulative factor.

Rural urban migration forms a part of internal migration and inter-State migration forms a part of external migration which adds to the total population of Hyderabad Metropolitan population since 1961 to 2011. It is seen from Table 4.12 that since 1961 the migration pull is on an increasing scale and Telangana region has no exception to it. Major contributions of population of such is from Seema Andhras and the external also is population is from other States. Six census years over a period of 60 years, Seema Andhra contributes to a total of 58.78 per cent whereas other States contribution as

Table 4.12: Telangana Region—Migrations

Sl. No.	Year	Source Andhra	Percentage	Other States	Percentage	Total Population
1.	1961	3,02,540	55.22	2,45,337	44.70	5,47,877
2.	1971	3,76,466	55.22	3,05,285	44.78	6,81,751
3.	1981	4,80,228	55.20	3,89,607	44.80	8,69,835
4.	1991	7,06,031	60.50	4,60,907	39.50	11,66,938
5.	2001	8,65,169	63.30	5,01,019	36.68	13,66,188
6.	2011	9,84,501	63.26	5,71,645	36.74	15,56,146
	Total	37,14,935	60.02	24,73,800	39.98	61,88,735

Source: Sakshi, Rashtreeyam, p.10; Hyderabad Friday, September 26, 2014.

migration has grown to 41.72 per cent. Migration as well as natural increase (i.e. No. of Births—No. of Deaths = Natural Net Increase) has an impact on Hyderabad Urban Metropolitan Region. It is attributed that metropolises are magnetic centres to attract population from different districts not only due to the internal pull but also the external population has to be considered as an external pull factor to the increase of total population. We conclude that total population means the net increase of population besides the two dominant pulls of internal and external forces, finally adds to final population figures.

Urbanisation Scenario in India

"India is largely a rural country with about 73 per cent of its population living in rural villages. The growth of urban population as well as the pace of urbanization has been generally slow compared to most of the other African countries. Recent urban population rose from 17.3 per cent in 1951 to a mere 25.7 per cent in 1991. An anlaysis of the growth rate of urban population in India in 1981-1991 indicates that 58 per cent of this growth was due to natural increase (births minus deaths) and 42 per cent due to rural-urban migration. It may be understood that though urban population in India may be only 26 per cent, this seemingly low percentage is a large population, number wise. Therefore, quality of life in urban areas means the lives of large number of people. Therefore, this population groups requires urgent consideration".[6]

In metropolitan and mega cities, have also been experiencing the main problem. These cities are presenting urban slums enriched with urban poverty who are living below the poverty line (BPL). It is a never ending process and it could be seen from Figure 4.1. It is seen from the figure that natural increase (i.e. births—deaths = net increase adds to total population (effect) with 52 per cent, besides this, rural migration (from rural to urban) almost it is grown to a tune of 48 per cent (according to one study). This is the second stage. The third stage is efforts. The urban governance has to take necessary steps to activate them through their constant efforts totally for new ventures (micro-enterprises).

The above efforts may yield fruits over a period of time and present a positive change in the socio-economic life of the people living in urban slum environment. This State and status of study is termed as "impact study".

Vision and Mission: Never ending process model: The vision and mission is necessary to curb urban poverty through UPA programmes.

Vision: The vision of the nation is to generate employment opportunities and also disseminate knowledge through skills through a harmonious blend of science and technology and to serve the society by developing themselves as well as to others with human sensitiveness, besides changing the environment. Central to this vision, is a constant and concerned efforts with commitment to regional and national development through plans for development (nation/state/region).

Mission

1. To identify, recognise and improve the skills of people to further develop human resources.
2. To cultivate collectivism, (mission) for development and also eliminate/eradicate urban poverty environment through urban spatial planning for infra development in order to achieve quality (norms) of life in an urban environment. It is seen from six stages environment Figure 4.1.

Six staged work is examined. They are: (1) Population, (2) Migration, (3) Efforts, (4) Activation, and (5) Effects; The five stages will present a changed view in total environment and (6) Positive change. It is examined through the following model to handle urban poverty as well as urban slum improvement in the total framework of increase of population in an environment. The most important problems are: (1) Slum Population, and (2) Urban Poverty. Through these programmes only by governance, it is possible to achieve human development in a changing environment and it is a Never Ending Process.

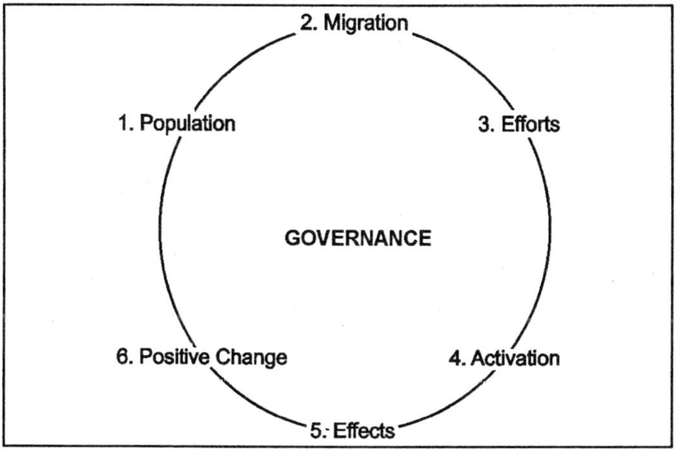

Fig. 4.1: Changing Environment and Never Ending Process

Conclusion

1. If we examine Census of India 2011, provisional population totals and also population with decadal growth rate by residue persons, there is a growing need to examine the micro-level data i.e. sub-units of Andhra Pradesh in order to identify and recognise the causes for its variations in general and income generating population on the other end.
2. Further, it has been identified that there is every need to know the trend in total population, rural population and urban population by district or even in small units in order to recognise a definite pattern in the composition and structure which helps the policy makers to identify the norms for a development plan.
3. GIS mapping is a tool to identify and plan health care facilities in Andhra Pradesh, keeping in view of the mounting growth of population, as health is a key factor

for human growth to generate human power for growth, etc.

NOTES

1. Dr. Bharat Singh "Population and Urbanization: Changing Perspectives, Aarti Prakasan, New Delhi, 2001, p. 1.
2. *Ibid.*, p. 76.
3. N.K. Varma, "Population, Poverty and Employment", Published by Mahveer & Sons, New Delhi, 2006, p. 27.
4. *Ibid.*, p. 18.
5. Jabir Hasan Khan, Samshad and Tarique Hasan, "Determinates of Rural-Urban Migration of Male population in India", *Annuals*, 31, Vol. 1, June, 2011, p. 57.
6. Subha Singh "Urbanization—An emerging humanitarian disaster in *Concepts in Urbanization*, Published, ABD Publishers, Jaipur, pp. 166-167, 2014.

5

Urban Poverty Alleviation: An Environmental Impact Assessment

A Methodological Perspective

T. Aishwarya

Introduction

In an Urban environment, Urban Spaces/Places are considered as important focal points to generate growth in the field of urban economy and urban processes. These Urban Spaces/Places vary from one to another genetically besides its potential, socio-economic, cultural and even political aspects have their impact on human life. 'Urban Environment' presents as a system in a total system and it is treated as a system within the systems which could be identified by different factors such as its growth and interaction of nearby settlements with the main settlement/settlement system over space in spatial functioning also. Environmental geographical studies have channeled into sub-systems. They are classified as follows: (1) Evolution of urban and environmental systems, (2) Functional and administrative classification, (3) Critical study of urban fringe, (4) Urban and Environmental ecology, (5) Demography and occupational structures are combined with urban spatial inequalities, and (6) Urbanization and Methodological dimensions including applied urban environmental systems.

Methodology for urban studies was developed by many geographers, economists, sociologists, demographers and practitioners of public administration and public policy for its design and implementation. Land transformation in relation to distance in developing an urban environment in such a way that, "Urbanization process took off in developing countries in a highway but it is significantly different from the developed countries because of inherent social-economic and environmental differences. They spread concern in these countries regarding the expansion and land reorganizations in and around urban centres".

Keeping in view of the urban and environmental status, structural studies and scenarios that environment and poverty have an active, reactive and interactive roles in the spatial distribution of Topological urban environmental phenomena relating to urban slums, urban poverty and the poverty estimates are equally important dimensions in order to identify and recognize as a need to pay special attention by governance through their policies and programmes for augmenting planned development over a period of time. The present study relates to urban environmental studies, urban poverty and the poverty estimates besides urban poverty alleviation programmes with a list of potential areas of research.

A detailed account of poverty therefore relates to: (1) Urban process and economic growth; (2) The proportional growth of total population composition (the incremental growth over a period of time) turns to enhance poverty; (3) Poverty and its geographic variations and estimates of poverty ratio of the national level (from past to the present period of time) including official estimates; and (4) Percentage of people living below the poverty line in India besides total poverty ratio and poverty reduction at the state are presented. It has been identified that urban poverty alleviation programmes and its effect on people and administrative units have a positive impact and reduce the poverty or a bearing for achieving economic sustainability including identified vulnerabilities.

Poverty: An Overview

"Poverty has a multi-dimensional phenomenon such as, minimum standard of living that is to say that people do not have the basic minimum necessities of life". If we analyze the same (i.e.) when people don't get basic needs like, food, clothing and shelter, they are said to be living below the subsistence level and suffering from poverty. When a large section of people in a geographic region live in such miserable conditions, the region/nation had registered mass poverty.

The 'Poverty' concepts differ from region to region or country to country depending upon the country's stages of economic development. While poverty is defined with reference to a reasonable standard of living in developed countries, it is defined with reference to a minimum lower standard living in developing countries like India.

According to the Government of India, economic survey 2001-02, "a high poverty level is characterized by a poor quality of life, deprivation of minimum needs, malnutrition, illiteracy and low human resource development".[1]

Genesis of Poverty

The genesis of poverty has been germinated from three important areas such as: (1) Social inequality, (2) Economic inequality, and (3) Political inequality. It is seen from the following.

G.P = Social inequality + Economic inequality + Political inequality (Genesis of Poverty)

To attain equity the bridging word is justice (i.e.) Social justice; Economic justice and Political justice. Social and Economic inequality is seen when there's absence of richness in (i.e.) (1) Poor in Resources (P.R.), (2) Economic productivity (E.P.), (3) Technology (T) For example a country is poor in resources, but occupies good position even among the other nations (i.e.) Japan with better technology occupies good position. It is written as.

$$D = E.P + Tech - P.R$$

Income-calories-food items – Deprived off setting them.

(1) Life expectancy, (2) Lack of literacy, (3) Long term unemployment Heath care, Education and nutrition may also present poverty in some cases for example.

"Many of the poor are found to dwell in areas suffering from environmental degradation which has resulted chiefly from expanding population pressure and adverse affects of traditional growth strategies" (Clem Tisdell).[2]

The conclusions of various studies arrived at are different because they have adopted different methodologies to reach their estimates. However, there is a consensus on same points. Firstly, poverty in urban area is largely the result of the overflow of the rural poor into the urban areas. Secondly, the incidence of poverty is the greatest among small farmers and landless workers in rural areas. To antidote the above situation, there is every need to introduce the Poverty Alleviation Programmes, these may to some extent solve the poverty partly but not completely. The 'Poverty' is the same whether it is urban rural poverty.

World Development Report (WDR)

The World Bank's World Development Report (WDR) for 1990 (World Bank,1990) with poverty as it's thematic focus, made a bold attempt to provide a grand, unified and general theory of poverty reduction, a replicable model in its own terms, partly because of which it came under a great deal of criticism from certain quarters during its 'Public defense'. However, the World Bank—Since 12 years down the line—had this to say about poverty reduction, "There is no blue print for building a poverty reduction strategy; rather the process should reflect specific circumstances and characteristics. Further, the multi-dimensional nature of poverty (low income, poor health and education, gender insecurity, powerlessness etc.) needs to be carefully considered: (World Bank, 2002).

A number of focal points of research have been identified. They are:

1. How to set in motion mechanisms for community participation and collaborative activities to understand the specific needs of the community in the process of design of anti-poverty programmes and projects.
2. Methodology of improving channels and levels of communication between community and development agencies/government officials.
3. Creation of feed-back mechanisms on the basis of local perspectives for shaping of projects.
4. Mutual identification of ways to improve and create economic and social responsibilities.

5. How, Why and effective community participation helps create successful project intervention.
6. Identification of community—level strengths and weaknesses.
7. Involvement of local leaders and entrepreneurs for human resource development.
8. Identification of appropriate end—objectives, such as, equitable access to resources, services and opportunities, particularly marginalized communities.
9. Implementation process to be based on local-level coordinating agencies.
10. Proper matching and dialogue between local/community participation/institutions and policy/regulatory frame work."[3]

Studies at the meso- and micro-levels seek to shed light on casual factors impacting on chronic poverty and which have been able to identify several economic, social, political and environmental factors that have a crucial bearing on chronic poverty (Human and Shepherd, 2001).

Studies at the national level show that the descent into poverty is associated with life cycle changes, demographic characteristics, and human capital indicators, common shocks as well as idiosyncratic shocks, social exclusion etc. (Baulch and McCullchao, 2001, Jalan & Raviallion, 2000; Sen, 2003; Bhide and Mehta, 2004).

Urban Sprawl and Sustainable Development

It is observed that better living environment or calm and peaceful life in the peripheral areas, decaying of central areas; cheaper land and housing cost in the suburban; weak administrative controls or less restrictions in comparison to cities, increase in disposable income, poor regional planning; upcoming of economic activities due to foreign investment etc. are some of the factors which support urban sprawl. Such areas, generally, do not have access to or one devoid of physical and social infrastructure provided and maintained by the city government".[4]

They opined that, "it is the area having mixed characteristics of rural and urban land use because of spread of cities due to various push and pull factors".[5]

D. Rajasekhar[6] (S.H.G.)

Self-Help Groups (S.H.G.) has presented a detailed study entitled, "Does good governance work for poverty reduction at the ground level? A study of Self-Help Groups in Karnataka and Madhya Pradesh" by the author analysed that poverty in India has a strong gender dimension. In order to reduce poverty, interventions should aim not only at improvement of the material conditions of women but also lead to their empowerment. The government has been formulating and implementing policies and programmes during the post-independence period for development and empowerment of poor women. The study further opined that SHG's are considered to be having great potential in building social capital and promoting collective action and achieving equitable, effective and sustainable delivery of financial and other development services to the poor women. This helped the government to formulate programmes, for women's development and empowerment through SHG's since1990's. The programmes adopted the strategy of micro-finance as an instrument of development and empowerment of women. The assignment of functions to multiple agencies reflects the global and Indian thinking on promoting good governance in poverty reduction programmes.

Urbanization and Economic Growth

The current population of India is 1.21 billion. The population is expected to grow at the rate of 1.8-1.5 per cent per annum by 2030. Therefore, the estimated population of India by 2040 will be in the range of 1.5-1.7 billion.

Where as income growth and incidence of poverty have been extremely uneven across States, a slowing down in the rate of urbanization and concentrations of demographic growth in developed states seem to be logical outcome. The process of urbanization has also become exclusionary in nature, as only a few large cities with a strong economic base are able to raise resources for development, leaving small and medium towns (in the Lurch & Kundu, 2003). India is 30 per cent urbanized and is expected to reach 40 per cent by 2040".[7]

Any State or nation has to plan for balanced development taking urbanization activity and economic functions to help to generate growth. Thus, the government should have to take necessary steps to augment economic activities by involving rural migrants who have stepped into urban spaces and their potential should be used systematically by providing skill training for employment in urban areas.

Hypothesis

1. The city size increases, share of population living in slums also increases.
2. The share of urban poverty decreases with an increase of Urban Poverty Alleviation Programmes (Impact Analysis).

Urban Poverty is a major problem and many Urban and Metropolises have been facing the problem as a result of rural-urban migration, Nick Devas[8] has identified that crude statistics are not available for Urban Poverty. The United Nations Human Settlements Programme (UN-Habitat) (UNCHS, 1996) based on country studies suggests, that between a third and a half of the Urban Population could be regarded as living in Poverty. That would suggest a figure between 700 million and 1 billion in 2000. In terms of trends, there is some evidence to suggest that the proportion of the Urban Population in Poverty declined during the 1970's and 1980's, at least in Asia (Pernia,1994) although the absolute numbers living in poverty did not decrease (and in many cases went up) as a result of urban population growth. More recently, the proportion of the Urban Population living in Poverty has probably been increasing, with the absolute numbers in poverty increasing substantially, as a result of structured adjustment and the economic downturn in Asia.

Further, observed that, "even where the percentage of the urban population below the poverty line has fallen significantly the numbers of poverty can increase and increase substantially. This encapsulates the problem for governments, even where they are successful in promoting economic growth and implementing policies which enable the poor to escape poverty, in immigration of rural poor continues to add the numbers of the poor in cities Indeed, the greater the success of the cities in dealing with poverty, the more attractive these places become for the rural to migrate for the rural poor to migrate.

Research among the urban poor has demonstrated the complex arrangements and networks which those in poverty use in order to survive. These networks often cross the Urban Rural divide. A useful Analytical approach here is the assets-vulnerability framework (Moser, 1998, Rakodi, 1999). This identifies the Various forms of 'Capital'—Natural, Physical, financial and Social—which the poor make use of in maintaining their livelihoods, and the ways in which these forms of capital are Vulnerable to risks and shocks. The framework enables an analysis to be made of how assets can be increased and vulnerability reduced".

Analytical View

Bhalla has identified that, "A considerable fraction of this agrarian work force also ends up operating very small and fragmented land holdings with widespread under employment and low labour productivity; degradation of land and water resources may only worsen the situation. It should therefore come as no surprise that a substantial proportion of those engaged in agriculture in India do not wish to continue with farming as their primary sources of revenue (Bhalla, 2006). This is a glaring example of what could be termed "truncated pattern of sectored shift" where in a large division of the rural population is stuck between stagnant agricultural opportunities and inadequate demands for higher quality employment in urban areas. The poor, especially in rural environments, thus continue to depend considerable on natural resources to sustain their basic livelihoods."[9] As a result, the rural population with less capabilities, capacities and caliber were driven out from rural areas and were forcibly made to enter into a new urban environment apart from metro/mega urban environment where in urban slums are visible.

Further, it has been identified that, more than 40 per cent of population lives in poverty, as per international norm of less than $1.25 a day. Long-term migration is a limited option for most people in rural areas given the high cost of migration and a dearth of job opportunities in the non-form sectors. Circular migration for casual work remains the main stay for substantial fraction of the rural population".

Micro-Regional Planning

Micro-regional planning has a holistic approach that goes far beyond conventional service delivery by sector agencies. Development should be multi-sectoral and holistic in character. A region (Urban slum) is complicated and complex web with a large number of inter-related problems that can only be solved by an integrated approach. India does not only need a persistent high growth rate of its GDP, but the fruits of growth must reach to every section of the society and to every nook and corner of India.

Inclusive growth instead of growth alone has been used for the first time in eleventh five year plan. The Planning Commission has shifted its focus from time to time from highly centralized to the indicative, sectoral perspective plan approach and integrate it with planning from below because the problems of specific regional (slum) and much too complex to allow for a simple patent remedy, 73rd and 74th amendments are an example to strengthen the planning at gross roots level".[10] "Sustainable development is concerned with the continued existence and well-being of human kind and that of environment. However, in seeking harmony between these two requirements there remains a gulf between environmentalists, whose aim is to protect natural environment from destruction or deterioration, and those whose concerns include reducing environmental hazards for human populations and promoting environmental justice for those lacking healthy environment and an adequate natural resource base for their livelihoods".[11]

Governance

Directive Principles of State Policy: These Principles whether form part of our Constitution (Part IV). "Fundamental Rights and Directive Principles leave no doubt about the concern and commitment of the Constitution to the rights of the citizens to enjoy social security. The social security that is envisaged is not only against aggression and violation of sovereignty by other countries, but also security against deprivation. The concept of social security and the commitment to social security are thus implicit in the Constitution. The judgment of the Supreme Court that clearly declares the right to life includes the right to livelihood which should remove any doubt about the national commitment to social security. The right to livelihood includes the right to work, and the right to education that equips us with the skills that we need for employment as well as the ability to fulfill one's civic and social responsibilities".[12]

As per the directive principles of state policy as well as fundamental rights, besides the pronouncements of Supreme Court Judgments, it makes a way forward for people to acquire the required skills which are to be provided by the government and ultimately makes people to secure employment without any hindrance. The Urban Povertical People should have to be covered with Social Security in reaching the equity on social and economic front with their counter parts wherever they are living in the hierarchy of Cities, Metro cities, Mega cities or towns in India.

Total and Slum Population: (Stochastic increase in Population)

A significant proportion of Urban Population in Indian cities remains outside the formal planning process. People living in informal settlements dependent on informal economy for survival in the city are an integral part of Indian cities. As observed earlier the share of slum population in selected cities in India has increased in proportion to the city size increases as we can see from the following table.[13]

It is seen form table that the total population has been on an increasing scale and the slum population also increases with percentage of slum population to total population.

Total and slum population in million plus cities in India, Census, 2001, is presented in Table 5.1. It is seen form the table that 10 cities are categorized as million plus cities. They are: (1) Greater Mumbai, (2) Delhi Metropolitan Corporation, (3) Kolkata, (4) Bangalore, (5) Chennai, (6) Ahmedabad, (7) Hyderabad, (8) Kanpur, (9) Pune, and (10) Surat.

(1) It is observed that Greater Mumbai contributes highest population in both ways (i.e.) the total population as well as slum population with 54.06 per cent of slum population to total population.
(2) Delhi Metropolitan Corporation secures second place next to Mumbai with 98,79,000 total population with 1851000

Table 5.1: Total and Slum Population in Million Plus cities in India Census 2001

Sl. No.	*Million Plus Cities*	*Total Population (in '0000)*	*Slum Population (in '0000)*	*Percentage of Slum to Total Population*
1.	Greater Mumbai	11,978	6,475	54.06
2.	Delhi M. Corp	9,879	1,851	18.74
3.	Kolkata	4,573	1,485	32.48
4.	Bangalore	4,301	431	10.02
5.	Chennai	4,344	820	18.88
6.	Ahmedabad	3,637	474	13.46
7.	Hyderabad	3,520	627	17.23
8.	Kanpur	2,551	368	14.42
9.	Pune	2,538	492	19.39
10.	Surat	2,433	508	20.89
	All India	73,346	17,697	24.13

slum population, attain 18.74 per cent of slum population to the total population.

(3) It is further examined that Kolkata and Mumbai exceeds the all India figure 24.13. Whereas, other cities are placed below the all India figure. It is attributed that rural urban migration is the causative factor with its highest contribution. In south India, Chennai and Hyderabad occupy first and second place both in total population as well as the share of slum population. Their contributions are to a tune of 18.88 per cent and 17.23 per cent respectively. This migration processes further strains the respective states to plan for anti-poverty programmes.

(4) The patterns of development in Indian mega cities are an amalgam of planned and organic (Self-organizing) growth.

Survival compulsions may force poor population to evolve as self-organized systems. These systems rest on the innovative skills of people struggling to survive in a hostile environment and meet their mobility and accessibility needs. Housing, employment and transport strategies adopted by this section of the society are often termed as informal housing, informal employment and informal transport.

Many of the economic development programmes completely miss the link between housing location, livelihoods of the poor and transport. Access to affordable transport is one of the most important factors in determining livelihoods for the urban poor.

Some of the urban poor have to make a different trade-off by accepting long travel distances form a peripheral location in order to obtain affordable but secure housing".[14]

Eight Basic Features of Urban Poverty in India

'Urban Poverty' reveals that the problems that are being faced by the poor in small urban areas are different from that of large cities. The Urban Poverty manifests in the form of inadequate provision of housing and shelter, water, sanitation, health, education, social security and livelihoods along with special needs of vulnerable groups like women, children, differently abled and aged people.

Even when segments of the urban population are not income poor, they face deprivation in terms of lack of access to sanitary living conditions, and their well being is hampered by discrimination, social exclusion, crime, and violence, insecurity of tenure, hazardous environmental conditions and lack of voice in governance. These deprivations are often cumulative in nature (i.e.) one dimension of poverty is often the cause of or contribution to another dimension.

Eight Points

Informalization

Informalization of urban market: The Urban Poor working in informal sector often face relatively poor working conditions, lack of social insurance, job insecurity and are more prone to economic shocks no work-no-wages.

Migration Patterns

Migration patterns among the migrants in the urban areas, nearly 59 per cent migrated from rural areas and 41 per cent from urban areas. Employment and livelihoods of the high numbers of male migrants, living in temporary shelters in the labour force is a common future of urban life.

Poor Living Conditions

In many urban areas, a large number of people live in cramped, over-crowded and often unsanitary conditions especially in slums which are prone to environmental natural hazards such as (floods, landslides etc.) and man-made disasters like (e.g. fire, accidents, pollution etc).

Problem of Housing

Most of the urban poor live in deplorable housing conditions with high implicit and explicit costs of housing. The census, 2011 data reveals that 3.1 per cent of the urban population does not have an exclusive room for living, while 32.1 per cent live in one room house. Another problem faced by urban poor is the lack of entitlements on property and assets. There are also houseless people without any address. This number and proportion is difficult to estimate.

Lack of Access to Education

The poor face a lack of access to quality education which results in higher proportions of the monthly income of the urban poor being spent on basic education for their children.

Lack of Access to Health Care

Urban slums and Low Income Settlements [LIS] are faced with a multitude of health problems. Increasing number of communicable and non-communicable diseases, malnutrition among children, inadequate water and sanitation facilities etc. add to poor health conditions of the urban people about 29.4 per cent of the urban population does not have access to tap water and 18.6 per cent have no latrine facility within the house.

Lack of Access to Financial Services

The standard of living and lack of basic services is aggravated by the limited access to financial services. The urban poor work largely in the unorganized sector, which has not received priority from the formal financial sector in the absence of secured income, assets and lack of credit history.

Lack of Social Safety Nets

In the Urban areas, some slums residents live in clearly defined occupational or caste based groupings, however most of them do not have clearly defined safety nets. The social fabric of the urban poor is strained as support from family, community based networks and safety nets are limited where as in the rural areas such social networks do exist and provide the necessary support. This social exclusion restricts people from participating on fair terms in local and national social life.[15]

Poverty Ratio at the National Level

Table 5.2: Population below Poverty line: Poverty Ratio (%)

Sl. No.	Year	Rural	Urban	All India
1.	1973-74	56.4	49.0	54.9
2.	1977-78	53.1	45.2	51.3
3.	1983-84	45.7	40.8	44.5
4.	1987-88	39.1	38.2	38.9
5.	1993-1994	37.3	32.4	36.6
6.	1999-2000	27.1	23.6	26.1
7.	2004-2005	28.3	25.7	27.5

Source 15: Ministry of Housing and Urban Poverty Alleviation G.o.I. compendium on Urban Poverty and Urban Slums, 2006.

Source 16: Household consumption survey, NSSO, G.o.I., Various Rounds.

Table 5.3: Estimates of poverty in India in 1999-2000

Sl. No.		All India	Rural	Urban
1.	Official Estimates	26.1	27.1	23.6
2.	Angus Deaton	28.8	30.2	24.7
3.	Sundaram & Tendulkar	28.0	—	—
4.	Datta & Revallion	34.0	—	—
5.	Surjit Bhella	15.0	—	—

Source: Compiled by the Author.

Poverty Ratio's at the National Level

Poverty Ratio at the National level both for rural, Urban and All India have been presented in table 5.2. The following are the gross observations:

1. It is seen from Table 5.2 that during 1973-74, rural poverty ratio per cent was to a tune of 56.4 and urban poverty ratio was 49.0 and the National figure was 54.9 per cent and the rural population below poverty line stood at 56.4 per cent thus is above the National figure by 2 per cent.
2. It is examined that the population below the poverty-line and it was grown to a tune of 45.7 per cent in the rural areas, where as in urban parts gained to 40.87 percentage, the rural per cent exceeds the all India figure. It is attributed that the poverty is decreasing in rural areas. As a result of the introduction of anti-poverty programmes, the poverty ratio is reduced. However, these anti-poverty programmes have its positive impact.
3. It is further examined that over a period of seven years, the rural poverty ratio has been reduced by half of the 1973-74 figure (i.e.) 56.4 and also the urban poverty ratio has been reduced to (i.e.) 25.7 per cent. It is attributed that the urban poverty ratio has been reduced by half of the figure 50.0 per cent during 1973-74 and it is due to the introduction SJSRY programme from 1997 onwards.

Estimates of Poverty Ratios

Estimates of Poverty in India in 1999-2000 is presented in Table 5.2. Data is presented not only relating to the nation but also the rural as well as Urban areas as about the estimates of poverty. It is seen from Table 5.3 that various persons have estimated the poverty at the national level and it may be accepted because of its uniformity in estimates. During 1999-2000, the estimates are spread over by official estimates by Angus Deaten, Sundaram and Tendulkar, Datta and Revallion and Surjit Bhella. It is noted that official estimates and Angus Deaten have estimated at these levels. They are: (1) For all India, (2) Rural and (3) Urban.

All India estimates of poverty vary perhaps due to different calculations and methodologies. It is presented in Table 5.3.

The following aspects are specially examined and identified quantitatively. They are:

1. Poverty Ratio at the National level,
2. Estimates of poverty in India (by different methods by persons and agencies),
3. Percentage of people below the poverty line in India from 1973-74 to 1999-2000,
4. Urban Poverty Ratio for 1983, 1994 and 2000,
5. Total Poverty Ratio, and
6. Per Annum Poverty Reduction at the state level.

Urban Poverty Ratio

Urban total Poverty Ratio is presented in Table 5.4. It is seen from table that the ratios for 1983-1993 and 2000 respectively the poverty is estimated at 30.81, 33.83 and 26.63 for Andhra Pradesh and the corresponding figures for Nation are to the tune of 40.03, 32.36 and 23.62. It is noted that for the years 1983 and 2000, that Andhra Pradesh Urban Poverty ratios are below the National level.

Table 5.4: Urban Total Poverty Ratio

				Ranks (in Per cent)		
	1983	*1993-94*	*2000*	*I*	*II*	*III*
Andhra Pradesh	30.81	33.83	26.63	12	5	6
All India	40.3	32.36	23.62			

Source: *Economic Survey*, Ministry of Finance, G.o.I., New Delhi: 2002-2003.

Table 5.5: Total Poverty Ratio

				Ranks		
	1983	*1994*	*2000*	*I*	*II*	*III*
Andhra Pradesh	30.44	22.19	15.77	13	14	10
All India	40.90	35.97	26.10			

Source: *Economic Survey*, Ministry of Finance, G.o.I., New Delhi, 2002-2003.

Table 5.6: Per Annum Poverty Reduction at the State level (%)

	Rural		*Urban*		*Total*	
	1983 -1994	*1994 -2000*	*1983 – 1994*	*1994 -2000*	*1983 -1994*	*1994-2000*
Andhra Pradesh	1.44	0.81	–0.75	1.95	0.83	1.07
All India	0.78	1.70	0.77	1.46	0.79	1.65

Whereas for 1993-94 it has increased by 3 per cent for A.P. Impact of SJSRY is more in Andhra Pradesh State is visible since urban poverty is reduced from 30.81 to 26.63. (It is presented in Table 5.5).

At the National level, the Urban Poverty ratio has been steadily on the path of decrease by 7.0 per cent (Table 5.6). The impact of anti-poverty programmes has a positive result upon urban poverty alleviation and reduction.

Total Poverty Ratio

Total Poverty Ratio's for Andhra Pradesh and all India is presented in Table 5.5. It is seen from the table that, alarmingly the total poverty ratio's over a period of 17 years, has been reduced from 30.44 (1983) to 15.77 (2000) and has gained a rank such as 13,14 and 10 ranks for the above years.

Per Annum Poverty Reduction at the State Level

Urban Poverty Alleviation Programmes have a Positive and telling effect on people in various political units. It is seen from table 5.6, from the year 83 to 94 at the state level, it has been marked by 1.44 per cent and 0.81 in rural areas, where as in urban areas, it has been registered that from-0.75 to 1.95 per cent. From 1983 to 1994 it is further reduced by 0.83 and 1.07 per cent for Andhra Pradesh State, and at the all India level, in rural areas it has been from 0.78 per cent to 1.70 per cent (1983 to 94-2000), where as in urban areas, it is on an increasing scale by 0.77 per cent to 1.46 per cent and at the sum total level, it reduced by 0.79 per cent to 1.65 per cent. Thus, the data above shows the Urban Poverty Alleviation programmes have a positive role to reduce the urban as well as rural poverty both at the state level and all India level.

Planning Commission Estimates of Poverty (See Annexure-I)

Impact Analysis of U.P.A.

Approach to Urban Housing and Poverty Alleviation

The Government of India has adopted a two-pronged approach to deal with the problems of slums and urban poverty in the country. These include provision of basic services and shelter to the urban poor and addressing concerns such as Skill development, employment and income generation. The first attempt to deal with Urban Poverty Started in 1958 with the adoption of community development (UCD) pilot project. This was done following the successful adoption of the community development approach in rural areas.

Major Thrust areas and Programmes in Five Year Plans

1. During the second five year plan (1956-61), Urban Community Development (UCD) pilot project which was started in 1958 based on, an area oriented approach later followed by a series of UCD pilot projects.
2. During the third five year plan (1961-66), major thrust was on housing programmes and co-ordination of efforts of all agencies and orienting the programmes to the needs of the low income groups (LIG). A scheme was introduced in 1959 to give loans to State governments for a period of 10 years for acquisition and development of land in order to make available building sites in sufficient numbers.
3. During Fourth Five Year Plan (1969-74), Housing and Urban Development Corporation (HUDCO) was established to fund housing and urban development programmes, especially for the poor. A scheme for environmental improvement of urban slums (EIUS) was launched in the Central sector from 1972-73 with a view to providing a minimum level of services like safe drinking water supply, sewerage, storm water drainage, pavements, community baths, and latrines, street lighting etc. to slum dwellers in 11 cities with a population of 8 lakhs and above. The scheme was later extended to 9 more cities.

4. During Fifth Five Year Plan (1974-79), The urban land (ceiling and regulation) set was enacted to prevent the concentration of land holding in urban areas and to make available urban land for construction of houses for the middle and low income groups. Environmental Improvement of Urban Slums (EIUS) was transferred to State Governments for implementation from 1974 onwards.
5. During Sixth Five Year Plan (1980-85), it was emphasized on integrated provision of services along with shelter, particularly for the poor. The integrated development of small and medium towns (IDSM) was launched in towns with population below one lakh for provision of roads, pavements, minor civic works, busstands, markets, and shopping complexes etc.

Urban basic services (UBS) programme was started in 1981 aiming at catering to the basic physical and social needs of the urban poor with a view to improving their living conditions.

During Seventh Five Year Plan (1985-90), made the first conscious attempt to directly address the urban poverty issues. In the very beginning of the seventh plan, G.O.I. decided to expand the programmes of Urban Basic Services (UBS) implemented during 1981-84 with collaboration of the UNICEF in 42 towns to 168 towns. The UBS aimed at catering to the basic physical and social needs of the urban poor with a view to improving their living conditions.

Subsequently, as a following of the recommendations made by the National Commission on Urbanization (NCU), the G.O.I. adopted a four pronged strategy for addressing the issues of growing incidence of poverty in urban areas. Comprising: (a) employment creation for low-income communities through promotion of micro-enterprises and public works; (b) housing and shelter up-gradation; (c) social development planning with special focus on development of children and women; and (d) environmental up-gradation of slums based on the above stated strategy, the G.O.I. adopted a comprehensive approach to urban poverty alleviation by launching two schemes, namely: (i) The Nehru Rozgar Yojana (NRY) launched in 1989, to cater to the economic needs of the urban poor by providing them employment opportunities through skill up-gradation and assistance to set-up their own-microenterprises; and (ii) The Urban Basic Services of the Poor (UBSP) which was a modified UBS programme, started in 1990. The UBSP programme envisaged fostering community structures comprising urban poor for ensuring their effective participation in their development activities.

During 1990-92, the annual plan was introduced, and the Constitution 74th Amendment Act was enacted. Article 243 of the Act mandated the setting-up of elected municipalities as 'institutions of self-government'—a third tier of government. The Act envisaged urban poverty alleviation, slum up-gradation and protection of interest of weaker sections as amongst the legitimate function of Urban Local Bodies (ULB's).

During the Eighth Five Year Plan (1992-97), the Prime Ministers Integrated Urban Poverty Eradication Programme (PMIUPEP) was started in 1995 for improving the quality of life of urban poor by creating a facilitating environment through community based planning and implementation. The objective of the scheme was effective achievement of social sector goals, community empowerment, employment generation and environmental improvement. The PMIUPEP incorporated within itself all the components of UBSP including the self-employment, physical infrastructure creation component and the shelter up-gradation components of NRY. The programme, however was applicable to 345 class 2 towns and 79 specifically identified district head quarters and hilly areas. The National Slum Development Programme (NSDP) was launched in 1996, Providing additional Central Assistance to States for the up-gradation of urban slums. The scheme covered the provision of physical amenities like water supply, storm water drains, sewer, community bath, community latrines, widening and paving of the existing lanes, street lights etc,. It also includes social infrastructure and community amenities like pre-school education, non-formal education, adult education, maternity, child health and primary health care including immunization etc.

During Ninth Five Year Plan period (1997-2002) G.o.I., New Delhi, as per the recommendations of the committee needed by Prof. S.R. Hashim all the three ongoing urban poverty alleviation schemes namely Nehru Rozgar Yojana (NRY), Urban Basic Services for the Poor (UBSP) and Prime Ministers Integrated Urban Poverty Eradication Programme (PMIDPEP) were subsumed in a new scheme, namely Swarna Jayanti Shahari Rozgar Yojana (SJSRY), which was launched with effect from 1-12. 1997.

Programme for Infrastructure Development for mega cities, called Mega City Scheme, was launched in 1997 covering Mumbai, Kolkata, Chennai, Hyderabad and Bangalore.

The Scheme of Valmiki Ambedkar Awas Yojana (VAMBAY) was launched on 15th August, 2001 with the objectives to provide or upgrade shelter to slum dwellers living below the poverty line and converge the same with environmental improvement of Urban slums. A National city sanitation project called National Bharat Abhiyan was also started as an integral component of VAMBAY.

During Tenth Five Year Plan period (2002-2007), Jawaharlal Nehru National Urban Renewal Mission (JNNURM) was launched on 3rd December, 2005 with commitment of Rs 50,000 crores as Additional Central Assistance to States for the provision of city wide infrastructure and basic services to the urban poor over the mission period 2005-12, with focus on an urban sector reforms agenda to be implemented by State governments and urban local bodies.

During the Eleventh Five Year Plan period (2007-2012), The President of India has announced a new scheme called Rajiv Awas Yojana (RAY) on June 4, 2009 for the slum dwellers and Urban Poor aimed at ushering in a 'slum free India' by encouraging States/ Union Territories to tackle the problem of slums in a definite manner. RAY calls for a multi-pronged approach focusing on:

- Legal framework for property rights to slum dwellers.
- Rajiv Awas Yojana for credit risk guarantee fund with an amount of Rs.1000 crores corpus for the purpose.

During the Twelfth Five Year Plan period (2012-2017), the following items were identified to provide for the urban poor.

1. To provide the urban poor affordable shelter and decent living and working conditions.
2. To make adequate provision of land for the poor in the master plan itself.
3. To address various vulnerabilities including residential, occupational and social vulnerabilities associated with urban poverty.

4. To provide basic services to migrant workers and their families and other vulnerable sections of society including women and children".[16]

The twelfth five year plan has identified the following primary causes of urban poverty and growth in slums.

1. Structural—which include socially constructed constraints to opportunities for low income groups;
2. Influx of large number of workers to cities without commensurate job opportunities and availability of housing and basic amenities;
3. High cost of living, including the cost of health care and medical facilities, housing, transport and education;
4. Lack of urban planning especially for housing low income categories and the provision of land for informal sector activities;
5. Absence of adequate regulation to protect the economic interest of the poor; and
6. Lack of involvement of the poor in urban planning and development processes.

Twelfth Plan—Objective for the Urban Poverty Alleviation

1. To provide the urban poor affordable shelter and living and working conditions;
2. To make adequate provision of land for the poor in the master plan itself;
3. To address various vulnerabilities including residential, occupational and social vulnerabilities associated in the urban poverty; and
4. To provide basic services to migrant workers, their families and other vulnerable sections of the society including women and children. [17]

Future Areas of Research

Future areas of research is 'Urban Fringe' which is the most prevalent state and at the same time, most problematic area of peri-urban region. This is the area of future growth, the area in which the city expands, yet, is often Subjected to a chotic development before it is finally merged in the city. An area of transition, between the rural and the urban, the 'fringe' has been the subject of study by different social scientists such as Economists, Geographers, sociologists, Regional planners and Public Administrators which helps the planners as well as administrators to design and prepare a policy document for implementation.

Conclusions

1. It is concluded that Poverty Alleviation programmes should have to be implemented intensively in tune with the growth of population whether it is rural or urban.
2. Poverty Alleviation Programmes, designed by experts at the National level, should have to be matched to the growing needs of the people as well as suitable to the area.
3. Keeping in view the reforms at the National and State levels, the UPA should be able to eradicate the poverty not only at the National level but also at the State level covering the urban areas.
4. People have been facing the problems such as lack of income, insufficient calories of food and food items. Lack of literacy besides long term unemployment by the people. Poverty is visible in multiple ways such as inadequacies in health care, education and nutrition. It is observed that many of the poor are found to live in areas of suffering from environmental degradation which inturn results chiefly from expanding population over a period of time. The expanding population pressure and the adverse effects of traditional growth strategies are the real problems. Keeping in view of the environmental degradation, Government of India or State should be able to uplift the people from degradation through the mechanism of urban micro level planning, as it may alleviate people from urban poverty and also improve the structural location in the fields of Health, education, nutrition and settlements. Finally, people may be able to achieve empowerment situation through 73 & 74 C.A.A. besides achieving entitlements for the tiny hutments in urban slums, where they live in.

REFERENCES

1. S.K. Dhage, "Poverty Alleviation Programmes in India: Issues and Challenges" in *Poverty, Poverty Alleviation and Social Disadvantage*, Clem Tisdell (Ed.), Serials Publications, New Delhi (2007).
2. Poverty, Poverty Alleviation and Social Disadvantage publshed by Serials Publication. Clem Tisdell.
3. Sakti Padhi and Aswini K. Mishra, "New Governance and Development, understanding poverty" H.S. Shylendra. (ed.) Academic Foundation, New Delhi, p. 150 (2009).
4. Ashwani Luthra and Swati Sharma, Urban sprawl and sustainable Development of Jaipur.
5. Spatio-Economic development record, Vol. 20, No. 3, May-June, 2013, p. 70.
6. D. Rajasekhar, "Does Good Governance work for Poverty Reduction at the ground level?—A Study of Self-Help Groups in Karnataka and Madhya Pradesh", in *Understanding Poverty*, H.S. Shylendra (ed.), Academic Foundation, New Delhi (2009), pp. 193/194.
7. State of the Urban Poor Report, 2013, pp. 65 and 66.
8. Nick Devas, "Urban Governance, Voice and Poverty in the Developing World," Earth Scan Publications Limited, First South Asian Edition, 2006, London, NWIOJH, UK.
9. A. Anitha Shah: Natural Resources and Chronic Poverty in India: Interface and policy imperatives. in, pp. 362 and 365. Environment and Development Economics (ed.) by Scott Barrett, Oxford, University Press, (2014).
10. Dr. Ghazan Ferullah, "Micro Regional Planning in India", A.K.Publications, Delhi, 2008. p. 1.
11. Roger Zetter and Rodney White, "Planning in Cities" Sustainability and Growth in the Developing World", ITDG Publishing, London, U.K. 2002, p. 25.
12. Meenu Agarwal, "Extent of Poverty and Alleviation Measures" (p. 109) in Economic Reforms, Unemployment and Poverty, Pub: New Centrury Publications, New Delhi, India (2008).
13. *Source*: Singh (2006).
14. State of the Urban Poor Report, 2013 Ministry of Housing and Urban Poverty Alleviation. G.o.I., New Delhi (Oxford), p. 67.
15. *Source*: Planning Commission (2012), Report of the Expert Group to Recommend the Detailed Methodology for Identification of families living Below Poverty Line in Urban Areas, Perspective Planning Division, New Delhi, pp. 17-20.
16. State of Housing in India—A statistical compendium, 2013, Published by Government of India, Ministry of Housing and Urban Poverty Alleviation, National Building Organization.
17. Twelfth Five Year Plan Document, Planning Commission of India, New Delhi.

PART TWO

6
Reducing Poverty in Urban India

Smt. K.V. Jagadamba

Poverty is rampant and it is varied and vivid Planning Commission in India has been paying full attention to eliminate/ eradicate poverty through various plans from its inception to the present day and the present Twelfth Five Year Plan also spelled out to form slum free city in order to eliminate slums in different geographic regions of Metropolitan to towns in hierarchy. This chapter has been divided into two parts. They are: (1) Mission for the Elimination of Poverty in Municipal Areas (MEPMA), Government of Andhra Pradesh, (2) Environmental Impact Assessment (EIA), (3) KUDUMBASHREE Urban CDS, (4) Environmental Impact Assessment (EIA), (5) Livelihood Generation Initiatives of Government of Gujarat (UMEED), (6) Environmental Impact Assessment (EIA), (7) Rajasthan Mission on Skill and Livelihoods (RMOL), Conclusions are presented in Part 'A' of the Chapter and Part 'B' deals with the four case studies reducing poverty in India.

'Reducing Poverty' in Urban India is an urgent task to Government of India. Under the 74th Constitution Amendment Act, Urban Poverty Alleviation has been entrusted to ULBs, as per the XII Schedule. However, most of the ULBs lack the financial resources to provide basic services or undertake comprehensive poverty alleviation programmes. Nevertheless, various State governments including Andhra Pradesh (MEPMA), Kerala (KUDUMBASHREE), and Gujarat (UMEED) etc. have evolved innovative solutions to creating choices for the urban poor besides approaches for urban poverty alleviation. A common element in these approaches has been the adopting of a Mission approaches, focus on building community structure and integration of skills and livelihoods as central components of the programme.

Mission for the Elimination of Poverty in Municipal Areas (MEPMA), Government of Andhra Pradesh

Andhra Pradesh Urban Services for the Poor (APUSP), a flagship programme (2000-08) of the Government of Andhra Pradesh addressed the challenges of municipal service delivery in 42 class-I towns and resulted in improvements in livelihoods and access to basic services for about 3 million poor people in the slums of Andhra Pradesh. There Government of Andhra Pradesh scaled up APUSP reforms across the state through creation of a Mission for the Elimination of Poverty in Municipal Areas (MEPMA). MEMPMA is nodal agency for convergence of all services targeted towards the urban poor (youth welfare, minority, BC, SC, ST, Labour, Health, Women and child welfare, civil supplies etc.) RAY, and the street vendors' policy among others.

The Mission adopted the following strategies to converge with various programmes:

- Building organization of the poor as CBOs;
- Empowering the poor by building their capacities;
- Creating highly trained social capital at grassroot level in health, education, livelihoods and vulnerability etc.;
- Access to credit for the poor by facilitating interface between CBO's and bankers (Town Level Bankers Committee with SHGs);
- Taking up placement linked livelihood programmes on continuous basis; and
- Services under 7-Point Charter (Security of land, improved housing, sanitation, water supply, health, education and social security system) etc.

Environmental Impact Assessment

The progress under this Mission has been remarkable and nearly, 25 lakh members are involved in 2.5 lakh Self-Help Groups spread across all the Municipalities in the state. 90 per cent of the Urban Poor living in 7520 slums in the state have been organized into

SHGs. Bank linkages of Rs. 1481.08 crores have been established. Around 5,100 micro-enterprises have been grounded[1].

KUDUMBASHREE—URBAN CDS

A community based, women oriented initiative to fight urban poverty in Kerala been designed and executed by T.K. Jose, Executive Director, SPEM, Government of Kerala.

1. Mission of KUDUMBASHREE
   "To eradicate absolute poverty in ten years through concerned community action under the leadership of local governments, by facilitating organization of poor for combining self-help with demand led convergence of available services and resources to tackle the multiple dimensions and manifestation of poverty holistically."
2. What is KUDUMBASHREE?
   - It is a multi-faceted women based participatory eradication programme jointly initiated by Government of Kerala and NABARD.
   - It is scaled up from two UNICEF assisted initiatives Alappuzha Municipality (UBSP) and Malappuram district (CBNP).
   - It is implemented by community based organization (CBOs) of poor women in co-operation with local self-government.
3. KUDUMBASHREE—History and Evolution
   An up scaling of an urban experiment
   - Initiated in 7 wards of Alappuzha Municipality with the support of UNICEF (1992-93).
   - Creation of Urban Poverty Alleviation Fund (UPA Fund). (As per section 284 of the Kerala Municipalities Act 1994).
   - 2 per cent of estimated annual revenue income of Municipalities.
   - 30 per cent of General Purpose Grant.
   - Alappuzha modal scaled up to the entire urban area under the leadership of UPA Cell (1995).
   - All these experiences were taken state-wide as 'KUDUMBASHREE' (1998).

- UPA cell merged with KUDUMBASHREE (1999).
- Expanded to all Grama Panchayats in a phased manner (3 phases)—2000-02.

4. Identifying poor—The Poverty Index—"Allappey Model"
   A Family
   - Living in a substandard house or hut.
   - No access to sanitary latrines
   - No access to safe drinking water (150 mts)
   - Getting only 2 meals a day or less.
   - Having children below 5 years of age.
   - Having no or only one earning member.
   - Belonging to socially disadvantaged groups.
   - Having an illiterate adult member.
   - Having alcoholics or drug addicts.

A family having at least four of the above factors is classified as a Family at Risks or a 'Poor Family'.

5. Linkage with the Local Body Advisory Committee—ADS level. Councilor of the concerned Ward as the Chairman ADS Chair Person as Convenor.
   - Monitoring and Advisory Committee—CDS level.
   - Municipal Chairman as the Chairperson.
   - All Elected Women Councillors.
   - All standing committee Chairpersons.
   - Municipal Secretary as the Convenor.
   - CDS Secretary as Joint Convenor.
   - Representatives from other Functional and Development Department.
   - CDS President.
6. Revised Poverty Index—Family with:
   - No land/less than 5 cents of land (1 cent = 40 m^2)
   - No house/Dilapidated house
   - No Sanitary Latrine
   - No access to safe drinking water within 150 meters.
   - Women/headed household/presence of a widow, divorce/abandoned lady/unwed mother.
   - No regularly employed person in the family
   - Socially Disadvantaged Groups (SC/ST).
   - Presence of Mentally or Physically Challenged Person/

Chronically ill member in the family.
- Families without colour TV.

A family having at least four of the above factors is classified as a 'Family at Risk' or a 'Poor Family'.

7. Relevance and Significance of 9 Point Index
   - Simple, transparent and easily understood.
   - Various manifestations of deprivations are included.
   - Do not depend much on income.
   - Large possible Combinations of poverty-9 C/4 and Combinations, 382 different possible ways of finding a poor family.
   - It facilitates to rational grading of poor families.
   - It Suggests possible corrective steps.
8. Nine point Index—Possible Combinations

No. of Risk Factors	*Combinations*
4 Risk Factors	126
5 Risk Factors	126
6 Risk Factors	84
7 Risk Factors	36
8 Risk Factors	9
9 Risk Factors	1
Total	382

9. Community Based Organisations (CBOs) 3 tier structure fully managed by the poor
   (a) Neighbourhood Group (NHG)
   (b) Area Development Society (ADS)
   (c) Community Development Society (CDS)

(a) Neighbourhood Group—The Building Block
- One Woman each from 15-40 families at risk-organized into Neighbourhood Group (NHG).
- Democratically selected committee of Five "Barefoot Specialists".
- Volunteer for Community Health Activities.
- Volunteer for infrastructure development.
- Volunteer for Income Generation Activities.
- Secretary—(The General Manager)
- President—(The Leader and Chief Coordinator)

(b) Area Development Society—ADS/Federation of all NHGs in a Ward.

(c) Community Development Society—CDS
- The Apex body at the local body level
- Registered under the Travancore—Cochin Literary Scientific and Charitable Societies Act of 1955.

Linkages with the local body
- Advisory Committee—ADS level
- Councillor of the concerned ward as the Chairman
- ADS Chairperson as Convenor
- Monitoring in Advisory Committee—CDS level
  - ➢ Municipal Chairman as the Chairperson
  - ➢ All the elected women Councillors
  - ➢ All standing committee Chairpersons
  - ➢ Municipal Secretary as the Convenor
  - ➢ CDS Secretary as Joint Convenor
  - ➢ Representatives from other functional and Development Department.
  - ➢ CDS President.

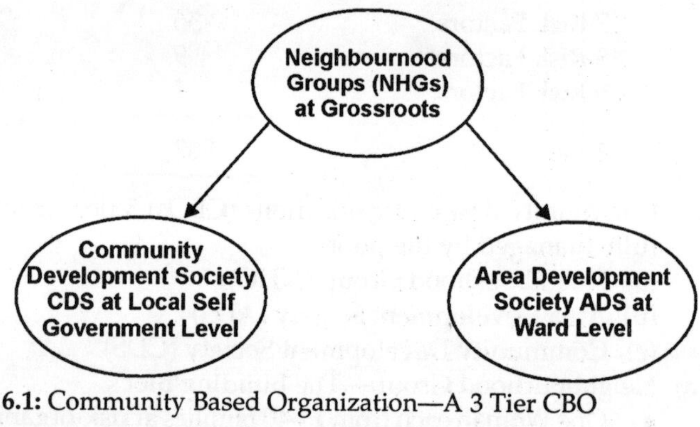

Fig. 6.1: Community Based Organization—A 3 Tier CBO

Focus on

- Human Resource Development
- Community Health
- Education
- 'Bala Sabha'—Children's NHG
- Micro-Finance

- Micro-Enterprise Development
- Destitute Rehabilitation—Ashraya
- Bhavana Shree
- Lease Land Farming

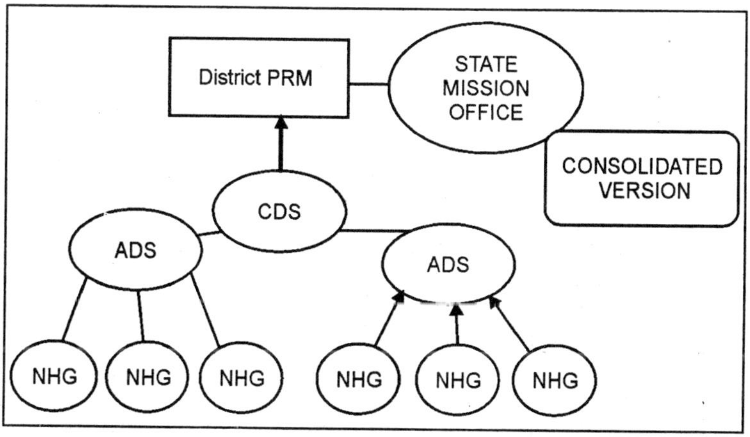

Fig. 6.2: Management of Information System in KUDUMBASHREE[2] Government of Kerala

Environment Impact Assessment (EIA)

It is one of the largest women's movement in Asia with nearly 37.37 lakh poor families brought under the Community Based Organizations (CBOs) consisting of 2.05 lakh Neighbourhood Groups (NHGs), 17,578 Area Development Societies (ADSs) and 1,061 Community Development Societies (CDSs) both in rural and urban. The Mission has mobilized a sum of Rs. 1,688 cores as thrift and disbursed loans amounting to Rs. 4,195 crores to the members of NHGs and allotted more than 25 thousand women to establish their individual enterprises in urban areas.

Comment (View)

Approaches Adopted for Urban Poverty Alleviation by both the Missions

Both the models emphasized the need for bottom-up and Convergent approach for Urban Poverty Alleviation through building and empowering organization to the poor.

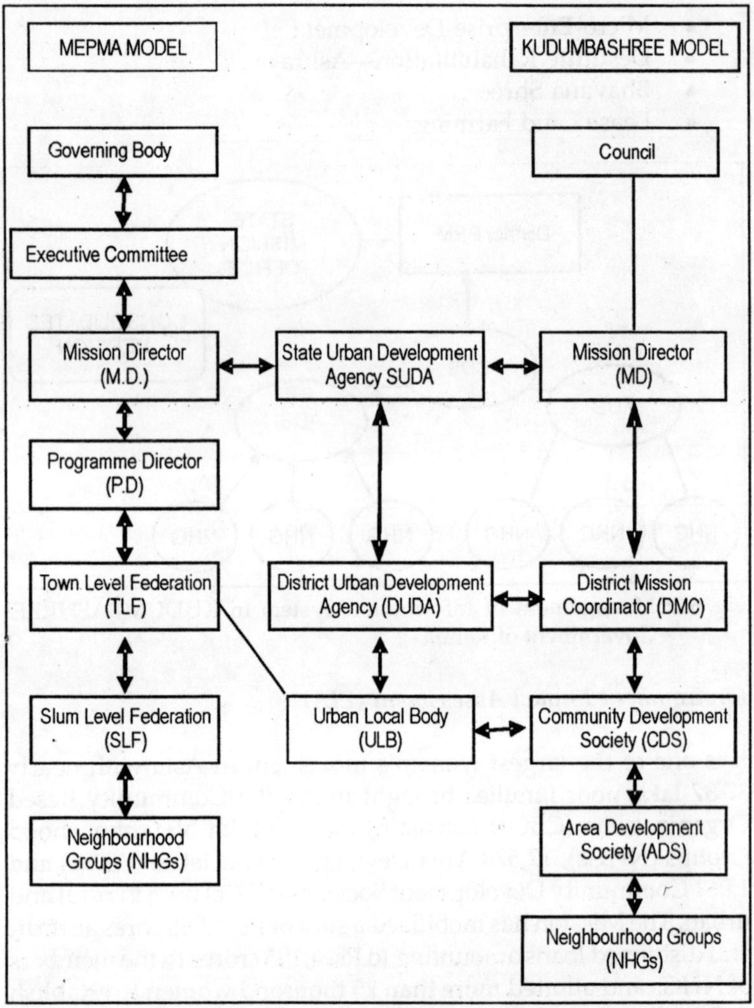

Fig. 6.3: Genesis of MEPMA and Kudumbashree Models

Source: Annexure-III, Reducing poverty in Urban India: Select State Level Approaches, pp. 83-86.

Livelihood Generation Initiatives by Government of Gujarat (UMEED)

UMEED is an ongoing initiative under the Rs. 13,000 crore Garib Samruddhi Yojana of the Gujarat Government. The programme aims at achieving sustained reduction in the vulnerability and poverty of the poor. In 2005, SAATH Partnered with Ahmedabad Municipal Corporation American India Foundation (AIF) to pilot an innovative employability—training programme called "UDAAN" aimed at under privileged youth ages 18 to 35 years. UDAAN successfully trained and placed over 900 youth in service sector domains like customer relations and sales, hotel management, bed side patient attendant and others.

After the successful pilot of UDAAN, on recommendation of the Government of Gujarat to replicate the programme across all major towns of Gujarat, it was renamed "UMEED". The programme runs on a Public-Private-Partnership mode, and is jointly run by four organizations—SAATH, CAP, Foundation, Aid-et-Action and skill pro Foundation. The programme adopts the following beneficiary selection criteria:

- The age of the student should be in the range of 18-25 years.
- The minimum qualification of the aspirant should be at least 7th class.

UMEED adopts the following Step-by-step Process for Training

Environmental Impact Assessment

Based on the market scan, the programme delivers trainings to youth from vulnerable families across Gujarat in areas like business process outsourcing, beside patient assistance, customer relations, and then places graduates at Indian companies. The three month training programme cost Rs. 4,500/-. Beneficiaries pay Rs. 500/- towards the cost, while the rest of it is borne by donors and the government. Over, 19,000 youth have been trained and placed in north and Cental Gujarat in 46 training centres. Placement rates are as high as 85 per cent and average starting salaries are Rs. 3,000/- per month.[3]

Rajasthan Mission on Skill and Livelihoods (RMOL)

A similar initiative has been undertaken by Government of Rajasthan named, "Rajasthan Mission on Skill and Livelihoods" (RMOL), which aims at creating a large number of livelihood opportunities for the poor, increasing labour force and to increase the income levels of working poor in the state. The Mission runs on a Public-Private-Partnership mode and collaborates with Government departments such as Technical Education Department, Fisheries department, Agriculture department of labour and employment department, as well as with NGOs and other National and International Organizations.[4]

Conclusions

1. It is concluded that individual states have designed their own mission mode approaches to eradicate/eliminate urban poverty to a large extent.
2. A common element in the approaches has been the adoption of mission approach, focus on building community structure and integration of skills and livelihoods as central components of the programme.
3. Keeping in view of the above location and situation, it is a felt need that the Nation should have to design exclusively the aspect of anti-poverty programmes intensively with a unified objective (i.e.) Urban livelihoods, the approach should be on a Mission mode at least by the Mo HUPA, New Delhi, Gender Budgeting is a tool to achieve women empowerment and it is possible through administrative reforms at the National Level.

Part 'B' deals with the four case studies relating to reducing poverty in India. These case studies are conducted at different regional levels to understand the startegy and the status of the units with a time tag before the year 2000 and 2008. They are presented in the following paragraphs:

The following aspects are dealt with:

(1) Micro-Level study of self-employment programme—A Regional Study;
(2) Urban Self-Employment Programme (USEP)—Action Plan with a critical appraisal;
(3) Establishment of Micro-Business Centres for SHG's for the year 2009-10—Social Development Strategy; and
(4) TLF in a total of 125 ULBS—Action Plan—Critical Appraisal.

Case Study—One

Micro-Level Study of USEP Progress—A Regional Study

An attempt is made to indentify the progress of USEP in Andhra Pradesh as case study and also to recognize the role of USEP as a programme and progress as contribution in the regional prospective.

Data: Data has been collected from website, both for Telangana Districts and Districts of Andhra Pradesh relating to USEP progress for the years (starting from) 2008-2009; 2009-2010; 2010-2011; 2011-2012; 2012-2013; and 2013-2014 as it is seen from Table 6.1. The particulars such as no. of application received: no of sanctioned grounded/not grounded, unit cost, Bank loan amount, subsidy amount and beneficiary and beneficiary contribution.

Observations (For Andhra Region)

1. Under category not grounded (the units) performance is seen from the column of 6 of Table 6.1, it is observed during the year 2009-2010, 2012-2013 and 2013-2014, the unit could not be grounded due to various reasons and for the remaining years, they have successfully grounded the units.

Comparative Study (2008-2009 and 2013-2014)

If we compare the state-wise report, for the years 2008-2009 and 2013-2014, the following are important observations.

Telangana:	(1) Increase of Applications—3105	
Andhra Pradesh:	(2) Increase of Applications—2476	
Telangana:	(1) Sanctioned Applications—1718	
Andhra Pradesh:	(2) Sanctioned Applications—2428	
Telangana: Grounded:	217	
Andhra Pradesh:	No Change	0
	Not Grounded	1501
	Unit cost	+4848.53
	Bank loan amount	33.94.7
	Subsidy Amount	1212.41
	Beneficiary Contribution	242.49

Table 6.1: Telangana Region and Andhra Pradesh Region. Regional Breakup of USEP Progress—All amounts in Rs. in Lakhs

Sl. No.	Year	No. of Applications	Sanction	Grounded	Not Grounded	Unit Cost	Bank Loan Amount	Subsidy Amount	Beneficiary Contribution
1.	2008-2009	1103	902	902	0	457.17	320.17	114.35	22.88
	Andhra Pradesh	4978	4978	3200	0	1185.94	830.16	296.49	59.31
2.	2009-2010	1854	1739	1738	1	838.85	1739	209.74	41.97
	Andhra Pradesh	6016	5764	5764	10	2632.98	1843.11	658.24	131.65
3.	2010-2011	2379	1846	1846	0	1370.77	959.53	342.7	68.54
	Andhra Pradesh	6708	5335	5335	0	3416.95	2391.88	854.25	170.87
4.	2011-2012	3012	1615	1615	0	1537.15	1076.01	384.31	76.88
	Andhra Pradesh	6698	4161	4161	0	3636.71	2545.71	909.21	181.84
5.	2012-2013	3011	2523	1614	909	2469.65	1728.77	617.42	123.49
	Andhra Pradesh	6804	6346	3848	2498	6789.57	4752.74	1697.39	339.46
6.	2013-2014	4208	2620	1119	1501	2654.15	1857.92	663.56	132.72
	Andhra Pradesh	7454	5628	3200	2428	6034.47	4224.86	1508.9	301.80
	2008-2009 Change after	+3105	+1718	+217	+1501	+2197	+1537.75	+549.21	+109.84
	2008-2009	TR1103	902	902	0	457.37	320.17	114.35	22.88
	2013-2014	TR4208	2620	1119	1501	2654.15	1857.92	663.56	132.72
	2008-2009	AP4978	3200	3200	0	1185.94	830.16	296.49	59.31
	2013-2014	AP7454	5628	3200	2428	6034.47	4224.86	1508.90	301.80
	2008-2009 Change after	+2476	+2428	0	+2488	+4848.53	+3394.7	+1212.41	+242.49
	2008-2009 Percentage Change after	49.73%	75.87%	0%	24.28%	40.91%	50.89%	40.89%	40.80%

Source: Annual Report on Urban Self-Employment Programme–Published by MEPMA.
MEPMA: [Mission for Elimination of Poverty in Municapl Areas.]

Gross Observations (Over 2008-09)

1. It is noted that No. of Application have been increased by 49.73 per cent.
2. It is observed that a net sanction by 75.87 per cent has been increased to the previous figures.
3. It is notated that all the sanctioned units are grounded.
4. It is further observed that 24.28 per cent units were not grounded. It felt that orientation classes should have to be conducted for the USEP candidates.
5. Unit cost has been increased by 40.91 per cent.
6. It is noted that 50.89 per cent has been increased as bank loan amount to the people seeking USEP.
7. 40.89 per cent component has been on an increasing side under subsidy amount.
8. Finally, it is seen that 40.80 per cent has been reduced under beneficiary contribution.

For Telangana Region, the increase or decrease has been worked out absolutely over 2008. The observations are stated below:

1. No. of applications have been increased by 3105.
2. No. of application sanctioned loan amount were to a tune of 1718.
3. No. of Units grounded was to a tune of 217.
4. It is noted that not grounded units have been on an increase by 1501.
5. The unit cost has been increased by 2197.
6. Bank loan amount has been increased by 1537.75.
7. The subsidy amount—amounts are a tune of 549.21 and
8. The beneficiary contribution by 109.84 when compared to the previous figure (base figure).

Urban Self-Employment Programme (USEP) for the year 2009-10 action plan is presented in Table 6.2. It is identified that the total composition relating 21 districts and the urban units of GHMC, GVMC and VMC are the contributory units of Urban Self-Employment Programmme (USEP) for the year 2009–2010. The observations are as follows.

Table 6.2: Urban Self-Employment Programme (USEP) Action Plan 2009-10

Sl. No.	Name of the District	Target		Total	S.C. Coverage	S.T. Coverage	Coverage
		SHG	PWDS				
1.	Ananthapur	485	165	650	105	44	99
2.	Chitoor	415	40	455	75	30	67
3.	Kadapa	270	120	390	60	28	59
4.	Kurnool	480	34	514	84	34	78
5.	Srikakulam	255	70	325	51	22	49
6.	Vizianagaram	275	50	325	52	22	50
7.	Vishakapatnam	267	50	317	52	21	47
8.	East Godavari	543	107	650	108	42	98
9.	West Godavari	550	100	650	105	44	98
10.	Krishna	335	107	442	70	29	67
11.	Guntur	1276	345	1621	263	106	246
12.	Prakasam	295	160	455	74	30	69
13.	Nellore	374	81	455	74	29	68
14.	Karimnagar	218	142	360	58	23	55
15.	Khammam	447	122	569	91	36	86
16.	Mahabubnagar	220	64	284	46	20	43
17.	Medak	247	115	362	59	25	54
18.	Nalgonda	178	50	228	37	16	34
19.	Nizamabad	293	130	423	68	29	64
20.	Warangal	365	116	481	78	32	72
21.	Ranga Reddy	300	19	319	51	21	48
	Mission Cities GHMC	1350	600	1950	316	129	293
	Mission Cities GHMC	6000	200	8000	130	53	120
	Mission Cities VMC	500	150	650	105	43	98
	Mission Cities Total	2450	950	3400	551	225	511
	Grand Total	10793	3207	14000	2263	930	2112

Source: Action Plan, 2009–2010 operational manual MEPMA, Hyderabad.

Observations

1. There are 10,793 S.H.G.C. (Target), PWDS (3207) and a total 14,000 units are identified and it is observed that GHMC, occupies highest position with 1350; whereas

Nalgonda gains with 178 (lowest). Among the Coastal districts, Guntur district gains with 178 (Lower) among the Coastal districts, Guntur districts gains highest with 1276 (SHG) 345 (PWDs) and a total 1621 units in the entire state.

2. It is further observed that Guntur district has a coverage 263 (SC) out of 2,263; Srikakulam (51) and the last being occupied by Nalgonda (37)
3. S.T coverage is highest 129 (GHMC) and the second place secured by Guntur with 106. The least being Nalgonda with 16.
4. Minority coverage highest has been recorded by Guntur district (246) and the lowest has been occupied by Nalgonda (34)

Establishment of Micro-Business Centres for SHGs, 2009-10 is presented in table 6.3. The data relating to all the districts in Andhra Pradesh and also those urban units of GHMC, VMC and GVMC Action Plan, 2009-10 is presented in the above table, for to have closer took upon the establishment of Micro-Business Centres for SHGs. Column 3 to 6, shows the per cent of SHG members in a regulated pattern are i.e., S.C., S.T., B.C., and Minorities. Column 7 shows the establishment of Micro-Business Centres for SHGs. Column 8 till shows the total, S.C., S.T and Minorities for the establishment of Multi-Purpose common Resource Centres (CRCs) in Andhra Pradesh. If we examine the data closely, the following are important observations:

1. Per cent of SHG Members, the highest is recorded as 21.75 Prakasam District), later has been occupied by 20.84 (Kurnool district) and GHMC (18 Circles) contributed to 19.80 per cent.
2. Per cent of SHG Members with ST's, Khammam occupies by 8.77 per cent, whereas Guntur occupies by 5.20 and the least occupies by East Godavari with 0.62 per cent.
3. Per cent of SHG is BC members, highest being Vizianagaram district 69.96, whereas Warangal with 68.50 and the least per cent with 37.28 as Guntur. It is noted that Costal Districts of Guntur occupies with this per cent.

Table 6.3: Establishment of Micro-Business centre for SHG's 2009-2010

Sl. No.	Name of the districts	% SHG Members				Establishment of Micro business centre for SHGs	Establishment of Multi Public Common Resource Centers (CRCs)			
		SC	ST	BC	Minorities		Total	SC	ST	Minorities
1.	Adialbad	16.25	2.30	53.15	15.66		7	1	0	1
2.	Anantapur	10.23	2.62	47.34	22.65	Minorities	7	1	0	1
3.	Chitoor	11.42	2.08	56.54	12.13		8	1	1	1
4.	East Godavari	13.17	0.62	61.72	1.59		9	1	1	1
5.	Guntur	17.93	5.20	37.28	15.02	SC	12	2	1	2
6.	Kadapa	15.70	2.11	37.69	21.49	Minorities	7	1	0	1
7.	Karimnagar	14.80	1.71	66.14	8.45		6	1	0	1
8.	Khammam	18.53	8.77	57.63	2.35	SC	7	1	0	1
9.	Krishna	14.35	2.61	45.70	8.61		5	1	0	1
10.	Kurnool	20.84	1.42	42.96	15.93	SC	5	1	0	1
11.	Mahaboobnagar	6.64	1.11	69.21	17.13		4	1	0	1
12.	Medak	13.57	0.97	52.68	23.31	Minorities	5	1	0	1
13.	Nalgonda	14.77	3.51	56.83	9.91	ST	4	1	0	1
14.	Nellore	18.74	5.55	48.61	10.89	SC	4	1	0	1
15.	Nizamabad	11.87	0.74	53.98	26.20	Minorities	4	1	0	1
16.	Prakasam	21.75	4.48	37.81	11.18	SC	4	1	0	1
17.	Ranga Reddy	15.06	3.53	44.85	18.34	ST	2	0	0	0
18.	Srikakulam	10.97	0.90	65.03	1.14		5	1	0	1
19.	Vishakapatnam	8.79	0.82	53.67	1.24		2	0	0	0
20.	Vizinagaram	11.90	1.24	69.96	1.01		4	1	1	1
21.	Warangal	15.83	1.89	68.50	7.85		2	0	0	0
22.	West Godavari	14.03	1.15	57.22	2.41		8	1	1	1
23.	GHMC (18 Circles)	19.80	2.63	52.13	11.62	Minorities	18	3	1	3
24.	VMC (3 Circles)						3	0	0	0
25.	GVMC (6 Circles)						6	1	0	1
	Action Plan 2009-2010					23	148	24	5	24

Source: MEPMA: Hyderabad, Andhra Pradesh.

4. Nizamabad district has 26.20 per cent with Minorities, as highest and the least being Vizianagaram with 1.01 per cent.

There are 211 TLFs in all 171 ULBs as on 5th November 2012. Hence, details are worked out to release Rs. 15,000/- to each TLFs existed in 125 ULBs as per the Action Plan towards conducting of GB meetings of TLFs for the year 2012-2013.

Table 6.4: Release of Funds to ULB's and TLF's

Name of the District	*No.of ULBs as per online dated 5.11.2012*	*No.of TLFs for which amount proposed in the existing 125 ULBs Now*	*Amount proposed for GB meetings @Rs.15,000/-per each TLF*
Adilabad	7	7	105000
Anantapur	12	8	120000
Chittoor	8	9	135000
East Godavari	12	16	240000
Guntur	13	16	240000
Kadapa	9	10	150000
Karimnagar	11	8	120000
Khammam	6	7	105000
Krishna	8	6	90000
Kurnool	10	7	105000
Mahabubnagar	9	4	60000
Medak	6	5	75000
Nalgonda	8	4	60000
Nellore	6	5	75000
Nizamabad	4	5	75000
Prakasam	8	4	60000
Ranga Reddy	2	2	30000
Srikakulam	5	5	75000
Visakhapatnam	4	4	30000
Vizianagaram	4	2	60000
Warangal	6	7	105000
West Godavari	9	7	105000
Cantonment	1	1	15000
GHMC	1	1	15000
GVMC	1	0	0
VMC	1	0	0
Total	171	150	2250000

Source: MEPMA—Action Plan, Hyderabad, A.P.
ULB: Urban Local Bodies
TLF: Town Level Federation

Action plan 2012-13, implementation of MEPMA activities such as conducting of General Body Meeting of TLFs for the year 2012-13 (release of funds) has been presented in Table 6.4.

It is seen that an amount of Rs. 22.5 lakhs @ Rs. 15,000/- to each TLF towards conducting General Body Meeting to 150 TLF under UCDN component of SJSRY and it is proposed to strengthen the existing slum level federations. CRP strengthen was being implemented in all the slums excluding mission Cities for strengthening SHGs and formation of Slum Level Federations (SLFs) through utilizing the technical expertise.

Observations

1. It is observed from Table 6.4, 22 districts one Cantonment, GHMC, GVMC and VMC and the major units ULBS. As on 05-11-2012, the No. of ULBs are shown in Column 3; in column 4, that No. of. TLFs proposed in the existing ULBS and the 5th column, an amount of proposed for General Body Meeting @ Rs. 15,000/-for each TLF.
2. It is seen that Guntur district is having 13 ULBs, later it has 16 ULBs and an amount of Rs. 2,40,000 (Rupees: Two lakhs and forty thousand) were sanctioned which is highest in Andhra Pradesh and the second place occupied by East Godavary with, 12 and 16 ULBs centres MEPMA has sanctioned an amount of Rs. 2,40,000/- (Rupees: Two lakhs and forty thousand) out of 22.50 lakhs for the entire Andhra Pradesh.

Conclusion

1. It is concluded that the Twelfth Five Year Plan also spelled out to form slum free city in order to eliminate slums in different geographical regions of metropolitan cities to towns in a hierarchy for poverty reduction.
2. For reducing the poverty in urban areas, Government of India has been designed and prescribed suitable approaches such as Mission for the Elimination of Poverty in Municipal Areas, Government of Andhra Pradesh. Environmental Assessments present a positive result in this direction.

Urban Self-Employment Progressive and its Progress

Financial Year: 2013-14

		USEP Progress for the Year				All Amounts in Rs. Lakhs	
Sl. No.	District	No. of Applications Registered	No. of Applications forward to Bank	No. of Applications consent given by Bank	Sanctioned	Grounded	Not-Grounded
1.	Anantapur	671	452	427	413	108	297
2.	Chittoor	664	618	617	607	366	241
3.	Cuddapah	663	544	462	436	243	193
4.	East Godavari	894	642	590	468	311	157
5.	Guntur	587	541	540	504	248	256
6.	GVMC	538	536	536	536	395	141
7.	Krishna	592	557	548	541	352	189
8.	Kurnool	591	543	542	488	130	358
9.	Nellore	500	437	435	435	370	65
10.	Prakasam	560	420	408	316	225	91
11.	Srikakulam	175	161	155	155	121	34
12.	Vishakhapatnam	160	133	132	132	117	15
13.	Vizianagaram	263	251	251	159	41	118
14.	VMC	110	110	110	110	14	96
15.	West Godavari	486	393	391	328	191	137
	Total	7454	6338	6144	5628	3240	2388

Source: MEPMA, Hyderabad, A.P.

Urban Self-Employment Progressive and its Progress

Financial Year: 2013-2014

Sl. No.	USEP Progress for the year							All amounts in Rs. lakhs		
	District	Target	No. of Applications	Sanctioned	Grounded	Not Grounded	Unit Cost	Bank Loan Amount	Subsidy Amount	Beneficiary Contribution
1.	Anantapur	550	671	413	116	297	379.80	265.83	94.95	18.99
2.	Chittoor	600	664	607	366	241	698.80	489.86	174.95	34.99
3.	Cuddapah	500	663	436	243	193	403.55	282.49	100.89	20.18
4.	East Godavari	600	894	468	311	157	567.05	396.94	141.76	28.35
5.	Guntur	600	587	504	248	256	464.82	325.37	116.21	23.24
6.	GVMC	800	538	536	395	141	717.15	502.01	179.29	35.86
7.	Krishna	500	592	541	352	189	549.15	384.41	137.29	27.46
8.	Kurnool	600	591	488	130	358	664.95	465.47	166.24	33.25
9.	Nellore	400	500	435	370	65	293.55	205.49	73.39	14.68
10.	Prakasam	300	560	316	225	91	284.10	198.87	71.03	14.21
11.	Srikakulam	200	175	155	121	34	162.30	113.61	40.58	8.12
12.	Vishakhapatnam	125	160	132	117	15	118.12	82.68	29.53	5.91
13.	Vizianagaram	200	263	159	41	118	161.15	112.81	40.29	8.06
14.	VMC	250	110	110	14	96	182.50	127.75	45.63	9.13
15.	West Godavari	400	486	328	191	137	387.48	271.24	96.87	19.37
	Total	6625	7454	5628	3240	2388	6034.47	4224.86	1508.9	301.8

Source: MEPMA, Hyderabad, A.P.

Urban Self-Employment Progressive and its Progress

Financial Year: 2012-2013

Sl. No.	USEP Progress for the year							All amounts in Rs. lakhs		
	District	Target	No. of Applications	Sanctioned	Grounded	Not Grounded	Unit Cost	Bank Loan Amount	Subsidy Amount	Beneficiary Contribution
1.	Anantapur	551	587	557	300	257	490.49	343.34	122.62	24.52
2.	Chittoor	648	804	769	528	241	834.99	584.49	208.75	41.75
3.	Cuddapah	500	554	496	322	174	482.65	337.86	120.66	24.13
4.	East Godavari	681	610	580	340	240	1022.65	715.86	255.66	51.13
5.	Guntur	603	695	645	451	194	655.82	459.07	163.96	32.79
6.	GVMC	804	365	322	129	193	308.84	216.19	77.21	15.44
7.	Krishna	509	562	496	317	179	502.35	351.65	125.59	25.12
8.	Kurnool	614	620	565	213	352	768.57	538.00	192.14	38.43
9.	Nellore	376	435	405	278	127	297.22	208.06	74.31	14.86
10.	Prakasam	332	355	303	174	129	279.05	195.34	69.76	13.95
11.	Srikakulam	200	122	122	121	1	109.85	76.90	27.46	5.49
12.	Vishakhapatnam	121	106	104	44	60	118.85	83.20	29.71	5.94
13.	Vizianagaram	208	212	211	140	71	216.61	151.63	54.15	10.83
14.	VMC	157	354	354	195	159	256.42	179.50	64.11	12.82
15.	West Godavari	421	423	417	297	120	445.21	311.65	111.30	22.26
	Total	6725	6804	6346	3849	2497	6789.57	4752.74	1697.39	339.46

Source: MEPMA, Hyderabad, A.P.

Urban Self-Employment Progressive and its Progress

Financial Year: 2011-2012

Sl. No.	District	USEP Progress for the year					All amounts in Rs. lakhs			
		Target	No. of Applications	Sanctioned	Grounded	Not Grounded	Unit Cost	Bank Loan Amount	Subsidy Amount	Beneficiary Contribution
1.	Anantapur	400	552	246	246	0	172.00	120.40	43.00	8.60
2.	Chittoor	500	696	560	560	0	548.02	383.61	137.01	27.40
3.	Cuddapah	450	616	441	441	0	406.55	284.59	101.64	20.33
4.	East Godavari	400	543	200	200	0	261.25	182.88	65.31	13.06
5.	Guntur	800	852	652	652	0	417.46	292.22	104.37	20.87
6.	GVMC	800	164	78	78	0	93.04	65.13	23.26	4.65
7.	Krishna	400	686	422	422	0	337.05	235.94	84.26	16.85
8.	Kurnool	500	573	352	352	0	395.99	277.19	99.00	19.80
9.	Nellore	450	477	313	313	0	287.40	201.18	71.85	14.37
10.	Prakasam	300	440	142	142	0	50.70	35.49	12.68	2.54
11.	Srikakulam	280	208	177	177	0	117.75	82.43	29.44	5.89
12.	Vishakhapatnam	150	134	80	80	0	93.79	65.65	23.45	4.69
13.	Vizianagaram	250	180	135	135	0	126.35	88.45	31.59	6.32
14.	VMC	700	194	165	165	0	129.26	90.48	32.32	6.46
15.	West Godavari	300	383	198	198	0	200.10	140.07	50.03	10.01
Total		6680	6698	4161	4161	0	3636.71	2545.71	909.21	181.84

Source: MEPMA, Hyderabad, A.P.

Urban Self-Employment Progressive and its Progress

Financial Year: 2010-2011

			USEP Progress for the year					All amounts in Rs. lakhs		
Sl. No.	District	Target	No. of Applications	Sanctioned	Grounded	Not Grounded	Unit Cost	Bank Loan Amount	Subsidy Amount	Beneficiary Contribution
1.	Anantapur	0	525	397	397	0	201.60	141.12	50.40	10.08
2.	Chittoor	0	465	387	387	0	308.70	216.09	77.18	15.44
3.	Cuddapah	0	396	347	347	0	162.55	113.79	40.64	8.13
4.	East Godavari	0	533	505	505	0	388.48	271.94	97.12	19.42
5.	Guntur	0	909	779	779	0	327.53	229.27	81.88	16.38
6.	GVMC	0	61	57	57	0	70.90	49.63	17.73	3.55
7.	Krishna	0	674	640	640	0	385.60	269.92	96.40	19.28
8.	Kurnool	0	476	418	418	0	336.10	235.27	84.03	16.81
9.	Nellore	0	321	308	308	0	180.75	126.53	45.19	9.04
10.	Prakasam	0	417	387	387	0	281.49	197.04	70.37	14.07
11.	Srikakulam	0	252	236	236	0	148.95	104.27	37.24	7.45
12.	Vishakhapatnam	0	172	105	105	0	102.61	71.83	25.65	5.13
13.	Vizianagaram	0	252	241	241	0	165.72	116.00	41.43	8.29
14.	VMC	0	714	35	35	0	6.85	4.80	1.71	0.34
15.	West Godavari	0	541	493	493	0	349.12	244.36	87.28	17.46
	Total	0	6708	5335	5335	0	3416.95	2391.88	854.25	170.87

Source: MEPMA, Hyderabad, A.P.

Urban Self-Employment Progressive and its Progress

Financial Year: 2009-2010

			USEP Progress for the year						*All amounts in Rs. lakhs*	
Sl. No.	*District*	*Target*	*No. of Applications*	*Sanctioned*	*Grounded*	*Not Grounded*	*Unit Cost*	*Bank Loan Amount*	*Subsidy Amount*	*Beneficiary Contribution*
1.	Anantapur	0	611	552	550	2	270.63	189.44	67.66	13.53
2.	Chittoor	0	436	382	382	0	185.52	129.87	46.38	9.28
3.	Cuddapah	0	249	247	247	0	101.97	71.38	25.49	5.10
4.	East Godavari	0	425	422	422	0	209.55	146.69	52.39	10.48
5.	Guntur	0	1080	1044	1044	0	373.89	261.72	93.47	18.69
6.	GVMC	0	72	72	72	0	32.65	22.86	8.16	1.63
7.	Krishna	0	458	443	443	0	185.10	129.57	46.28	9.26
8.	Kurnool	0	485	478	478	0	351.52	246.06	87.88	17.58
9.	Nellore	0	348	345	337	8	178.55	124.99	44.64	8.93
10.	Prakasam	0	484	478	478	0	246.63	172.64	61.66	12.33
11.	Srikakulam	0	173	173	173	0	73.85	51.70	18.46	3.69
12.	Vishakhapatnam	0	51	51	51	0	19.25	13.48	4.81	0.96
13.	Vizianagaram	0	114	111	111	0	52.09	36.46	13.02	2.60
14.	VMC	0	496	494	494	0	122.85	86.00	30.71	6.14
15.	West Godavari	0	534	472	472	0	228.93	160.25	57.23	11.45
	Total	0	6016	5764	5754	10	2632.98	1843.11	658.24	131.65

Source: MEPMA, Hyderabad, A.P.

Urban Self-Employment Progressive and its Progress

Financial Year: 2008-2009

			USEP Progress for the year					*All amounts in Rs. lakhs*		
Sl. No.	*District*	*Target*	*No. of Applications*	*Sanctioned*	*Grounded*	*Not Grounded*	*Unit Cost*	*Bank Loan Amount*	*Subsidy Amount*	*Beneficiary Contribution*
1.	Anantapur	0	501	338	338	0	157.03	109.92	39.26	7.85
2.	Chittoor	0	198	198	198	0	73.80	51.66	18.45	3.69
3.	Cuddapah	0	390	234	234	0	56.11	39.28	14.03	2.81
4.	East Godavari	0	402	400	400	0	159.41	111.59	39.85	7.97
5.	Guntur	0	352	351	351	0	81.76	57.23	20.44	4.09
6.	GVMC	0	72	72	72	0	28.49	19.94	7.12	1.42
7.	Krishna	0	190	185	185	0	77.37	54.16	19.34	3.87
8.	Kurnool	0	2015	651	651	0	224.31	157.02	56.08	11.22
9.	Nellore	0	47	47	47	0	23.50	16.45	5.88	1.18
10.	Prakasam	0	319	315	315	0	145.40	101.78	36.35	7.27
11.	Srikakulam	0	148	148	148	0	55.23	38.66	13.81	2.76
12.	Vishakhapatnam	0	26	26	26	0	5.55	3.89	1.39	0.28
13.	Vizianagaram	0	3	3	3	0	1.00	0.70	0.25	0.05
14.	VMC	0	0	0	0	0	0.00	0.00	0.00	0.00
15.	West Godavari	0	315	232	232	0	96.98	67.88	24.24	4.85
	Total	0	4978	3200	3200	0	1185.94	830.16	296.49	59.31

Source: MEPMA, Hyderabad, A.P.

Urban Self-Employment Progressive and its Progress

Financial Year: 2008-2009

USEP Progress for the year							All amounts in Rs. lakhs			
Sl. No	*District*	*Target*	*No. of Applications*	*Sanctioned*	*Grounded*	*Not Grounded*	*Unit Cost*	*Bank Loan Amount*	*Subsidy Amount*	*Beneficiary Contribution*
1.	Adilabad	0	59	57	57	0	27.60	19.32	6.90	1.38
2.	GHMC	0	31	31	31	0	6.40	4.48	1.60	0.32
3.	Karimnagar	0	0	0	0	0	0.00	0.00	0.00	0.00
4.	Khammam	0	125	105	105	0	50.05	35.04	12.51	2.50
5.	Mahabubnagar	0	53	53	53	0	19.75	13.83	4.94	0.99
6.	Medak	0	175	162	162	0	76.40	53.48	19.10	3.82
7.	Nalgonda	0	67	47	47	0	22.36	15.65	5.59	1.12
8.	Nizamabad	0	522	437	437	0	248.31	173.82	62.08	12.42
9.	Rangareddi	0	10	10	10	0	6.50	4.55	1.63	0.33
10.	Warangal	0	61	0	0	0	0.00	0.00	0.00	0.00
	Total	0	1103	902	902	0	457.37	320.17	114.35	22.88

Source: MEPMA, Hyderabad, A.P.

Urban Self-Employment Progressive and its Progress

Financial Year: 2009-2010

			USEP Progress for the year							*All amounts in Rs. lakhs*
Sl. No.	*District*	*Target*	*No. of Applications*	*Sanctioned*	*Grounded*	*Not Grounded*	*Unit Cost*	*Bank Loan Amount*	*Subsidy Amount*	*Beneficiary Contribution*
1.	Adilabad	0	167	131	131	0	72.15	50.50	18.04	3.61
2.	GHMC	0	4	3	3	0	1.50	1.05	0.38	0.08
3.	Karimnagar	0	177	177	177	0	89.60	62.72	22.40	4.48
4.	Khammam	0	162	162	162	0	80.90	56.63	20.23	4.05
5.	Mahabubnagar	0	298	271	270	1	152.78	106.95	38.20	7.64
6.	Medak	0	201	170	170	0	78.35	54.85	19.59	3.92
7.	Nalgonda	0	204	191	191	0	102.70	71.89	25.68	5.14
8.	Nizamabad	0	208	203	203	0	93.70	65.59	23.43	4.69
9.	Rangareddi	0	235	233	233	0	75.52	52.86	18.88	3.78
10.	Warangal	0	198	198	198	0	91.65	64.16	22.91	4.58
	Total	0	1854	1739	1738	1	838.85	587.2	209.74	41.97

Source: MEPMA, Hyderabad, A.P.

Urban Self-Employment Progressive and its Progress

Financial Year: 2010-2011

USEP Progress for the year										*All amounts in Rs. lakhs*
Sl. No.	*District*	*Target*	*No. of Applications*	*Sanctioned*	*Grounded*	*Not Grounded*	*Unit Cost*	*Bank Loan Amount*	*Subsidy Amount*	*Beneficiary Contribution*
1.	Adilabad	0	278	233	233	0	324.26	226.98	81.06	16.21
2.	GHMC	0	339	102	102	0	47.70	33.39	11.93	2.39
3.	Karimnagar	0	261	240	240	0	174.09	121.86	43.52	8.70
4.	Khammam	0	271	270	270	0	164.40	115.08	41.10	8.22
5.	Mahabubnagar	0	260	222	222	0	152.32	106.62	38.08	7.62
6.	Medak	0	237	181	181	0	88.82	62.17	22.21	4.44
7.	Nalgonda	0	270	225	225	0	198.23	138.76	49.56	9.91
8.	Nizamabad	0	218	174	174	0	87.00	60.90	21.75	4.35
9.	Rangareddi	0	94	76	76	0	36.80	25.76	9.20	1.84
10.	Warangal	0	151	123	123	0	97.15	68.01	24.29	4.86
	Total	0	2379	1846	1846	0	1370.77	959.53	342.7	68.54

Source: MEPMA, Hyderabad, A.P.

Urban Self-Employment Progressive and its Progress

Financial Year: 2011-2012

All amounts in Rs. lakhs

Sl. No.	District	Target	No. of Applications	Sanctioned	Grounded	Not Grounded	Unit Cost	Bank Loan Amount	Subsidy Amount	Beneficiary Contribution
1.	Adilabad	450	453	365	365	0	405.29	283.70	101.32	20.26
2.	GHMC	978	791	189	189	0	137.36	96.15	34.34	6.87
3.	Karimnagar	250	285	182	182	0	190.50	133.35	47.63	9.53
4.	Khammam	250	222	176	176	0	117.65	82.36	29.41	5.88
5.	Mahabubnagar	250	261	152	152	0	118.55	82.99	29.64	5.93
6.	Medak	251	266	149	149	0	103.90	72.73	25.98	5.20
7.	Nalgonda	250	206	77	77	0	81.50	57.05	20.38	4.08
8.	Nizamabad	250	254	157	157	0	166.90	116.83	41.73	8.35
9.	Rangareddi	146	81	41	41	0	23.00	16.10	5.75	1.15
10.	Warangal	245	193	127	127	0	192.50	134.75	48.13	9.63
	Total	3320	3012	1615	1615	0	1537.15	1076.01	384.31	76.88

Source: MEPMA, Hyderabad, A.P.

Urban Self-Employment Progressive and its Progress

Financial Year: 2012-2013

All amounts in Rs. lakhs

Sl. No.	*District*	*Target*	*No. of Applications*	*Sanctioned*	*Grounded*	*Not Grounded*	*Unit Cost*	*Bank Loan Amount*	*Subsidy Amount*	*Beneficiary Contribution*
1.	Adilabad	359	477	463	327	136	584.90	409.43	146.23	29.25
2.	GHMC	733	534	340	76	264	251.37	175.96	62.84	12.57
3.	Karimnagar	471	209	186	85	101	194.00	135.80	48.50	9.70
4.	Khammam	419	377	347	267	80	281.00	196.70	70.25	14.05
5.	Mahabubnagar	327	355	280	223	57	213.80	149.66	53.45	10.69
6.	Medak	190	200	191	167	24	136.85	95.80	34.21	6.84
7.	Nalgonda	241	423	313	147	166	362.03	253.42	90.51	18.10
8.	Nizamabad	234	189	176	142	34	148.30	103.81	37.08	7.42
9.	Rangareddi	112	87	76	55	21	27.85	19.50	6.96	1.39
10.	Warangal	141	160	151	125	26	269.55	188.69	67.39	13.48
	Total	3227	3011	2523	1614	909	2469.65	1728.77	617.42	123.49

Source: MEPMA, Hyderabad, A.P.

Urban Self-Employment Progressive and its Progress

Financial Year: 2013-2014

All amounts in Rs. lakhs

Sl. No.	District	Target	No. of Applications	Sanctioned	Grounded	Not Grounded	Unit Cost	Bank Loan Amount	Subsidy Amount	Beneficiary Contribution
1.	Adilabad	375	473	386	243	143	472.30	330.61	118.08	23.62
2.	GHMC	780	663	279	103	176	190.51	133.36	47.63	9.53
3.	Karimnagar	470	726	479	0	479	512.20	358.54	128.05	25.61
4.	Khammam	400	427	328	244	84	249.10	174.37	62.28	12.46
5.	Mahabubnagar	350	464	310	218	92	263.95	184.77	65.99	13.20
6.	Medak	200	156	128	82	46	102.27	71.59	25.57	5.11
7.	Nalgonda	250	605	171	14	157	210.05	147.04	52.51	10.50
8.	Nizamabad	250	324	222	164	58	208.90	146.23	52.23	10.45
9.	Rangareddi	100	114	99	51	48	53.27	37.29	13.32	2.66
10.	Warangal	200	256	218	0	218	391.60	274.12	97.90	19.58
	Total	3375	4208	2620	1119	1501	2654.15	1857.92	663.56	132.72

Source: MEPMA, Hyderabad, A.P.

3. KUDUMASREE urban CDS and its Environmental Impact as a positive sign for poverty reduction.
4. Livelihood generation initiatives of Government of Gujarat has left an indelible mark on the poverty reduction.
5. Finally, it is concluded Rajasthan Mission for Skill and Livelihood gives an exemplary status of poverty reductions in urban areas.

NOTES

1. Report of the working group on Urban Poverty, Slums and Service Delivery System, Steering Committee on Urbanization, plg.com U.D. 3rd October, 2011, p. 83.
2. Proceedings of the National Conference on Urban Poverty Alleviation 18th & 19th June, 2005, Srinagar, Jammu & Kashmir, Government of India, Ministry of Urban Employment and Poverty Alleviation, pp.73-76.
3. Source http://www.srrth.org/saater/indes.Ph.d?option=com-content & view=article &id=71&itemid=78.
4. Ref.http://rajasthanlivelihoods.org/index.html

7

Social Mobilization—A Strategy for Poverty Alleviation

T. Aishwarya

Introduction

Social mobilization is defined as the mass movement to engage people's participation in a process and is used by grassroots organizations to achieve a common goal. Social mobilization is the process of bringing together all feasible and practical inter-sectoral allies/partners to raise awareness of and demand for a particular programme, to assist in the delivery of resources and services and to strengthen community participation for sustainability and self-reliance. The process of social mobilization has a definite objective. Following the strategy of social mobilization SHGs are created with a view to achieving savings mobilization, obtaining credit for emergent requirements, mutual help and economic upliftment through income generating activities.

Social mobilization as a panacea for poverty alleviation the government embarked upon a major programme of organization of women into SHGs in many states for the last two decades. Having seen the experiences of United Nations Development Programme (UNDP), South Asia Poverty Alleviation Programme (SAPAP), District Poverty Initiatives Programme (DPIP), and Rural Poverty Reduction Programme (RPRP) in AP and finally Swarna Jayanthi Shahari Rozgar Yojana (SJSRY) in urban areas has given a fillip to the strategy of social mobilization for poverty alleviation. Now, it is time for us to take stock of the situation and identify the bottlenecks in implementation of the SJSRY and overcome with a view to mobilize the poor into self-sustained and self-reliant communities with sustainable livelihoods.

Further, it is essential to highlight the lessons learnt from SJSRY which clearly pointed out that the weak delivery mechanisms due to inadequate participation of the communities apart from lack of convergence among stakeholders, lack of capacity building of poor, lack of flow of credit to the urban poor for self-employment among others. Hence, National Urban Livelihood Mission (NULM) which is going to subsume SJSRY emphasized the need for demand driven paradigm for distribution of funds instead of allocation based strategy and facilitating the building of institutions of the poor and their capacities to implement the programmes by themselves with the support of government and civil society. Hence, the idea is to address the gap areas and implement the NULM in a much more meaningful way so that the communities get benefit from the government initiative.

The Change

Social mobilization approach has yielded positive results in organizing poor women into self-help groups and linking them to banks for small credit and thus enabling them to improve their livelihoods. Consequently, concrete social capital has been created among women in the state and social empowerment is on the rise. Further, the groups in Andhra Pradesh became central to the development process as the government cannot think of implementing any new initiative without their role and participation. AP being educated society women became active participants of development especially in health, education and livelihood promotion among others. Besides, this poverty levels are reduced drastically owing to the five components of SJSRY in the state though STEP-UP has been used to some extent. SJSRY has opened up new opportunities to the women belonging to SHGs and many are utilizing the bank linkage and social empowerment initiative taken up by the State government.

A serious attempt has been made to strengthen the capacities of SHG women through CRP strategy. Visit to ULBs has revealed that the women are in the process of moving towards empowerment by learning from training programmes. In fact, they became confident in speaking with the officials, even with the district level officials, while trying to secure government benefits. However, the level of confidence and capacities vary across different ULBs in a district and again from district to district.

The issue of social capital has been examined in our study in understanding the process of empowerment of women in the state. Many women who became members of the group began developing their levels of understanding and awareness on various issues. There is a close relationship among group members and a kind of bond existed; they showed solidarity when there is a problem to fellow members. There are instances wherein the group members contributed for the exigencies of their members. Their self-confidence and self-esteem levels are high after the participation in SHGs which is something remarkable that made Andhra Pradesh as unique compared to other states in the country.

Emerging Challenges

The results of social mobilization and poverty alleviation have resulted in the formation and nurturing of SHGs which are so impressive in terms of their functioning that it is attracting a lot of attention from all corners of the society. However, some challenges that need to be addressed encountered by SHGs that can significantly contribute to participatory urban development are outlined below:

- Group formation of women through social mobilization and their capacity building in urban areas on a saturation basis should be the agenda that should be given priority.
- Monitoring regularly by a team of experts by designing a framework of indicators would be useful in knowing the implementation arrangements, the process, output and outcomes. It can also enable us to suggest mid-course corrections if the programme is off the track.
- Community based trainings, by senior members of the group, should become an in-built activity of SHGs over a period of time.
- A decision by MEPMA may help the groups in reducing the interest rate on internal lending among groups would go a long way in improving the economic condition of poor women.

- Preparation of necessary guidelines such as restrictions in taking loans from other private agencies/NBFCs and awareness generation with a view to explain the adverse effects of MFI loans and finally avoiding taking MFI loans.

Social Mobilization and Community Development: The Role of Women

The status of women in the society is quite important and their role in society whether it is urban or rural occupied a superior place. The population composition in a State/Centre, almost nearly have equal size or sometimes to a tune of 51 per cent with male population and 49 per cent with female population. It is understood that women's participation in community development work has been started straight from 1958 onwards and it was the beginning of Urban Community Development Projects (UCD Projects), Government of India, New Delhi. In the process of Social mobilization, compared to man, women have an active, reactive and predominantly an interactive role in community development works.

Social Mobilization

Social mobilization is a pre-requisite for community development and it requires the following characteristics. They are: (1) homogeneity of individuals with common interest, (2) common need, (3) common opportunity, and (4) collective strength. Therefore, Homogeneity + Common Need + Common Opportunity +

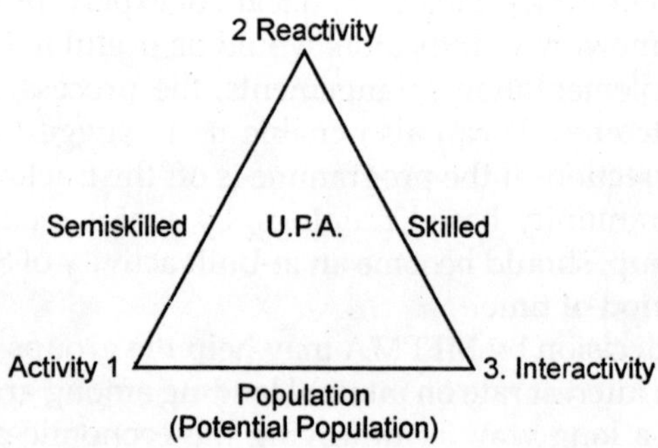

Fig. 7.1: Social Mobilization Women

Collective Strength is brought out through social mobilization. The process could be seen in the following Figure.

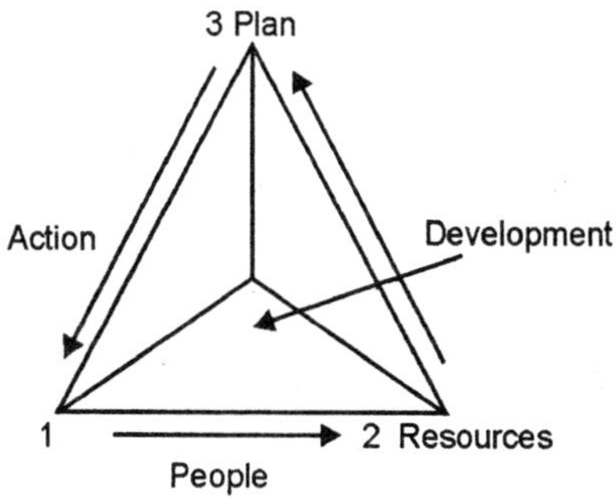

Fig. 7.2: Community Organizational System.

According to Fig. 7.2 Community Organizational System has its own mechanism where in peoples activity (role) with resources in accordance with a specific plan and the activated activity gives fruits. That is to say that people plus resources combined and systematically (mini plan) if envisaged may leads to development not only to the individuals but also to the group of individuals spatially and temporally. This is a spatio-temporal model yields/ gives development. The role of women in social mobilization is presented in the following paragraphs. The views expressed by Mrs. S.K. Pandet, B.S. Bennie, D. Pulla Rao, Nivedita Nath and *et al.*; K. Saritha; K. Saritha and Venkateswarlu, M., Rajasekhar, E.M., Raji, Mandakini Pant and Sobhita Rajagopal's works were considered as the backdrop of the present chapter and also dealt with historical perspectives with identified gaps in literature, Hypothesis, objectives and benefits of Social Mobilization involves several steps for meeting the objectives and targeted results were also presented.

Historical Perspective

Historically, it is evident that women are able and stable to do the necessary work at house besides her roles from sun to moon (i.e.) metamorphosing her roles vary from youth, mature and old stage. They are baby; daughter, sister, wife, daughter-in-law, mother, mother-in-law grandmother and great grandmother etc. we can identify her roles according to her age and stage of development over a period of time. We can view this as a temporal change. Women's role in the family as wells as in the society are quite useful and could not be measured by any means. They want to be independent but circumstances warranted them to be dependent in view of the non-earning capacity situation existed in the old society and contemporary location and situation of urban and rural systems. In addition to this, according to Manu, "Nastree Swatamtramarnayet". It means that women should not be given independence and current situation warrants any society or individual should have to extend the power of independence to act according to her own choices. Traditionally her place at home was cooking, child bearing, rearing, catering to the relatives, family members comprised of her work and life activities. Current situation has changed the entire scenario. Besides the above, in the modern period, women additionally have to perform their duties in employment. More and more women are employed in new avenues of employment and new occupations. In modern times, we have been witnessing women Chief Ministers, women Prime Ministers and ambassadors at state, the National and International levels in political life besides becoming Professors/Principals/Head of the Departments/Dean/Director and also like Vice-Chancellor to the great Universities brining fame to the society as well as to the mother land. They enjoy more and more opportunities. It is apt to identify that no gender discrimination is there for any post-carrying equal rights and opportunities current situation spells-out that ***equal rights and equal opportunities*** on par with the other (Male) gender. This is the contemporary situation exists for both the genders. Women may be able to become an entrepreneur as well as ready for empowerment with all her capacities, capabilities and caliber.

Empowerment of Women through Collectivization

Groups and federations are inextricably woven together into the realm of urban poverty alleviation in India today. With the ever-increasing awareness on the role of the user groups in the sustainability of all development initiatives, social mobilization and subsequent collectivization of homogenous groups within the community is often taken as the first step in scheme implementation. The formation of Self-Help Groups (SHGs) started in India way back in the early 90's with the NABARD promoting rural SHGs as a pre-requisite for financing them for various initiatives. Similarly, the Rashtriya Mahila Kosh (RMK) as an initiative of the government sought to make available micro-credit to groups for a series of initiatives of income generations through Non-governmental organizations. It might be mentioned that these institutional initiatives have gone a long way in the development of the earliest groups.

Mrs. S.K. Pandit (1998)[1] has identified and stated that, "the directive principles are fundamental in the governance of the county and are to be applied in enacting legislation, they are not judicially enforceable". "That the State should not discriminate against any citizen on grounds of sex, among other things, it provides that nothing in this article shall prevent the state from making any special provision for women and children. So, there is a constitutional provision in India permitting the state to discriminate in favour of women, if such discrimination is found necessary. "Finally opined that women claim to be largest majority in India with a variety of social and economic disabilities which prevent them from exercising their human rights and freedom in society".

Pulla Rao, D. (2012)[2] has identified that, "though women share equally with men in population, they are treated unequally in all other aspects. Even in the urbanized and sophisticated countries they are treated as the second rated citizen with subordination to men and further presented that, in the recent past, women entrepreneurs have been playing an increasingly important role in promoting growth and economic development of the country". Nebedita Nath[3] presented in a paper on "problems and prospects of emerging entrepreneurship among women in slums of Western Orissa" had expressed that the absence of the traditional economy women in slums are now adhering themselves to different new forms of economic activities. The SHGs are playing a major role in promoting entrepreneurship among the women in slums. According to the authors courage will make women self reliant providing new avenues followed by economics, security and empowerment. Saritha, K.,[4] and *et al.*; have presented a scenario on "Socio-economic conditions of women Micro-entrepreneurs of Tirupati Region, Chittoor, district particularly mentioned that women constitute an integral part of socio-economic life and actively participate in socio-economic development women are the victims of poverty and unemployment. The problem of poverty and unemployment cannot be solved unless women are able to participate fully in the economic and social development of the country". Saritha, K. and Venkateswarlu, M.,[5] have presented in their paper on "Impact of Success of Micro-Enterprises on the Women Micro-Entrepreneurship of Tirupati Region, Chittoor district—A study on Women Empowerment" made further an attempt to analyze the impact of the success of the micro-enterprises on the women—micro-entrepreneurs in Tirupati Region of Chittoor district. The authors found that the Micro-enterprises and the resources generated thereby had a positive impact on the status of the women and it lead to economic development of women. T. Rajasekar[6] and *et al.*; have stated in their paper on "Muslim Women Empowerment through Mat Weaving" revealed that majority of them are getting below Rs. 3,000/- per month, getting disease from mat weaving and they are not at all aware of the medical facilities for its treatment. Their exquisite silkan mats have won the admiration of celebrities for over a century. Paradoxically the Shrinkage tribe remains in search of support and wider recognition. They have recommended policy oriented measures for the upliftment of the conditions of the mat weavers". "Micro-finance and women empowerment" by E.M. Reji[7] where in argues that there is an evidence that micro-finance programme have contributed significantly to women's empowerment by helping them to develop the habit of saving and accessing credit at an affordable rate besides helping members to gain confidence and self respect. While most micro-finance programmes target women, and aim at their empowerments, only a few have attempted to measure empowerment in the context of micro-finance. In this article the author presents findings of a study which attempts to provide a framework for assessing empowerment in the context of micro-finance programmes. The five key elements used to explain empowerment in this framework involve. Power, autonomy and reliance, participation, capacity building and entitlement. The author concludes that micro-finance creates an enabling environment for empowerment and the framework presented in this article it can be used for empowerment and that the framework projected in this article can be used for empowerment in other programme contexts with suitable modifications.

According to Reji, "the concept of empowerment has broadened to include the growing concern of women's movement for gender equality and social justice. Thus, empowerment is viewed as a process where powerless gain greater control over circumstances and their lives. It includes control over both resources and ideology, greater self confidence and an inner transformation of one's consciousness to overcome external barriers. Empowerment is a continuous process and takes place in three steps involving dependency independence and inter-dependence. The first stage has been channelized by the dependence of individuals on others for everything. The second stage involves the development of the ability to take individual or collective decisions without the intervention of any intermediaries or external forces. In this stage, individuals develop confidence and the abilities to raise one's voice, when it is considered the basic element of one's empowerment. In the third stage, individuals develop an increased consciousness among them" (p. 560). This increased mobility leads to attaining a greater sense of self-confidence (Khaand Kar and Pith, 1966). He has presented three paradigms. 3 distinct paradigms are as follows: (1) feminist empowerment paradigm, (2) poverty alleviation paradigm and (3) financial self-sustainability paradigm.

The 'Poverty Alleviation Paradigm' is based on the principles of self-help to build sustainable livelihoods and sustainable communities; micro-finance is often an integrated part of the strategy for poverty alleviation. Gender lobbies have argued for women because of higher levels of poverty and responsibility among women. Under the poverty alleviation paradigm, "empowerment is frequently used and often synonymously with a multidimensional definition of poverty alleviation" (p. 563). The women's name is a symbol of their own independence and medium through which they exercise collective citizenship. The women claimed that after the Sangha's name had been constructed, the groups have become more cohesive and as a result, they feel empowered. Mandakani Pant's[8] Study of Self-Help Groups (SHGs) from the economically backward areas of three States about their role in the planning process in Panchayati Raj System. It was found that SHG's are providing a supportive lease to the women from the marginalized communities by mobilizing community level activism. SHG's can enhance women's participation by ensuring accountability to Gram Panchayats mobilizing Grama Sabha, support to elected representatives, and creating social capital. Sabita Rajgopal also stated that, the women development programmes exercise in Rajasthan clearly established that the poor, non literate woman given space and support could reflect, articulate and challenge injustice. The Sathins developed skills of communication, mobilization and reflection. They grew to become leaders assuming a greater degree of control over their lives. There was a clear recognition that catalyzing change would necessitate a change in the self-image, leading to change in the social image. However, the challenge is to build capabilities and abilities wherein marginalized groups can become agents of social change and action and gain meaningful opportunities as citizens. Women's resource based livelihood in the wider context of development viewed through lens of citizenship rights. It is emphasized that there is much to be learnt from emphatic interaction with the collective struggle of poor women and from action and dialogue on the ground. The aim is towards recasting citizenship for a gender just development that ensures women's livelihood rights.[9]

Collectives have more Strength

It is a well accepted pheonomena that the collectives have more strength than individuals and this is the theory as to how women of homogenous backgrounds having similar objectives and needs are formed into groups to emancipate themselves from the poverty. Acknowledging the importance of social mobilization, 13th Five Year Plan, added two buzz words inclusive growth and convergence. The newly introduced NULM seeks to strengthen the poor in community in a "Right-Based Approach" rather than benefit receiving mode. This is definitely an additional improvement over the existing paradigm of bottom up and 'demand-responsive" approach. The opportunities could be tapped only when the community plays an important role and take active part in identification of the right individuals for the training, keeping in view of the strong infrastructure within which there are embedded. This will lead to the ownership of the initiatives and their identification with the impacts that the programme inputs create in terms of better employability, skill and knowledge base. This helps to achieve equal development of all segments of the poor community, namely women, youth, children, different categories of literates, skilled and semiskilled and self-employed.

Social Mobilization
1st Step

1 → **1. Accounting and Book keeping Maintenance of records for**
- i. Meeting like agenda, resolutions, visitors
- ii. Passbook, Thrift, of interest rates Internal lending, Repayment and defaults

2 → **2. Groups & Federations**
1. Maintenance of Books
2. Thrift and Credit System
3. Repayment
4. Community Based Recovery Management (CBRM)
5. Micro Credit-Plan (MCP)

2nd Step

3 → **3. Bank Linkage**
1. Revolving fund
2. Community investment fund
3. Credit guarantee fund
4. Universal financial inclusion
5. Basic savings bank account

4 → **4. Best Practices**
1. Community based capacity building
2. Social Action Committees
3. Food security/Rice Credit line
4. C.R.P. strategy

3rd Step

5 → **5. Livelihood Promotion**
1. Concept of livelihood
2. Innovation strategy
3. MBCs and Self-Employment
4. Sustainable livelihood promotion through groups

6 → **6. Sustainability Issues**
1. Rating
2. Community based Mobilization and evaluation
3. Self reliant community groups

Fig. 7.1: Social mobilization involves several steps for meeting the objectives and targeted results (Structure)

Community Mobilization in SJSRY and NULM

NULM: Social Mobilization and Institution Building

An important focus of NULM is the component of Social Mobilization and Institution Building that is built into the principles, values and strategy of the Mission. This makes social mobilization assume paramount place in the implementation of the NULM. Starting with core belief that the poor are entrepreneurial by nature having an innate desire to come out of poverty, the NULM cites motivation of the urban poor to form their own institutions as the very first step, followed by capacity building in order to manage the external environment, access finance, expand their skills, enterprises by offering them continuous and carefully designed handholding support, duly induced by a dedicated and sensitive support structure right from the national to city and community level. The core values of the NULM prioritizes prominence to the community Owner ship and productive involvement of the urban poor and their institutions in all processes strengthened through transparency and at the same time holding the government functionaries and the community equally accountable. These would ultimately work towards the community achieving self-reliance, self-dependence, self and mutual help.

The NULM strategy includes building the capacity of the urban poor and their institutions as well as the institutions involved in implementation of the mission through support on which the further structures of stabilization and enhancement of livelihood options, build skills to access market-based job opportunities and establishment of micro-enterprises. On this foundation are built the components of permanent shelter with basic infrastructural facilities.

UPA through Community Development Society

In the area of Urban Poverty Alleviation (UPA), the formation of SHG's started with the UBSP wherein the concept of Community Development Society (CDS) as a viable structure through which all activities related to the provision of basic amenities was initiated. This three tier structure representing the community (usually a slum or Basthi) was envisioned to be initiated with the presence of a Resident Community Volunteer (RCV) who would initiate the process by formation of groups called as Neighbourhood Groups (NHGs) That may also function as Thrift and Credit (T & C) Groups which would take up various works/Supervision of works related to the provision of basic services. The NHGs were further federated at the slum level into Neighbourhood Committees (NHCs) and further at the ULB level into community Development Society (CDS). In case of large municipalities, an Area Development Society (ADS) was also envisioned at the intermediary level of the ward.

The organization of the community in Kerala as part of the Kudumbashree has coincided with the introduction of the SJSRY and therefore, the implementation of the programme has created model for the rest of the country. The major point is that while this is so, the CDS structure grew into a vibrant module for Social Mobilization Close at the heels of Kerala, the AP government also developed strong CDS structure, further strengthened through the initiation of the Andhra Pradesh Urban Services for the Poor (APUSP) initiated in 32 class-I towns and further extended to other towns in the state. Other southern states and some of the states like Gujarat and West Bengal also achieved commendable success in the implementation of the program. The APUSP, which has implemented from 2000 to 2008, subsequently got integrated into the government as a Mission programme implemented by a dedicated nodal organization called Mission for the Elimination of Poverty in Urban Areas (MEPMA) as an autonomous body under the direct control of the C & DMA empirical strategies presented in the 7th chapter inclusive of testing of Hypothesis.

The NULM in its concept and thrust is focused on social mobilization as an important element of implementation. In a way, it is the evolution of the programme to the current stage which leverages the learning's as well as the successes achieved in the earlier versions into this version. The effective implementation of the SJSRY is dependent on the involvement of the community in utilizing the provisions therein. The third objective of the SJSRY Guidelines relates to "empowering the community to tackle the issues of urban poverty through suitable self-managed community structures like Neighbourhood Groups (NHGs), Neighbourhood Committees (NHC), Community Development Society (CDs) etc." The concept of groups and federations has emerged out over a period of time.

The encouraging part of these programs including SJSRY was that people's participation constituted the basic principle in designing and implementing these programs. This approach is no doubt a breakthrough in the strategy of improving the lifestyle of the Urban poor and to prepare the Urban Community to shoulder higher responsibility in improving the Socio-Economic and political picture of India.

In SJSRY programme formation of Neighbourhood groups (NHG), Neighbourhood Committees (NHC) and Community

Development Society (CDS) as the apex and coordination body have been establishing far-reaching impact on the overall development. The responsibility of the community structure envisaged and developed in the SJSRY Programme is mainly restricted to poverty eradication through a set of given and innovative programme now being implemented. The functioning of these Community Organization manned by women selected by the community from below the Poverty line and named as Resident Community volunteers (RCV) has already attracted attention and it is expected that this strategy will revolutionize the Urban Development in foreseeable future.

SJSRY rest on foundation of Community empowerment and its implementation is through community organization for the purpose. Community Organization like Neighbourhood Group (NHG), Neighbourhood Committees (NHC) Community Development Societies (CDs) have been set up in target areas on prescribed pattern. The CDS is the focal point for purpose of identification of beneficiaries, preparation of applications monitoring or recovery generally for providing whatever other support is necessary to the programme. The CDS also identify viable projects suitable for the particular area. The CDS may also set themselves up Thrift and Credit societies to encourage community savings as also other group activities. CDS is a registered body, hence has been authorized to have access to funds under various schemes as also wider finance and credit base. CDS is the nodal agency of this programme. CDS lay emphasis on providing the entire gamut of social sector input to their areas including health, welfare, education etc. Thorough establishing convergence between schemes implemented by different departments.

Since 1992, UBSP has grown from a handful of cities and women participating to a network in 25 States and Union Territories and over 1,30,000 women volunteers organized in 30,000 Neighbourhood associations, recognized by the Government. Many of these women have said that before UBSP they were in their homes and could not interact with outsiders. Now, through the training and guidance provided, they are more confident, articulate and unafraid to make their needs and demands known both within and outside their homes. Over 100 of these volunteers have contested municipal elections (1995) with over 60 elected to date! One of the UBSP cities, Alleppey in Kerala received the UN "We the Peoples Award" in 1995 (September) for its remarkable achievements in women's organization for children and women's needs.

(i) Institutional Framework: At the national level, UBSP is one of several programmes under the Ministry of Urban Affairs and Employment's (MOUA&E) Urban Poverty Alleviation Programme (UPA), with specific objectives of women's empowerment; attainment of social sector goals; and convergence with other Government schemes for long-term sustainability. State Urban Development Agencies or Cells manage the programme with structures also at the district level, especially those which have many cities and towns.

Within this overall national framework, the community organizational system is what makes UBSP a unique government effort for facilitating peoples participation, beginning in urban poor Neighbourhoods. One (or more) RCVs (Resident Community Volunteers) are elected by her Neighbourhood (15-40 households) as a focal point for communication and interaction forming a Neighbourhood Group (NHG). Units of NHGs (around 10 groups) from Neighbourhood Committees where mini plans are prepared, resources mobilized, and action taken. When formally registered, they may receive programme resources for direct management of activities. In some States, Community Development Societies at city or ward level are registered for advocacy, planning and resource mobilization especially for thrift and credit. Through UBSP, one paid Community organizer is generally available for initial organization and planning work for 2000 households (10,000 persons), expected to work intensively in the communities for several years, helping the women towards self-reliant action. After some time, Community Organizers initiate efforts in other Neighbourhoods, often with the help of RCVs. At city level, Urban Poverty Alleviation Committees/Units are formed for convergence among departments and overall management.

Development of Social Capital—Family Counseling Centres

To empower women in legal matters and rights of women, the Family Counseling Centres (FCCs) are established to provide training to poor urban women to enable them to resolve their family disputes by adopting various methods of counselling and thereby save expenditure on court litigations. FCCs were initiated in 21 towns and so far 8410 cases have been resolved. The process includes identification of paralegal workers, formation of Social Action Committees and Capacity Building of paralegal workers. The impact of FCCs has been that the number of disputes have been reduced resulting in happy families.

Deployment of Highly Trained Nagardeepikas

The Nagardeepikas are active and experienced members of the Self-Help Groups trained in various aspects like SHG concepts, Insurance, Family budget plans and solid waste management. Around 4400 Nagardeepikas have been trained and positioned in ULBs. These Nagardeepikas who are knowledge workers and change agents are readily available for taking up various community based services like Insurance and recovery mechanisms.

Citizen Resource Centre

To sensitize the urban poor about their needs, a citizen resource centre is set up in each town wherein all kinds of information can be made available and disseminated. The functions of the centre includes: drop in facility, learning centre, meeting place for social gatherings, venue for various trainings and centre of information and knowledge on services available with the Government and NGOs. Self-Help Groups are mostly informal groups whose members pool savings and re-lend within the group on rotational need basis. These groups have a common perception of need and impulse towards collective action. Most of these groups got formed around specific production activity, promoted savings among members and use the pooled resources to meet emergent needs of members, including consumption needs. Since the SHGs were able to mobilize savings from the poor who were not expected to have any savings and could also recycle effectively the pooled savings among members, they succeeded in performing/providing banking services to their members, may be in a primitive way, but in a manner which was cost effective, simple, flexible and available at the door step of the members.

Issues of Skill Development

Issues of skill development, Affordable Housing Schemes, BSUP & IHSDP HIGHLIGHTS OF PROGRESS BY 31.12.2011, Progress of Reforms, Progress on 3 Pro-Poor Key Reforms, Internal earmarking with in local body budgets for Basic Services to the Urban Poor, Progress of Reforms, High Level Committee and Rajiv Awas Yojana (RAY) are discussed and presented for understanding the process and the action which await legal functionalities (i.e.) from proposed (Bill) and Reform (Act) to implement them into for the welfare of the citizens. Indian economy is marked with low levels of skills base: in 2004-05, only 2 per cent of individuals of employable age of 15 to 29 years had received formal vocational training and 8 per cent of individuals received non-formal training. In contrast, many of the developed economies have 60 to 80 per cent of skilled workforce (e.g., Korea, 96% skilled work force). The country has 9039 Industrial Training Institutes/Centres with seating capacity of 12.16 lakh, which needs to be increased. An important aspect related to this is the availability of relevant skills. The skill development system needs to be driven by the current demand in the industry to make it relevant and reduce the mis-match. One of the important reasons for the mis-match is the lack of a proper mechanism for collect information on the labour market. Further the trainings have a need to be accepted beyond the local institutions in order to offer scope for the individual aspirant to search for employment outside. Often skill development trainings suffer the limitation of being offered only to suit the specific requirement of the industry seeking incumbents and the trainings are tailor-made for the purpose and may become limited beyond the given scope. Certification and accreditation of trainings on a larger scale (which is recognized at the state and national levels and beyond) would help address this issue effectively. This certification, based on concrete criteria like curriculum (that is in keeping with the employers' requirements as well as the current needs), consistency of trainer capability, mandatory number of hours of training and a third-party evaluation of candidates' performance would add to the authenticity of the training imparted. On the other hand, many skill development initiatives are given by training institutions that are purely theoretical with limited practical applicability. In both cases there is limited scope for the trained individual to secure the employment suitable to the training.

There is a need to develop a mechanism of defining the skills related to the sector broadly at the bare minimum, which are defined by reputed councils of vocational and skill development. These councils can play the important role of standardizing the minimum requirements of training in any sector, which can be further built upon by the employing institutions to suit their specific requirements.

Last, but not the least, traditional skills that have retained their relevance in the contemporary market which are passed on across generations should be preserved while seeking to formalize this system so as to retain and perpetuate the cultural weave in which they are embedded. Toy-making, brass and other metal curios, food dye based fabric making etc. to name a few, which reflect the culture and heritage of the area from which they originate, need to be preserved, and made exclusive through mechanisms like Geographical Indication (GI) protection and certification.

It is worthwhile mentioning that the National Skill Development Policy, formulated in early 2009 targets creation of 500 million skilled people by 2022. The vision clearly focuses on reduction of socio-economic divisions among Indian workforce through matching emerging skill demands and evolving a national system of vocational qualification, developing a standard certification system of quality skills, achieving greater stakeholder convergence and facilitating enhanced earnings of skilled workers. Towards realization of the vision, the immediate measures and targets include the following:

1. At least 2.5 per cent employment growth per year;
2. Achieve quantitative employment growth targets by promoting labour intensive sectors;
3. Focus on inclusion of individuals with their skill and training needs, as well as on provision of social security and improved work conditions and compensations, re-skilling, and development and regular update of employment data.

As strategies in the mid-term, focus on self employed and casual workers, creating more opportunities in the organized sector, social security coverage of unorganized sector, diversification of rural workforce, concentration on areas with more social disadvantaged, mapping of skills, developing a robust mechanism of accreditation, promoting PPP mode, creating skill development institutions, sector skill councils and national level vocational qualification framework are the important ones.

Women Empowerment—Reforms

Social Mobilization of women is a necessary prerequisite to protect and safeguard the interests of women as well as their roles and development in different fields which they choose to enter into it. From the time immemorial, 'women' were considered as secondary though they are primary in every aspect. It is seen from Manu to modern times, 'women' as a gender and she is supposed to perform her duties for which they have assigned. But, the situation warrants any government to think seriously and plan for their development in the overall plan for development.

1. Women, Demographic Situation and Technology

Statistically, women were precisely out-numbered the male population. But during the new millennium, female population is less in number comparatively with male population. Technology is one of the reasons for slowing down or less in number than the male population. The medical tests such as the gender tests often have been playing an important role and to that effort, and it shows the overall effect female on population leading to less in number.

Women's Participation and Community Development

The Population Composition in a State/Centre, is almost nearly have an equal size or sometimes to a tune of 51 per cent with male population and 49 per cent with female population. It is identified that women's participation in community development work has been in its offering since 1958 onwards.

2. Women as Event Managers

Women have an active, reactive and predominantly an interactive role in community development besides her social role in the family. Though women are primarily interested in social life but the economic situation compulsorily made them to enter into some profession through which economically she should be benefitted. As an individual she may not be able to deliver the goods but collectively, she may be quite successful in performing her duties. This situation may be seen in the solid mobilization process and community development and she should be termed as 'event manager'.

3. *Equal Rights and Equal Opportunity—Entrepreneur*

'Equal Rights' and 'Equal Opportunities' should have to be provided to women by the respective governments such as G.O.I., New Delhi and Government of Andhra Pradesh, Hyderabad in order to achieve development in various sectors. Women may be able to become an entrepreneur as well as ready for empowerment with all her capacities, capabilities and caliber.

4. *Women and Law*

Law has not succeeded in playing its role of Social Engineering and changing certain deeply rooted and noted social attitudes.

5. *Women and Employment*

More and more women are employed in new avenues of employment and in new occupations. They enjoy more opportunities than ever before as individuals, workers, wives and mothers. The phenomenal progress in education has made them capable of working in important fields like engineering, Medicine, Administrative services, Law, Judiciary, Journalism, and Politics etc.

6. *Women and Social Action*

It is observed that, the role of women in this field of "Social action" is now increasing as against her subservient position in the past. To fulfill this role, women must make certain adjustments, occupational roles, she is likely to develop certain attitudes, values and habits neither to unknown to her and to her family.

7. *Women and Special Ability*

It is further observed that there are women who have reported that things wanted to use their education and special abilities and there are some who worked to serve the society.

8. Women and Empowerment

A Study on women empowerment, Saritha *et al.*, have attempted to analyze the impact of the success of micro-enterprises on the women-micro-entrepreneurs and thus found that micro-enterprises and the resources generated thereby had a positive impact on the status of women and it leads to economic development.

From the above analysis, the following areas are emerged out and the same may be taken up for action research for the furtherance of thematic and goal oriented research. They are urban poverty and its prevalence is considered as an urban shadow region of the entire urban region. Keeping in view of the situation, Planners should be able to plan the programmes for urban development relating to urban slum, wherein people are living within adequate infrastructural facilities like Sanitation, Education and Nutrition. Generally, these people belongs to B.P.L. and the studies may be taken up for further research and development in order to alleviate urban poverty. To tune with the G.O.I. programmes, there is every need to uplift and alleviate urban poverty thereby government has to provide the necessary skill training programmes and vocational training programmes leading to employability of the skilled and semiskilled people in different sectors of economic development: Action plan for skilled and semi-skilled—A study from Andhra Pradesh. Entrepreneurial programmes and women empowerment activities should have to be designed and activated for their upliftment for economic progress includes social development. It is concluded and apt to stated that, "social mobilization is a complex problem of activity of people (women with a particular identified activity as a response to a common cause and reactive with process and thereby finally interact with semi-skilled people to fullfill the common goals and objectives within a timeframe to achieve economic ability with social stability of development over space with social engineering activity" (Quotation Mine please).

Conclusions

From the foregoing discussion, it is clear that the strategy of social mobilization of women has yielded positive results in organizing them into groups and enhancing their capacities and finally linking them to bank loans and thereby leading to improvement in their quality of life. It goes without saying that the organization of poor women into groups has established the fact that the generation of social capital has further resulted in empowerment of women socially and economically. It needs to be mentioned that the Self-Help Groups (SHG) have made strides in achieving expected results over a period of time. It should be emphasized that the grass root level work relating to formation, nurturing of women groups resulted in generation of social capital and concomitant empowerment of women at the micro level is possible to a great extent. It is a fact; in fact that the SHG model could be adopted by others also with a view to alleviate poverty in urban areas.

It is concluded that keeping in view of the above scenario, there is every need to identify the Self-Help Groups its evolution and evaluation. There is every need to identify with the basic premise that "collectives have more strength than individuals". It is apt to identify the correlating objectives with subject of urban poverty alleviation some modifications in the name of administrative reforms for adopting them in various environments is a necessary prerequisite whether it is urban "or rural" or rural-urban.

NOTES

1. Pandit, S.K. *"Women in Society"* Rajat Publications, Agra, 1998, pp. 1-5.
2. Pulla Rao, D., *"Women Entrepreneurship in India—Problems and Prospects"* Published by Abhijeet Publications, New Delhi, 2012, p. 1.
3. Nepedita Nath, "Problems and Prospects of Emerging Entrepreneurship Among Women in Slums in Western Orissa", *Ibid.*
4. K. Saritha Set eds., "Socio-Economic Conditions of Women-Micro-Entrepreneurs of Tirupati Region, Chittoor District, AP. 2012, pp. 256-263.
5. K. Saritha and Venkateswarlu, M. "Impact of success of Micro-Enterprises on the Women Micro-Entrepreneurs of Tirupati Region—A Study", 2012, pp. 256.263.
6. T. Rajesekhara Set.Ch, *"Muslim Women Empowerment through Mat Weaving"*, 2012, pp. 227-290.
7. Reji, E.M., "Micro-Finance and Empowerment: A General

Framework for Assessment of Women Empowerment", *Indian Journal of Social Work*, Vol. 70, Issue 4, October, 2009, pp. 557-570.

8. Mandakini Pant, "Study of Self-Help Groups (SHG's): A Study from three states of India. Published in *Women's Livelihood Rights: Recasting Citizenship for Development* (2nd Sumi Krishna; P.C. Bankal 1053-1054, Sage Publications, New Delhi, 2007.
9. *Indian Journal of Public Administration*, Vol. LVI, No. 4, October-December, 2010.

8
Gender Budgeting—Issues—Priorities—Way Forward for Policy Makers

S. Umapathi

A democratic nation is mandated to take up public service for the citizens. More particularly, when women and girl children constitute about 60 crores in our country and based on **'Healthy Child is Nation's Pride'** concept, the Central and State Governments are duty bound to take care of have not's i.e., people below poverty line (BPL) and those who hold a 'White Ration Card' that entitle them for subsidized rations pre-natal, post-natal care, free education upto the age of 14 years and free medical care at Corporate Hospitals and other benefits. Rough estimates indicate 30 per cent of Indians live BPL.

The Ministry of Women and Child Development (MWCD) Gender Budget Cell (GBC) of Government of India, New Delhi does prepare Annual Action Plan (AAP) engendering programmes, policies and Schemes of Central Ministries/Departments. For Gender Budgeting to be effective, it is important to look beyond more allocation of resources for women and to track their utilization and undertake analysis of their impact and beneficiary incidence.

"The Twelfth Five Year Plan emphasizes the same and states that the process of GB will further be strengthened in the Twelfth Plan and its reach extended to all Ministries, Departments and State governments. Steps will be taken to further institutionalize the GB processes by strengthening and empowering the Gender Budget Cells (GBCs). To ensure this, the suggested area of work in the Charter for GBC will be included in the quarterly/half yearly/annual plan of action. A comprehensive evaluation of GBC will also be undertaken."

The Department of Expenditure, Ministry of Finance, Government of India in its "Charter of Gender Budget Cells" elaborates that the General Responsive Budgeting is essential to tackle **gender imbalances,** promote **gender equality** and development and to ensure that public resources through the Ministry Budget are allocated and managed accordingly.

GRB or GB is a means of ensuring that public resources are allocated in an equitable way so that the most pressing needs of specific gender groups are satisfied. GRB is followed by conducting 'Performance audit' at the end of the year for reviewing the actual physical, financial targets of the programme, the constraints if any, in implementation, the need for strengthening delivery of systems, infrastructure/capacity building etc.

The performance audit is inter-woven with the concept of organizing meetings/discussions/consultations with GBCs of related departments, within the Government, field level Organization/Civil Society Groups/NGOs working in the sector for **exchanging ideas** and getting feedback on the efficiency and sectoral policies and programmes.

GRB envisages inbuilt training/sensitization/capacity building workshops for officials concerned with formulation of policy/ programme implementation and budget and accounts at the Government level and also in the implementing agencies.

In essence, the GB (Gender Budgeting) may be defined as—addressing gaps between policy commitment and allocation and gender sensitive programme formulation and implementation, main streaming of gender concerns in public expenditure and policy gender audit of public expenditure programme implementation and policies relating to public expenditure, fiscal and monetary matters etc.

Recently a separate Ministry called "**Ministry of Drinking Water and Sanitation**" has been created in Government of India with the objective of enabling all rural households to have access to and use of adequate safe drinking water, and to enable all households to have access and to use toilets. The Ministry is also mandated to ensure all Government schools and Anganwadis have functional toilets and urinals and access to safe drinking water, besides ensuring sustainability of drinking water sources and systems. The Ministry has to provide enabling environment for Panchayati Raj Institutions/Gram Panchayats/Village Water and

Sanitation Committees and other Self Help Groups to manage their own drinking water sources, systems and sanitation in their villages.

To know the gaps in Policy and Implementation an index called Gender Inequality Index (GII) has been formulated for policy makers.

The five key sectors short-listed by the Government of India are:

1. **Education and advocacy** (Compulsory Primary Education, Mid-day Meal, Technical Education, Girl Child protection/preference, Equal treatment for girl/boy child etc.) for example: *save the girl child campaign.*
2. **Women in need:** Sanction of pensions, creating old age homes in every district/revenue sub division, starting destitute/homes for mentally retarded/disabled in every district, Institutionalizing State after care homes/Grant in aid to voluntary organizations, Establishing functional Rescue Homes with counseling/skill development professionals for trafficked victims, Ensuring interim payment of immediate relief amount to victims of crime etc.
3. **Health** (Sanction of funds for maternity care, Special diet for pregnant women, pre-natal and post-natal care, Budget for hospital community health programmes, Family planning operations, Spacing child births, Preventing girl child abortions, Taking care of treatment for STD/AIDS etc.)
4. **Training:** Training and capacity building of both the village-level Anganwadi Teachers, Mid-wives, Nurses, PHC staffers, Taluk level officials, Project officers of Sarva Shiksha Abhiyan, officials of PRIs (Panchayati Raj Institutions) and PDs of ICDS.
5. Women empowerment programmes (running safe working Women's Hostels, supporting SHGs, Women Cooperative Banks etc.)

NOTE: As policy makers we can assess how much budget is required for all the above tasks and the convergence of various departments like, Department of Finance and Planning, Department of Women and Child Welfare, Department of Education, Department of Health and Sanitation, Department of Revenue, Department of Technical Education, Department of Rural Development, Department of Panchayati Raj and others. A single window for general budgeting is the need of the hour.

UN Dakar Framework for Action 2000

It was an important mile stone in GB (Gender Budgeting) and we can visualize the international community's thinking process as well. It is pertinent for us to take a look at the UN Dakar frame work for Action 2000 which *inter alia* discusses the following achievable/doable objectives for member Nations. India is one of the signatory countries. The action plan is

- To eliminate gender disparities in Primary/Secondary Education by 2005
- To achieve gender equality in Education by 2015 (good quality basic education)
- Results demonstrated positive impact of Girls Education (Child Activist *Malala Yousafzai* Winning Nobel Peace Prize of 2014)
- Improved maternal health, fertility rates, poverty reduction and economic growth.

FAO's 10 Year Strategic Framework 2009

The Food and Agriculture Organization of UN at Rome has charted a 10 year strategic framework in 2009 which among other goals include.

To ensure gender equity in access to resources, goods, services and **decision making in rural areas.**

The Eleventh Five Year Plan of our country (2007-2012) envisage the following main objectives both for the Centre and States namely: GB beyond traditional areas like health, education etc., into Gender neutral sectors like Transport, Power, Telecom, Defence, Para-military, Armed Police etc. Engendering important national Macro-economic policies and strive for inter-sectoral convergence.

All of us agree that we want our girl child to be treated on par with boy child. Though in urban scenario we have no issues, but in the rural areas where Panchayati Raj Institutions (PRIs) function, we have been noticing gross inequalities.

Issues that bother us:

The following five issues namely:

(i) Son-preference doctrine
(ii) Female foeticide (940 females: 1000 males in 2011)
(iii) Daughter 'social-burden theory'
(iv) Trafficking/bonded labour
(v) Rural male-dominated society do bother us.

But the main issue is lack of commitment on the part of PRI mechanisms. The institution of apolitical Sarpanch has become political that resulted in a chasm in the village administration. Panchayats always look up to Government for funds under various heads instead of achieving self-sufficiency from the house taxes, 'royalty' accrued from market yards/mines/registration and sand mining etc. People and officials have to develop ownership of a village/town/school/tank and other utilities.

Gender Responsive Budget would have

(i) Targeted expenditure of women's needs (Health, Education, Credit Programmes—Mana Vooru, Mana Badi, Mana Cheruvu). It is pertinent to refer to the National Rural Health Mission which was launched in 2005 to bring about dramatic improvement in the Health system and Health status of Rural India and seeking to provide universal access to health care, which is affordable, equitable and of good quality.
(ii) Expenditure on programmes for Women's Empowerment —Training for women members of PRIs (ZPTC, MPTC, Panchayat Ward members, Anganwadi members etc.) economic programmes for grass root women, education on XX, XY chromosomes theory making rural people specially women aware of the genetics that, it is a male who donates x or y chromosome. While xx will result in female baby xy will be a male. This would reduce marital

violence of daughters-in-law in urban/rural areas and reduces abortion rate of girl child foetus.

(iii) Equitable distribution of DIT (Direct Income Transfer).

(iv) Mandatory reservation for women in Government jobs.

(v) Food for work programmes enhanced support to public services that meet women's practical needs.. For example, the MGNREGS (Mahatma Gandhi Rural Employment Guarantee Scheme Focuses on rural poor).

(vi) Drinking water supply (Telangana State Government's resolve to provide one drinking water tap to each household and to improve all the water bodies in Telangana State).

(vii) Fuel (subsidized gas, VRS-Vana Rakshana Samithi, aforestation), Fodder supply/availability, fertilizers, market price for forest produce, Girijan product support mechanism.

(viii) Public health issues as already discussed.

Training of Rural Development Professionals

1. To empower people locally to guide the growth process through a sub district-citizen centric approach, where governance and development is activated at grass-root level (i.e. Community-driven development approach).
2. To draw upon the internal capacity of the stakeholder community to activate a *self-driven transformation process.*
3. To manage self-propelling and people-driven process of change that contributes to sustainable livelihoods and the transformation of rural economy.
4. To adopt a demand-driven, community-driven approach and rights-based development/strengthening the communities.
5. To facilitate institutional development/strengthening the communities.
6. To formulate Standard Operation Procedures SOPs
   (a) How to perform the task,
   (b) Who is responsible for it,
   (c) What resources are needed,
   (d) How frequently the SOP is required to be followed, and
   (e) SOP identification no.

All these deliverables need budget for implementation at the village/Panchayat/Taluk/Division and District level in the State. This involves the policy-makers to re-balance the economy, create more equitable and sustainable growth and boost social services sector.

Translating gender commitments to public commitments. For example let us take the *Swatcha Bharat Mission* mode project of Government of India of Department of Ministry of Drinking Water and Sanitation (formerly under the Ministry of Rural Development), 6.88 crore tonnes of waste is produced per year in our country, 4.1 crore are missing toilets, 59.7 crore people are defecating in the open in our country i.e., 48 per cent of country's population. Fewer toilets result in more disease. In open defecation-feces percolate in ground water that in turn spreads diarrhea, encephalitis and, therefore causing loss of income in terms of productivity. We understand good sanitation could ***boost annual per capita income by Rs. 6000/- per year,*** besides enhancing International image of our country. In underdeveloped countries like Afghanistan only 15 per cent defecate in the open, in Congo 8 per cent, in Bangladesh 3 per cent. We also know that open defecation results in tainted water and food, consequently bacteria and intestinal worm enter into the body causing poor absorption of nutrients resulting in unhealthy people. What a social cost!! It is a pity that we spend 260 times more on Food than Sanitation.

Therefore, it is imperative that the policy-makers, stakeholders, district, Taluk and Panchayat level officers and political functionaries, Self-Help Groups and NGOs have to sit together and prepare achievable and doable objectives for making our nation proud of our human resources. Proper Gender Budgeting is the key.

REFERENCES

1. Ministry of MWCD, Government of India, New Delhi Gender Budget Cell (F.No. 1-17/2014GB) dated 8th May, 2014.
2. Department of Expenditure, Ministry of Finance, Charter of Gender Budget Cells 8th March, 2007.
3. Dr. R.R. Prasad, Head of the Centre for Equity and Social Development, NIRD, Hyderabad. Published on article 20th August, 2014 in *The New Indian Express*, AP Edition.

9
Self-Help Groups (SHGs) and Bank Linkages

Smt. Simhadri Kalyani

The status of women in India during the Vedic period have had equal positions with their counter parts (Men), inheriting and possessing properties and participating in cultural activities and State functions. It is observed that poverty has remained the biggest challenge in India's development efforts to get or secure about a perceptible change in the equality of life of its teeming population.

B. Samba Siva Rao and Y. Indira Kumari have identified that, "Women Self-Help Groups have often been considered as a strategic way to organize the poor women into homogenous groups and make way for channelizing services like micro-finance, micro-enterprise and micro-insurance with necessary linkages to technology, market support and other needed and required inputs." The main objective and positive influence of women Self-Help Groups on additional or incremental income of the poor families and their increased awareness and the levels of participation may lead to homogeneous benefit.

Utmost care has been taken by various governments to wipe out Gender inequality in order to attain gender equity. Almost 50 per cent of the India's development sector, almost half of the population and previously, they were considered as receivers of the benefit than they were producers of the commodities. They contribute to a tune of 2-3 of the World's Bank work norms; they earn nearly to a tune of 1/3rd of the total income and cannot disown the 1/10th of the world's resources. At the global level (international), the governments are very keen to ensure that women are empowered both economically and socially and they are equal partners in the National development along with the other gender (men). In this context, they may also important equally in designing the policy for the betterment of women in India.

It is opined that, though India being a developing country, 3/4th of its human resources (population) suffers from malnutrition, unemployment and poor health care. Provision of employment opportunities and income to urban women in one way, to improve their nutrition, health, education, and social status. The State governments as well as Government of India (GoI) has been trying with continuous efforts simultaneously in order to improve the status of urban women especially those living below the poverty line through different schemes of urban development.

One of the most important items in the agenda of national development is women's empowerment, which helps, not only for themselves but also helping the Nation. In 1977, as per Human Development index, out of 146 countries, India ranked 118th position and similarly in the gender related index too it gained to a rank of 118. According to Sambasiva Rao[1] and Indira Kumari that the aggregation of the human development gap by gender disparities explains the need to empower women with information and knowledge beside allowing them to emerge as leaders with confidence to guide their own destinies.

The effective training and extension services may be able to arise from the gradual decrease of Urban Poverty in Urban places, increasing population pressure and ever growing environmental degradation which has a telling effect and implications for food and nutritive scarcity in future. Keeping in view of the existing scenario, it is found that, empowerment of women is in dispensable for rapid transformation of urban economy society and for protection of environment and regeneration of Natural resources.

Malnutrition, maternal and child mortality have a bearing on poverty and it is inextricably linked with the effective strategy should aim at the following aspects. They are:

1. Physical accessibility of services should be closer to women.
2. Planner should be able to involve women while

formulation, designing and management of programme which should affect them

3. Make women (individually or in group) the contact point in order to deliver services directly to the beneficiaries and receivers (Ministry of Agriculture, Ghana, 1990).

"The sixth plan document began with an admission that the weaker sections (SC/STs, women) were still lagging behind in terms of incremental development targeting. Poor women in particular, the plan declared that, a fair share of employment opportunities would have to be created through poverty alleviation programmes. The assumption continued to be that employment and income generation would automatically lead to improvement in the status of women had not been commensurate with the inputs made. Hence, a separate ministry for women and children was created in 1984. And it appears that, "awareness has to be the starting point for women's empowerment."

Emphasis is laid on the empowerment of the women focusing on the following:

I. Dirrct involvcmcnt of women in programming and management
II. Effective collaboration of women's Self-Help Group's.
III. Organized and Strengthening of Women's Self-Help Groups.
IV. Substitution and for gender just society.
V. Identifying women's needs and priorities while generating employment.
VI. Organizing women in different groups to undertake certain productive activities to earn their livelihood and to develop the Urban Community."

Women empowerment means, the idea that giving women power over their economic, social and reproductive choices, which will raise their status, promote development and reduce population growth. Women empowerment can be viewed as a continuum of several inter-related and mutually reinforcing components such as awareness building, capacity building and skill development, participation and greater control and decision-making power in the home, community and society and also action to bring about greater equality between men and women.

The formation of Self-Help Group Concept, recognizing the merits of this approach, mainly voluntary organizations are implementing Self-Help Group Concepts in different ways. Homogeneity, in terms of socio-economic status, specific economic activity and people having almost similar problems and needs were the cohesive factors for this collective approach.

Self-Help Group (SHG) is a small group of people (mostly women) who are living in the same area engaged in similar or varied activities, maintaining almost equal living standards, a political and secular, aiming to achieve a common goal that is prosperity through thrift and credit. The immediate necessities of joining a group should be felt by the potential members. These common factors can be:

(a) Financial insecurity or poverty.
(b) Social problems.
(c) Area specific problems faced by women folk.

Thus, Self-Help Groups are consisting of members from neighbourhood families proved to be an alternative strategy for women empowerment.

The objectives of the study are presented and reflected in all the papers (chapters).

1. To study and functioning of SHG in an Urban environment.
2. To study the structure of municipal towns SHG's.
3. To assess the structural competentcy.
4. To evaluate the structure of TLF's.
5. To study the bank-wise SHG linkage.

The women member form groups of 10-15 women each for taking up economic activities suited to their skill, aptitude and local conditions. Through the strategy of group formations this programme aims to improve women access to basic services like health, education, child care, nutrition, water and sanitation.

"The financial institutions (Nationalized Banks) provide credit as per the norms of poverty alleviation programmes, linkages with allied development sectors, industry, dairy, social access to productive resources on both individual and collective basis. Groups of poor women are assisted through a package including subsidies, loans for skill upgradation, groups Revolving fund etc."

To reduce poverty through interventions viably and vulnerably of the urban poor households especially the gender (women and children) by enabling them to make accessible to gainful self employment and skilled employment opportunities, resulting man appreciable improvement in their self (livelihoods) on a sustainable basis, though building up strong grassroots level institutions of the poor (SHGs). The mission would aim at concentrating and centering on their capabilities, capacities and caliber to the utmost level usage to urban population where they live in urban areas as well as urban slums to achieve Quality living"—(Quotation Mine Please).

Self-Help Groups are defined as, "it is a homogenous group of heterogeneous people governed by the rules and regulations and there by act truly for a common cause (i.e.) to attain and achieve a designed level of development through their intensive efforts to affect their life, goals, ambitious for their betterment continuously over a period of time, these are registered for a common goal with common objectives: (Quotation mine please).

The author has attempted to present the functioning of Self-Help Groups in Andhra Pradesh as a case study Table 9.1 indicates that a macro-level study of SHG's structure, process and stage of development. Primarily the SHG structure is composed of 15 units. They are: (1) Ananthapur, (2) Chittoor, (3) East Godavari, (4) Guntur, (5) Greater Viskhapatnam Municipal Corporation, (6) Kadapa, (7) Krishna, (8) Kurnool, (9) Nellore, (10) Prakasam, (11) Srikakula, (12) Visakhapatnam, (13) Vijayanagaram, (14) Visakha Municipal Corporation, and (15) West Godavari. At the second level, East Godavari and Guntur districts have 13 municipalities respectively and occupies first position in Andhra Pradesh, whereas Ananthapur district has 12 municipalities, which occupies the second position and Kurnool occupies 3rd position with 10 municipalities, it is noted that Rayalaseema region has 30 municipal towns out of 114 municipalities Andhra Pradesh. East and West Godavari districts have 13 municipal towns and 9 municipal towns respectively. This is the Mission Structure.

1. Municipal Towns

Observations

- Number of SHG's are highest and ranks first with a total 22,298 out of 1,86,734 SHG's.
- Visakhapatnam has only 4 units with 4,380 SHG's out of 1,86,734 SHG's. Visakhapatnam occupies the last rank in the order.

2. *SHG's (nos. corpus)*

- It is observed that a total of 54,701.34 as corpus and Chittoor occupies dominantly with 7536.92.
- It is noted that Srikakulam occupies last rank with 845.77 which is located at the tip of the North Coastal Plain.

3. *SLF's (nos. and corpus)*

- It is a fact, that GVOCC has 810 SLFs with no corpus. It is highly deplorable to note that SHG people should be well counseled for achieving a good amount as target for corpus.
- It is further observed that the total SLFs in Guntur is to a tune of 655 and the corpus is highest in circar districts corpus of Rs.1764.12.

4. *TLF's*

- It is observed that there are 10 TLFs and has a corpus of 120.00 out of 443.28 Chittoor district occupies first position in corpus though it has only 10 TLFs.
- It is observed that VMC and Vizianagaram predominantly takes the last rank with 4 and 3 units respectively. But their corpus turns to a tune of 0.06 and 0.00 respectively.
- In table 9.2 data relating to total SHG, Updated SHGs' SHG's running and SHG s defunct are presented. The Gross Observations are presented in the following paragraphs.
- It is observed that Guntur has a total of 22,298 no's, and the present status is to a tiune of 21,742 (updated status).

Out of these units, there are 21,348 SHG's are running and the defunct are to a tune of 394 out of 6,476.

- It is observed that there are 1,86,748 total SHG's are existed as on date and the updated SHGs are to a tune of 1,85,368. The SHG running are to a total of 1,78,893 with defunct SHGs to a total of 6,476.
- It is further observed that there are 4,380 total SHG's and with an updated SHG's are to a tune of 4,377. The running SHG's are to a tune of 4,351 with 26 defunct SHG's and GVMC has 18,718 total SHG's with 18,484 updated SHG's. The running SHG's are with 18,468 and with 16 SHG's are defunct.

Bank-wise SHG Linkage: relating to Bank, total SHG's valid SHGs, invalid SHGs and duplicate SHG's are presented in Table 9.3. The following are the gross observations.

1. Nearly 41 banks have been providing financial assistance to SHGs and Indian Bank has stood first position by providing loan to a total number of 15,585 and the valid SHGs are to a tune of 13,509. The invalid SHGs are 222 and the duplicate SHG's are to a tune of 1788.
2. It is observed that Dena Bank has a total SHG's to a tune of 56 and 53 valid SHGs and invalid SHG and duplicate SHG's are 1 and 2 respectively.
3. Punjab and Sind Bank has only one SHG and it is not valid because it is a duplicate SHG.
4. State Bank of BK and Jaipur have only 3 SHGs and there's no valid SHG. There is one invalid SHG and two are duplicate SHGs.
5. It is observed that the city bank has one and only one SHG, but it is a duplicate SHG. There is no need to extend financial assistance.

Conclusion

Keeping in view of the financial linkage of SHG with bank, the gross observations suggests the following:

Table 9.1: Total No. of SHG's SLFs and TLF's and Corpus

District	Municipal	SHGs		SLFs		TLFs	
		Nos	Corpus	Nos	Corpus	Nos	Corpus
Anathapur	12	15491	5430.71	547	2102.13	14	27.96
Chittoor	8	11451	7536.92	429	1764.12	10	120.00
East Godavari	13	18792	6995.97	607	891.47	18	40.33
Guntur	13	22298	4261.67	655	1050.91	17	47.82
GVMC	1	18718	2726.11	810	0.00	0	0.00
Kadapa	9	13696	5309.26	460	903.61	12	56.11
Krishna	8	9548	3720.31	300	397.18	9	24.44
Kurnool	10	18506	4931.04	682	836.81	13	20.63
Nellore	7	10133	2370.12	390	415.28	7	31.44
Prakasam	8	9033	2123.88	331	339.89	9	44.78
Srikakulam	6	4875	845.77	165	185.51	5	7.55
Visakhapatnam	4	4380	899.41	133	143.07	4	5.74
Vizianagaram	5	6743	1732.52	224	178.08	4	0.06
VMC	1	11712	1738.06	195	13.98	3	0.00
West Godavari	9	11358	4079.59	332	358.68	8	16.42
Total	114	186734	54701.34	6260	9580.72	133	443.28

Source: MEPMA, Hyderabad, A.P.

Table 9.2: Classification of SHG's and their structure

District	*Total SHG*	*Updated SHGs*	*SHGs Running*	*SHGs Defunct*	*SHGs Double Entry*
Anathapur	15491	15392	14575	817	
Chittoor	11451	11451	10997	454	
East Godavari	18792	18535	17383	1152	
Guntur	22298	21742	21348	394	
GVMC	18718	18484	18468	16	
Kadapa	13698	13698	12847	851	
Krishna	9548	9428	9049	379	
Kurnool	18514	18514	18394	120	
Nellore	10133	10133	9712	421	
Prakasam	9035	9033	8709	325	
Srikakulam	4875	4875	4597	278	
Visakhapatnam	4380	4377	4351	26	
Vizianagaram	6743	6704	6436	268	
VMC	11712	11712	11357	355	
West Godavari	11360	11290	10670	620	
Total	186748	185368	178893	6476	

Source: MEPMA, Hyderabad, A.P.

Table 9.3: Bank-wise SHG Report

Bank	*Total SHGs*	*Valid SHGs*	*In Valid SHGs*	*Duplicate SHGs*	
Unmapped to any Bank	11001	0	2632	8328	41
Andhra Bank	45297	38077	961	5964	295
Allahabad Bank	1284	1138	55	89	2
Bank of Baroda	1901	1689	37	166	9
Bank of India	9433	7842	167	1352	72
Bank of Maharashtra	161	144	0	17	0
Canara Bank	8193	7484	101	588	20
Central Bank of India	2909	2480	64	328	37
Corporation Bank	3266	2861	83	299	23
Dena Bank	56	53	1	2	0
Indian Bank	15585	13509	222	1788	66
Indian Overseas Bank	3831	3473	74	263	21
Oriental Bank of CCOMR	205	168	5	25	7
Punjab National Bank	1173	868	168	131	66
Punjab & Sind Bank	1	0	0	1	0
Syndicate Bank	8871	7782	201	854	34
UCO Bank	1955	1392	14	535	14
Union Bank of India	10549	8955	164	1302	128

(*Contd.*)

Table 9.3 (*Contd.*)

United Bank of India	189	116	5	47	21
Vijaya Bank	2606	2240	66	291	9
State Bank of India	40123	34290	514	5040	279
State BK of BIK & Jaipur	3	0	1	2	0
State Bank of Mysore	234	216	6	11	1
State Bank of Trivancor	23	16	1	1	5
Reserve Bank of India	25	0	2	22	1
City Bank	1	0	0	1	0
City Union Bank	20	14	5	1	0
Development Credit BK	1	0	0	1	0
Federal Bank	1	0	0	1	0
HSBC	1	0	0	1	0
IDBI	1	0	0	1	0
ING VYSYA Bank	276	183	35	58	0
Karnataka Bank	209	160	6	43	0
Karur Vysya Bank	31	20	6	5	0
Axis Bank	8	7	1	0	0
Deccan Grameena Bank	1	0	0	1	0
State Bank of Hyderabad	11411	9907	188	1217	99
Chaitanaya Godavari Grameena Bank	2474	2235	41	178	20
AP Grameena Vikas Bank	14385	11363	167	2766	89
AP Pragati Grameena Bank	14722	12896	338	1465	23
Saptagiri Grameena Bank	5174	4293	67	798	16
DCC Bank	3595	3022	78	454	41

Source: MEPMA, Hyderabad, A.P.

1. The functioning of SHGs should have to be observed and supervised so keenly and also to avoid in valid SHG's at this juncture.
2. It is observed that there are duplicate SHG's are existing and these are enabled for financial assistance. It is highly objectionable to entertain such SHG's applications for processing at the bank level. They should have to be rejected then and there (i.e.) on the same day of submitting it should have to be rejected.
3. Invalid SHGs should be supervised properly and the queries should have to be answered properly and may be resubmitted for financial assistance.
4. Those SHGs who have progressed over a period of time,

should have to be assisted for the second and third dose for proper running of SHGs.

NOTE

1. B. Sambasive Rao and Y. Indira Kumari, "Empowerment of Women and Rural Development" Pub. Serials Publications, New Delhi (2008).

10
Urban Slums and Governance

K.L.N. Murty

The Census of India data base expresses and explains that urbanization has increased by 31.31 per cent between 1991 and 2001-05 compared to 16 per cent in 1951 and 26 per cent in 1991. It is expected to touch the mark of less than 40 per cent in 2021. Thirty five cities in India have already crossed the population to a tune of one million plus and Greater Mumbai with a population of 163.08 lakhs, occupied first three positions respectively in 2001. The increase in urban population in 2001 as compared to 10 problems for the local self-government, which has already been stepped up and causes stress and strain. According to 2001 Census, there are 40.6 million persons living in slums in 607 towns and cities and has been touched to 22.8 per cent of the population of these cities. The practice of notifying slums, under relevant laws is not attempted to follow, especially where the land involved belongs to government or any of its agencies. On an average, the slum and squatter population is increasing at more than double, the general growth rate of population of the cities. Currently, atleast 40 per cent of the population of our cities is living in slum settlements. Economy and technology are changing very rapidly. Better planning and efficient administration, may be able to solve the problems of people living in slums and some may of hope could be created and ensure quality living in urban slums[1].

Slums are considered to be the major (issue) problems related to transportation, population, health and safety. Keeping in view of the present scenario, considering today's poor urban environmental quality in India, the majority of families affected by urban development projects are located in slum areas which are under consideration for resettlements and rehabilitation.

Most of India's population is currently living in slums. Every year, hundreds of thousands of men, women and children die around the world and India alone is responsible for 25 per cent of the deaths. By 1980, slum dwellers were half of India's entire population (*Source:* Census of India 2001, circular No. 8) slum dwellers constantly deal with issues such as: lack of clean water, constant migration at slums, no sewage or waste disposal facilities, pollution and insanitary living condition. High level of population, lack of basic needs and room-crowding are some of the basic characteristics of slum housing. The Government of India has not been able to and yet, to solve the problems that are strengthening the entire population of Indian slums.[2]

Urban Slums and Government Programmes

Slums are defined as "the physical manifestation of facts like rapid and uncentralised urbanization, rural-urban migrations, acute poverty, ill-conceived policies, in appropriate urban planning and weak institutional capacity" (1990). "Slums are not just dumping ground or just a way status to the city, it is also a provider of goods and societies that are demanded by the non-slum population".

The policy interventions have to improve living conditions of slum dwellers. Slums are the areas or pockets within or outside municipal limits where poverty striken rural migrants find shelter and search for their work and livelihood make necessary adjustment with urban life and get minimum life supporting conditions at affordable rate (UN-HABITAT, 2002). Sometimes such areas are also turned as Urban Poverty Pockets. The definition encompasses as wide variety of low-income settlements and poor human living conditions and includes old residential areas (UN-HABITAT, 2034).[3]

Further, UN-HABITAT defines slums as, "areas characterized by inadequate access to safe water, overcrowding, and insecure residential statuses". Such slums include decaying inner city housing and dilapidated structures and there is a common agreement on the diatum that a slum is an area in which social and physical environment is so unhealthy as to constitute and made to every aspect of well being be it physical, mental, social or psychological.

Such slum areas can be found in or around urban areas in different commitments across the world.

Rapid urbanization and urbanization of poverty are the major factors which cause minimize of people to live in improvised or informal settlements often described as slums:

(i) Poor structural quality and durability of housing.
(ii) Insufficient living areas (more than 3 people sharing room).
(iii) Lack of secure tenure.
(iv) Poor access to water, and
(v) Lack of sanitation facilities.

In nutshell, urban slums are defined, "as part and parcel of Urban region, geographically isolated with the characteristics such as, poor structure quality and durability of housing, insufficient living areas besides having lack of secure tenure (during with) simultaneously rich with poor access to water and lack of sanitation facilities with the increasing slum population is the result of increasing urban population. (Quotation mine please) slum could be characterized as:

- Physically an area of the city with inadequate housing, deficient facilities, overcrowding and congestion;
- Society a way of life having its own sets of house and values, health practices, deviant behaviour and social isolation, and
- Legally as defined urban section 3 of the Slum Act (improvement and clearance) Act 1956.

Planning and Policy for Slum Improvement: EIA (A Perspective)

1. 'Slum clearance' was announced in Second Five Year Plan (FYP) of the 401 and consequently all the State governments were required to set-up the necessary organizations are enacting legislation for the same.
2. The Fourth FYP emphasized on urban planning and decongestion of cities in such as a direction, "Environmental Improvement of Urban Slum (EIUS) was undertaken in the central sector from 1972-73 and focus was on providing a

minimum level of seven basic amenities like water supply (One tap for 150 persons, sever (open drains with normal outflow to avoid water accumulation), storm water drain, community bath and toilets (one for 20-25 persons, widening and paving of existing lanes and street lighting (one pole for 30 meters apart). Integrated Low Cost Sanitation Scheme was launched in 1980-81 to provide proper sanitation in the slums. This scheme is being operated through Housing and Urban Development Corporation (HUDCO) by providing subsidy through the Central Government and loans by HUDCO.

The Urban Basic Services Scheme (UBSS) was initiated in 1986 on a Pilot basis with involvement of UNICEF, Government of India and the State government and operated in Urban Slums, which related to the provision of Urban Basic Services for the Poor households. The Urban Basic Services for Poor (UBSP) was modified into Urban Basic Services Scheme (UBSS) with focus an improvement of physical as well as social-cultural environment for the well-being of the target group. The Eighth Plan under scored the urgent need for urban development, environmental protection and provision of basic amenities to the urban poor like drinking water, sanitation, education, and health services. One of the key issues to be addressed was identified as the haphazard growth of the cities and shortage of housing resulting in the emergence of squatters, shanties and slums. The Government of India have introduced the National Slum Development Programme (NSDP) in August, 1996 with the objective to provide adequate and satisfactory water supply and sanitation, pre-primary and primary educational facilities, adult literacy and informal educational facilities etc.

JNNURM was launched in December, 2005. Its focus is planned development of identified cities including peri-urban areas, out growth and urban commodes leading to dispersed urbanization and provision of basic services to the urban poor including security of tenure at affordable prices improved housing, water supply, sanitation and ensuring delivery of other existing universal services of the government for education, health and social security. BSUP, a sub-mission of JNNURM, focuses on integrated development of slums through projects that provide shelter, basic services and other related civic amenities to the urban poor. As a part of JNNURM, Integrated Housing and Slum Development Programme (IHSDP) was launched with a view to ameliorate the dilapidated living conditions of the urban slum dwellers covering all the towns except the 63 identified mission cities covered under the programme for Urban Basic Services for Poor (UBSP). In these programmes allocation of funds among states is on the basis of the State's Urban Slum Population to total urban slum population in India, Government of India is the funding agency and the State's contribution is to a tune of 80:20. Further, the funds maybe spent by the Urban Local Bodies, separate agencies of the States for this purpose as well as MP/MLA, Local Area Development Funds (LAD).

The Government of India announced Rajiv Awaas Yojana (RAY) under the MoHUPA in the budget relating to the year 2009-10 aimed at promoting slums in India within five years and with a focus to accord property rights to slum dwellers.

The focus of Eleventh FYP (Five Year Plan) (2007-12) is an inclusive growth. The report, working group on Urban Housing (Planning Commission, Government of India), New Delhi with focus on slums has reviewed various programmes of the Government of India for the slum dwellers.

It is concluded that, the data on living conditions and demographic profile of the slum dwellers has been collect by the NSSO in its 65th round and compared with its 58th round reveals and highlights the fact that there has been a considerable improvement in the living conditions in the slums and squatters in India over the last one decade. In the light of the above scenario. "The rate at which the slums are growing as a result of unplanned urbanization in India multiuse the slum problems at a rate much faster than they are resolved or taken care of".[4]

Sanitation is closely associated with environment as in absence of proper sanitation, a large segment of children are prone to water borne diseases. A large segment of households do not have sanitary latrine and in the absence of safe toilets, they are forced to defecate in open public places. In view of the improving urban sanitation, integrated low cost sanitation programme, the flagship scheme has been implemented by the MoH&UPA in association with HUDCO and urban local bodies, is a major initiative that is expected to improve the physical quality of life in urban areas, particularly in small towns.

The current approach of the Government of India to tackle urban poverty is the pegged. (1) to provide urban poor with housing and infrastructure.

(2) To ensure institutional reforms to facilitate decentralization as envisaged in the 74th CAA and to ensure accountability of Urban Local Bodies (ULBs) to the citizens.

(3) To facilitate access to livelihoods/employment—through policies like the National Policy for Urban Street Vendors (NPUSV) and programmes like the SJSRY, recently revamped as SWARUP, Swarojgar for Urban Poor.

These are aimed to strengthen the ULBs by facilitating exchange of information at various levels, setting-up of urban poverty resource centres and developing an organized institutional framework within the State and ULBs that will lead to proper implementation of the 74th CAA.

It is important that strategies for poverty alleviation are appropriately targeted, involve community participation in the UPA programmes. Rapid urbanization has put a strain on already stressed urban sanitation sections. Slums are rarely connected to cities sanitation infrastructural conditions of social infrastructure.

- The coverage of educational institutions, health facilities and other necessary social infrastructure facilities are grossly inadequate in slums.
- The banks are hesitant to provide towns to the urban poor for starting self employment ventures. The urban poor find it difficult to receive subsidy for self employment and there is considerable leakage in loans meant for the urban poor. The absence of collateral further accentuates their lack of credit worthiness.

Urban poor seem to suffer most due to poor availability of credit facilities for self-employment ventures. The constitution and participation of Self-Help Groups (SHGs) of the Urban Poor could be quite successful introducing linkages in the delivery system. At the same time, it could create a sense of ownership among the people benefitting from centrally sponsored Slum Development and Poverty Alleviation Schemes. Across cities, slum dwellers have expressed their willingness to pay for housing, water supply, sewage, drainage, solid waste management, roads, street lights, toilets, education, health services and also for skill improvement.

(i) The network of physical infrastructure required in slums has to be linked-up with the city-wide network. No city level investment in infrastructure should be covered unless it is linked-up with all slums.
(ii) It should be demand driven.
(iii) The strategy has to be physically and financially sustainable (recovery of cost sustainability).

Physical sustainability means as long as the land tenure issues are resolved between the slum dweller and the ULB, the ULB should be allowed to tax the slum dwellers for the services provided.[5]

Mridula Bhatnagar has put in an effort, "to understand and comprehend the social reality of slums. Focusing upon the structural and processed dimension as they exist and operate in the slums, centred to delineate deprivations and sufferings as an interdependent dominant realities experienced by the slum dwellers. The structures and processes of social deprivations, sufferings and exploitations were discussed, analysed and presented as they exist in socio-ecological structure of slums".[6]

Further, she has presented social inequalities are diverse and complicated, especially in the complex nebulous contemporary societies besides social inequalities, thus it can be discarded both subjectively and objectively. The objectives dimension imply the sources, extent and forms of actual inequalities as projected through the material possessions, economic activities nature of occupations and the residential location of people subject to social inequalities. Finally, arrived at that "living around affluence, the slum dwellers are constantly made acutely aware of their deprivations and their inability to break away from the visions circles of deprivations results in channelization of their frustrated energies into negative direction and has also identified, emergence and creation of New occupations as the result of process of industrialization and urbanization had led to mass migration from rural to urban centres over congestion in cities and in slums.

Rajiv Awas Yojana (RAY) envisages a "Slum Free India" with inclusive and equitable cities in which every citizen has access to basic civic infrastructure and social amenities and decent shelter.

Mission

Encourage States/Union Territories (UTs) to tackle slums in a definitive manner, by focusing on:

1. Bringing all existing slums, notified or non-notified (including recognized and identified) within the formal system and enabling them to avail the basic amenities that is available for the rest of the city/UA;
2. Redressing the failures of the formal system that lie behind the creation of slums by planning for affordable housing stock for the urban poor and initiating crucial policy changes required for facilitating the same.

Objectives

1. Improving and provisioning of housing. Basic civic infrastructure and social amenities in interned slums.
2. Enabling reforms to address some of the causes leading to creation of slums.
3. Facilitating a supportive environment for expanding institutional credit linkages for the urban poor.
4. Institutionalizing mechanisms for prevention of slums including creation of affordable housing stock.
5. Strengthening institutional and human resource capacities at the Municipal, City and State levels through comprehensive capacity building and strengthening of resource networks.
6. Empowering community by ensuring their participation at every stage of decision making through strengthening and nurturing Slum Dwellers Association/Federations.

RAY is to be implemented in a mission mode and will provide financial support to States/UTs/Urban Local Bodies (ULBs) Central Government Agencies, hereafter called implementing agencies, for providing housing and improvement of basic civic infrastructure and social amenities in each selected slums. Rental and transit housing will be admissible under the scheme. Operation and maintenance (O&M) of assets created under this scheme will also be eligible for funding.

RAY will also extend financial support to States for creation of affordable housing stock through public-private-partnership (PPP) under the Affordable Housing in Partnership (AHP) component of the scheme.

The scheme is applicable to all slums within a city, whether notified or non-notified (including identified and recognized), whether on lands belonging to Central Government or its Undertakings, autonomous bodies created under the Act of Parliament, State government or its Undertakings, Urban Local Bodies or any other public agency and private sector. It is also applicable to "urbanized villages" inside the planning area of the city, urban homeless and pavement dwellers.

Rajiv Rinn Yojana

Rajiv Rinn Yojana (RRY) is an instrument to address the housing of the EWS/LIG segments in urban areas, through enhanced credit flow. It is also formulated to channelize institutional credit to the poorer segments of the society and increasing home ownership in the country along with addressing housing shortage. RRY has been formulated by modifying the Interest Subsidy Scheme for Housing the Urban Poor (ISHUP) piloted in the Eleventh Plan period with enhanced scope and coverage. RRY is a Central Sector Scheme applicable in all the urban areas of the Country.

RRY provides for interest subsidy of 5 per cent (500 basis points) on loans granted to EWS and LIG categories to construct their houses or extend the existing ones. The upper limit of the loan is Rs 5 lakh for EWS and 8 lakh for LIG; interest subsidy would, however, be limited to the first Rs 5 lakh of the loan amount, in case the loan exceeds this amount.

Rajiv Rinn Yojana is a target driven scheme. The overall target for the Twelfth Plan period is 1 million (or 10 lakh) dwellings across country including slum and non-slum dwellers. The Targets for the States for the current Financial Year (2-13-14) are periodically fixed and conveyed to the concerned department(s).

Housing and Urban Development Corporation (HUDCO) and National Housing Bank (NHB) have been designated as the Central Nodal Agencies for the Scheme.

Twelfth Plan Strategy

- There are Short Term and Medium Term Challenges
- **Short Term:** Reverse the current growth slowdown: 5.5 per cent to 7 per cent in 2013-14.
- **Longer Term:** Get back to high growth. This requires accelerating from 5.5 per cent in 2012-13 to over 9 per cent in last two years.
- This is very difficult, especially given the global situation.

Growth must not only be rapid, but also more inclusive

- Inclusiveness is a multi-dimensional concept:
  - Reduce poverty
  - Improve regional equality across States and within States
  - Improve conditions for SCs, STs, OBCs, Minorities.
  - Generate attractive employment opportunities for youth
  - Close gender gaps
- Twelfth Plan lists 25 monitorable indicators.

25 Monitorable Targets, e.g.

- Average GDP Growth of 8 per cent.
- Agriculture Growth of 4 per cent.
- Reducing head-count poverty by 10 percentage point.
- Generating 50 million work opportunities.
- Eliminating gender and social gap in education.
- Reducing IMR to 25, MMR to 100 and TFR to 2.1.
- Enhance infrastructure investment to 9 per cent of GDP.
- Achieve universal road connectivity and access to power for all villages.
- Access to banking services for 90 per cent households.
- Major welfare benefits and subsidies *via Aadhaar*.

Strategy for Achieving Inclusiveness

- There are two routes to inclusiveness
  - ➢ Through higher growth which expands income and employment opportunities.
  - ➢ Through government pro-poor programmes which target poorer groups.
- Both are important. Twelfth Plan combines the pro-poor programme approach with efforts to get a growth pattern which is faster and inherently more inclusive.
- Two routes are mutually reinforcing
  - ➢ High growth generates more revenues, to finance inclusiveness.
  - ➢ Many inclusiveness programmes (health and education) contribute to growth.

Macro-Economic Challenges in Achieving High Growth

- Must increase the rate of investment, especially in infrastructure.
- Domestic savings must increase even more to reduce the investment saving gap which is necessary to keep the Current Account Deficit under control.
- Government dis-savings must be eliminated. This means fiscal deficit must be reduced.
- Growth of subsidies has to be contained.
- 75 per cent of the investment in the economy is private investment (household plus corporate).
- Both the Centre and the States have to create an eco-system that encourages private investment.
- Infrastructure, especially quality of power, and availability of skills is critical.

Effectiveness of Plan Programmes

- Twelfth Plan sets ambitious targets for Flagship Programmes in areas of Health, Education, Rural infrastructure, and Livelihood Development etc.
- Too much focus on the level of expenditure in these programmes. Not enough on effectiveness in terms of end results.

- Implementation in the field is the responsibility of State government agencies. However, programme guidelines are set by the Central Government.
- There are demands for greater flexibility from States. We are responding as follows:
  - Guidelines are being made more flexible to meet the requirements of individual States.
  - 10 per cent flexi-fund within each scheme for innovations.

Energy

- 8 per cent GDP growth requires 6 per cent growth in energy supply from all sources.
- Our fossil fuel resources are limited, and our import dependence is already high.
- Enhanced Energy Efficiency in all sectors.
- We need to push for renewable Energy: Wind, Solar and Storage Hydro.
- Difficult Policy Issues:
  - Coal *vs.* Forest Cover
  - Petroleum Price Distortions
  - Natural Gas Exploration Framework
  - All Energy Prices: Coal, Petroleum product, Natural Gas and Electric power are currently under priced. Fuel adjustment is needed.

Water

- Management of water resource is a major challenge. Estimates of water availability have been optimistic.
- Twelfth Plan proposes modified AIBP and expanded Watershed Management Programme.
- Water Sector needs better Regulatory Framework.
  - New Groundwater Law
  - Water Regulatory Authorities in each State.
  - National Water Framework Law.
- Agriculture accounts for 80 per cent of water use at present must shift to more water efficient agriculture practices.
- Manage urban and industrial water demand through water recycling and rationalize user charges.

Alternative Scenarios

- Twelfth Plan goal of 8 per cent inclusive growth is not a foregone conclusion.
- Depends on difficult policy decisions to be taken by Centre and States.
- For the first time Plan presents three scenarios

Strong inclusive Growth	**8 per cent**
Insufficient Action	**6 to 6.5 per cent**
Policy logjam	**5 to 5.5 per cent**

- Anything much less than 8 per cent will not satisfy aspirations of the people.

Conclusion

1. State-wise projected slum population from 2011 to 2017 is presented in Table 10.1. It is seen from Table 10.1, that at the micro level, the slum population has been on an increasing scale i.e. 8188002 to 8681318 for the years 2011 to 2017. At the national level, the same trend is seen. Contrary to this, Lakshdweep, records a low count for 2017 to tune of 1373.
2. It is concluded that slum dwellers constantly deal with issues such: as lack of clean water, constant migration at slums, new sewage or waste disposal facility, pollution and insanitary living conditions. High level population, lack of basic needs, and room crowding are some of the basic characteristics of slum housing. It is noted Government of India as well as State governments have been designing and implementing slum improvement programmes to alleviate their positions for a better qualitative life.
3. It is observed that about 40 per cent of the population of our cities is living in slum settlements. Economy and technology are changing very rapidly. Keeping in view of the above scenario, the respective State governments have to train and safeguard the slum population from the natural hazards, for that the disaster management unit is being constituted in the Twelfth Five Year Plan in order to achieve development over a period of time. Mission Mode Approach has been adopted to minimize or

Table 10.1: State-wise projected slum population from 2011 to 2017

States	*2011*	*2012*	*2013*	*2014*	*2015*	*2016*	*2017*
Andaman and Nicobar Island	33722	35294	36867	38265	39663	41060	42633
Andhra Pradesh	8188022	8273434	8357451	8440074	8521999	8602530	8681318
Arunachal Pradesh	98248	103459	108669	114127	119833	125788	131494
Assam	1070835	1100118	1129636	1159857	1190780	1222406	1253798
Bihar	1683954	1707378	1730148	1752590	1774376	1795671	1816639
Chandigarh	332473	348685	365154	381881	397321	411474	429744
Chhattisgarh	2111546	2169237	2228058	2287634	2347964	2409802	2470886
Dadra and Nagar Haveli	26083	28813	31542	34424	37305	40035	43219
Daman & Diu	9187	9316	9316	9445	9445	9575	9575
Delhi	3163430	3260984	3360874	3463999	3570716	3681745	3793313
Goa	154759	161494	168229	174815	180801	185741	192476
Gujarat	4662619	4759581	4866740	4954094	5051840	5149782	5245569
Haryana	3288292	3390907	3495059	3600364	3707207	3815202	3923582
Himachal Pradesh	87281	89143	91005	92983	94845	96707	98685
Jammu & Kashmir	494180	504243	514306	524369	534275	544180	553771
Jharkhand	931912	948949	966239	983530	1001202	1019382	1036673
Karnataka	3631147	3700490	3770161	3839998	3910162	3980656	4049341
Kerala	533278	536057	538776	541314	543671	545906	548021
Lakshadweep	1560	1560	1498	1435	1435	1435	1373
Madhya Pradesh	6393040	6523229	6654059	6785528	6917636	7050705	7181214
Maharashtra	18151071	18549628	18950624	19352665	19754009	20152914	20557046
Manipur	75197	75915	76514	76993	77592	78190	78789
Meghalaya	205176	208590	212003	215416	219209	222622	226415
Mizoram	105720	107700	109679	111659	113639	115619	117599
Nagaland	83220	84292	85365	86223	87295	88368	89226
Orissa	1736064	1770623	1805436	1840503	1876078	1912161	1948244
Puducherry	136899	143316	149876	156435	162282	167131	174118
Punjab	2798256	2864014	2930296	2996316	3062598	3128094	3193590
Rajasthan	3826160	3894590	3962311	4029561	4095395	4160049	4224939
Sikkim	13321	13803	14124	14605	14926	15408	15729
Tamil Nadu	8644892	8862969	9081045	9298651	9515080	9729624	9940165
Tripura	131080	134137	137003	140061	143118	146175	149232
Uttar Pradesh	10878336	11127210	11378552	11631376	11885434	12139739	12394291
Uttarakhand	826257	846181	866105	886615	906832	927342	947559
West Bengal	8546755	8640642	8733188	8825399	8918616	9014179	9106055
India	93055983	94977993	96907923	98845216	100786594	102729415	104668340

Source: Ministry of Housing and Urban Poverty Alleviation, 2008. Report of the Committee on Slum Statistics/Centres, New Delhi, India, Government of India, Ministry of Housing and Urban Poverty Alleviation.

eliminate urban poverty by designing suitable plans for development, both at the micro-level as well as macro-level. Definitely, it may bring development at all area levels for the identified population whether it is urban population or urban slum population with utmost accuracy and transparency.

NOTES

1. Research Paper—Public Administration—Urbanization and Urban Slums in India, A Study, Dr. Rajesh Kumar, *International Regional Research Journal*, March, 2011, ISSN-0974-2832, RNI-RAJBIL, 2009/29954, Vol. II, Issue 26.
2. Dr. Abir Bandyopadhyaya, Vandana Agrawal, "Slum in India: From Past to Present" *www.injes.com. International Research Journal of Engineering and Science* (IRJES), ISSN (online) 2319-183X, (print) 2319-1821, Volume 2, Issue 4 (April 2013), pp. 55-59, *www.irjgs.com*
3. Arun, K. Singh and Sharma Raj, *Urban Slums: An Enquiring into Concept, Characteristics and Policy Intervention, Urban Panorama*, Vol. XIII, January-June 2014, No. 1, pp. 37-52.
4. Atul Pratap Singh and Awadesh Kumar Sigh, *"Urban Sanitation and Rehabilitation of Scavengers in India"*, Vol. XIII, January-June, 2014, No.1, pp. 53-78.
5. Paramita Datta Dey, "Urban Poor, Poverty Reduction Strategy Approach", in Urban India, *A Journal of the National Institute of Urban Affairs*, New Delhi, Vol. 31, No. 1, January-June-2011, pp. 83-101.
6. Dr. Mridula Bhatnagar, *"Urban Slums and Poverty"*, Published by Ritu Publications, Jaipur (Rajasthan), India, 2010.
7. "Slum Population as percentage of Urban" http://mdgs.un.org/unsd/mdg/series details.ASPX?srid=710, Accessed 14th July 2014.
8. Special study: Dr. Rajesh Kumar, 'Urbanisation & Urban Slums in India: A Study' (in) International Referred Research Journals, March, 2011. ISSN-0974-2832, RNI.-RAJBIL, 2009/29954, Vol. II, *Issue-26.

11
Role of Technology in Achieving Slum Free Cities

M. Rama Rao

Background

According to the provisional Census 2011, the population in India is 121,01,93,422 of which 31.16 per cent (37,71,05,760) of population lives in urban areas and 68.84 per cent (833,087,662) in rural areas. The urban poverty in India is large and widespread; initially poverty remains large in rural areas, due to the rapid urbanization it is shifted and has been becoming a constraint for urban development. The share of the urban poor with the total urban population from 18.7 per cent in 1973 was increased to 26.8 per cent in 2004-05. On the other hand due to shortage of affordable housing stock the migrants' end up in informal settlements/ squatters resulting in growth of slum.

For the first time a detailed demographic data about slums across the country was collected during 2001 Census operations. A total of 52.4 million people living in 10.2 million households have been enumerated as slum dwellers from 1743 cities/towns of 26 States and Union Territories. The slum dwellers in 1743 cities constitute 18.5 per cent of the total urban population. Primary Census Abstract (PCA) 2011 States, out of 4,041 statutory towns' slums are reported from 2,543 Towns (63%). A total of 6,54,94,604 people residing in 1,39,20,191 with a household size of 4.7 are enumerated as slum dwellers. The decadal growth rate of slum dwellers for the period of 2001-11 is around 25 per cent. The 46

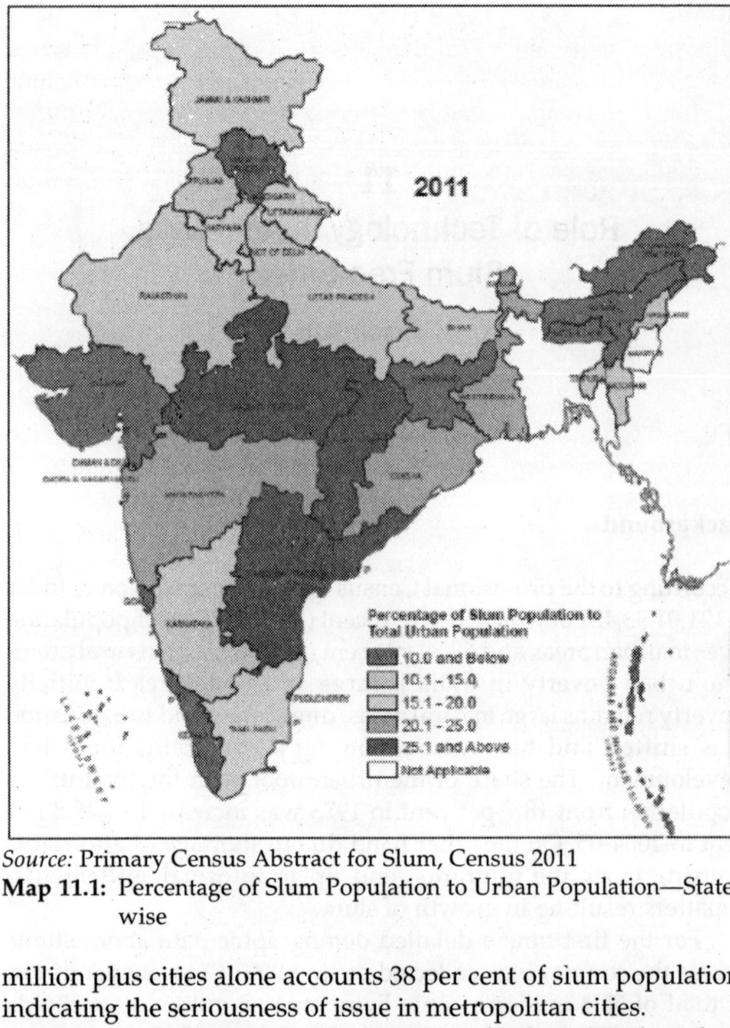

Source: Primary Census Abstract for Slum, Census 2011

Map 11.1: Percentage of Slum Population to Urban Population—State-wise

million plus cities alone accounts 38 per cent of sium population indicating the seriousness of issue in metropolitan cities.

To manage this situation Government of India in 2009 launched Rajiv Awas Yojana (RAY) with an aim to achieve the vision of a 'slum-free India' with inclusive and equitable cities in which every citizen has access to basic civic and social services and decent shelter. The plan preparation exercise under RAY is carried out in two phases i.e. Slum Free City Plan of Action (SFCPoA) on 'whole city' basis in first phase and Detailed Project Reports (DPR) on 'whole slum' basis for selected slums in second phase. Earlier schemes/programmes like Basic Service for Urban Poor (BSUP) and Integrated Housing Scheme and Development Programme (IHSDP) were implemented towards slum development in selected cities/towns. One of the unique difference between RAY and earlier programmes is ***using of technologies*** became essential in plan preparation process.

Technology is knowledge used to create tools or design programme and develop skills to extract or collect or store materials/data. In general it is the application of science to meet an objective or solve a problem. In present era, technical innovations representing progressive developments are emerging to make use of technology's competitive advantage. Its significance on humans is tremendous because technology helps them adapt to the situation.

The technologies prescribed by Ministry of Housing and Urban Poverty Alleviation (MoHUPA) in RAY guidelines are spatial information system i.e. Geographical Information System (GIS) and non-spatial data management tools *via* Management Information System (MIS). These technical applications strengthen the plan preparation process by overcoming challenges like beneficiary identification, boundary delineation and assessment of infrastructure gaps etc.

Geographical Information System (GIS) and its Role

It is a computer system designed to capture, store, analyze, manage and present all types of spatial or geographical data. In a general sense, the term describes any information system that integrates stores, edits, analyzes, shares, and displays geographic information. These information systems offer interpretation of physical data with other socio-economic data, and thereby providing an important linkage in the planning process and making it more effective and meaningful. With the help of satellite based maps and digital information all the required information is integrated in GIS based urban management system. This not only helps to unify information on common platform but also enables updating information as and when required with ease and precision. This has specific importance in the context of slums and informal settlements where accurate representation of the ground scenario with that of the socio-economic conditions of the people is a necessity for inclusive planning. The process of GIS application in the slum free cities plan preparation process is as follows:

The basic elements of a GIS

- Six Functions of a GIS:
  - ➢ Capture data
  - ➢ Store data
  - ➢ Query data
  - ➢ Analyze data
  - ➢ Display data
  - ➢ Produce output

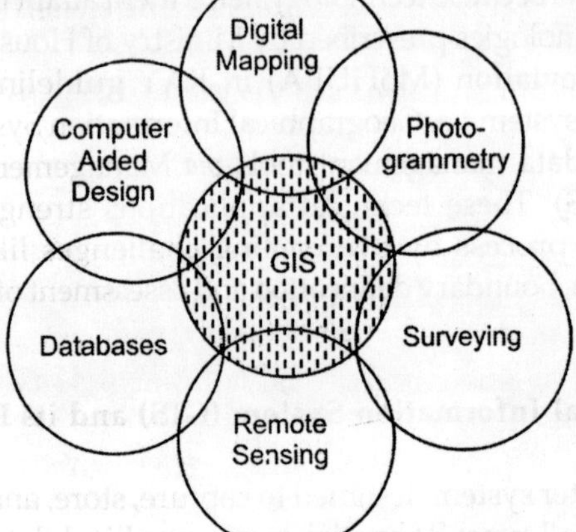

Fig. 11.1: Cross-disciplinary nature of GIS will help in decision-making

The foremost important aspect is that of preparing and updating a geo-referenced base map for the respective city or the study area for starting the Slum socio-economic survey. The preparation of slum level base map is the next vital component of the plan. The steps required to undertake for preparation of City and slum level Base Map using GIS is as follows:

Step I: Procurement of city level base map

A city base map between 1:2000—1:10,000 scale may be available with the concerned Urban Local Body or any other department of State government. In such cases, the first step will be collection of those base maps for the "planning area" including boundaries of municipal area, zones, wards and Slums. In case of unavailability of prepared city level base map the step II is initiated.

Step II: Inventory of satellite image

In some cases, high resolution satellite image (Cartosat–I, II, Quick bird, etc.) may also be available in ULB or any other department of State government. If the recent satellite images have been procured, preparation of city level base map can be initiated.

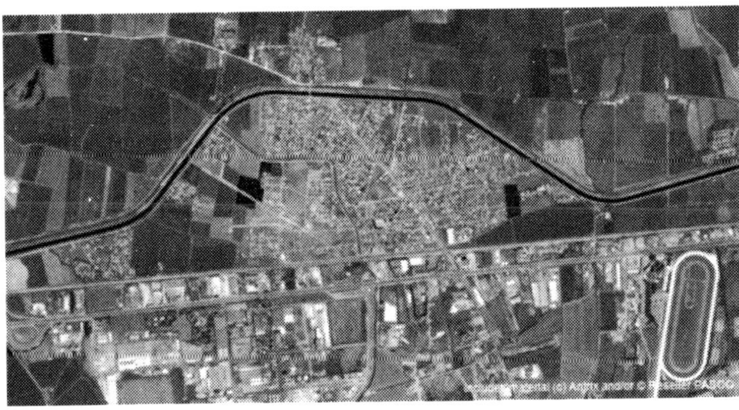

Fig. 11.2: Cartosat Image

Step III: Procurement of Cartosat I/II Satellite Image

If base map/GIS layers/high resolution satellite image are not readily available with the Cities/States, then Cartosat I/II image needs to be procured from National Remote Sensing Centre (NRSC) for the entire "Planning Area" of the RAY City. After procurement of satellite image city level base map will be prepared using GIS technology. The process is as follows:

The procured satellite image is added into GIS and geo-reference it. The process of defining the position of geographical objects relative to a standard reference grid is known as geo-referencing. It is a system that links information to a position on earth's surface. The task of updating and validating the geo-reference image is important wherever necessary. The process of digitization is carried out and a base map is generated at an appropriate scale.

Data Content for City Level Base Map

- Administrative boundaries (planning area, municipal, zones and wards).
- Major Roads.
- Important land marks such as major places of worship, major hospitals, all educational institutes, government offices, railway stations.
- Water bodies including canals and rivers and major drains and nallahs, etc. (Additional features will be incorporated with respect to site).

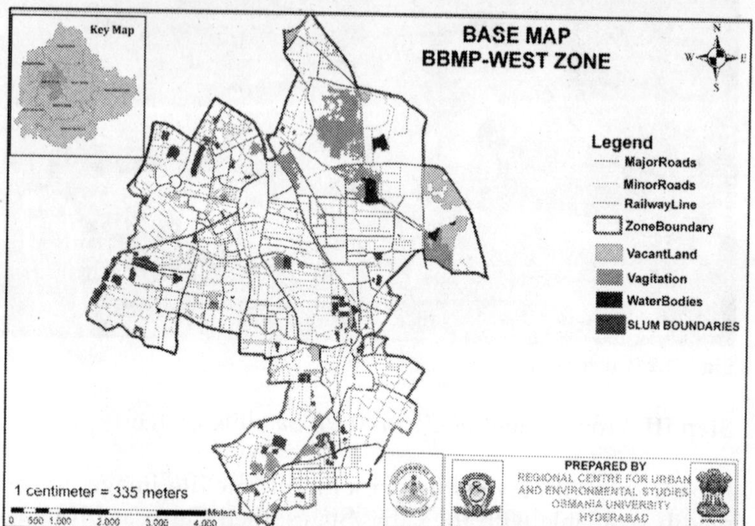

Map 11.2: Geo referenced Base Map (including slum bundaries) of West zone-Benguluru, Karnataka

Step IV: Delineation of Slum Boundary and preparing slum level base maps:

The list of slums within the city is available with the respective ULBs and it is finalized with the help of stakeholder, elected representatives and local dwellers. After finalization, each Slum will be marked on the city base map using Global Positioning System (GPS) survey points and satellite image. This information will be saved in a separate thematic layer (Slum Boundary), over the City Base Map. After demarcation of all the Slum boundaries in GIS interface, a unique Slum code will be allotted in the attribute field of Slum Boundary layer. It is an essential exercise, without which the SFCPoA is incomplete. This unique Slum code has to be identical with code provided on the slum profiling (socio-economic) surveys format, which will be used as common reference point for integration of socio-economic data and GIS data at Slum level. A detail mapping will be done for all the identified slums at 1:500 scales. After generating a detailed slum maps a unique id number is allotted to the each footprint/dwelling unit/Household. This id number has to be quoted on the household survey format for integration of surveyed data with GIS maps. This exercise is carried out during the preparation of Detailed Project Report (DPR).

Data Content for the Slum Map (1:500)

- Delineation of boundary using DGPS/TSS/GPS.
- Footprint of each structure and use (residential/ commercial/community centre etc.)
- Vacant Open spaces, green space both government/private,
- Major and Minor roads with cart track,

Fig. 11.3: Slum level GIS mapping; Bhavani Nagar Slum, Gulbarga, Karnataka

- Important landmarks in the slum
- Water supply pipelines/tube wells/community taps, community toilets.

Management Information System (MIS)

Having an appropriate, transparent and clean data base is the key for preparation of any plan. In the case of RAY, MoHUPA has prescribed three survey formats (Annexure I, II, III) designed by National Building Organization (NBO) to acquire enough information for preparing Slum Free Cities plan of Action reports (SFCPoA).

These questionnaires address the details regarding settlement profile, households' level and livelihood profile. After performing the ground surveys the data has to be verified and validated. The computerization of surveyed data is robust exercise and needs to perform for the healthy management of data. This whole process of computerization and management of data is termed as Management Information System (MIS). An online Monitoring System for Slum,

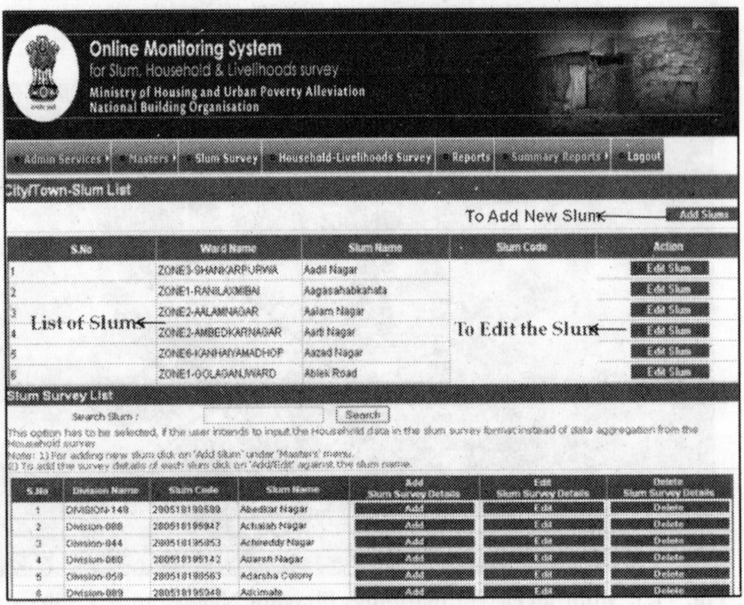

Fig. 11.4: An online ***MIS application*** developed by Centre for Good Governance as per the requirement of MoHUPA

Household and Livelihood Survey (Slum MIS) has developed by Ministry to achieve; easiness in accessing the data and quick analysis. User Manual has been prepared and made available in MoHUPA website. The surveyed details should be computerized using this Slum MIS. Once the data is entered, reports can be generated by using e-tools provided in the application.

As per MoHUPA guidelines, this Slum MIS will serve as a useful databank for various reports to be used for monitoring and implementation of all programmes of the ULB. Some of benefits could be as under:

- Baseline Information for Planning and Policy making.
- Identification of current levels of civic and social infrastructure, gaps therein so as to take appropriate steps to overcome shortcomings.
- Identification of livelihood needs such as training, employment etc. in each Slum area and decision-making on the same.

In the ULBs where it is not possible to use online system the ministry has facilitated an offline data entry module. The desired ULB may use the "Offline Services" by downloading the offline module, configure it on a single computer and enter the data and upload the data file to the online System. The ULB will have the access to see the details of upload and reports through online system.

GIS-MIS Integration for Preparation of Slum Free City Plan of Action (SFCPoA)

To achieve slum free cities, a systematic approach is essential for better designing and planning. The SFCPoA will be an overall action plan of the ULB with investment requirements projected for the next 10-15 years. Therefore, this task is performed in order to find appropriate and accurate solution for the challenged slums i.e. poor access of infrastructure and lack of *pucca* housing. An updated city base map prepared using high resolution satellite image and GIS will be integrated with MIS data at slum level data.

Integration of GIS with MIS means matching the common parameters (fields) from the attribute of the spatial data (Map)

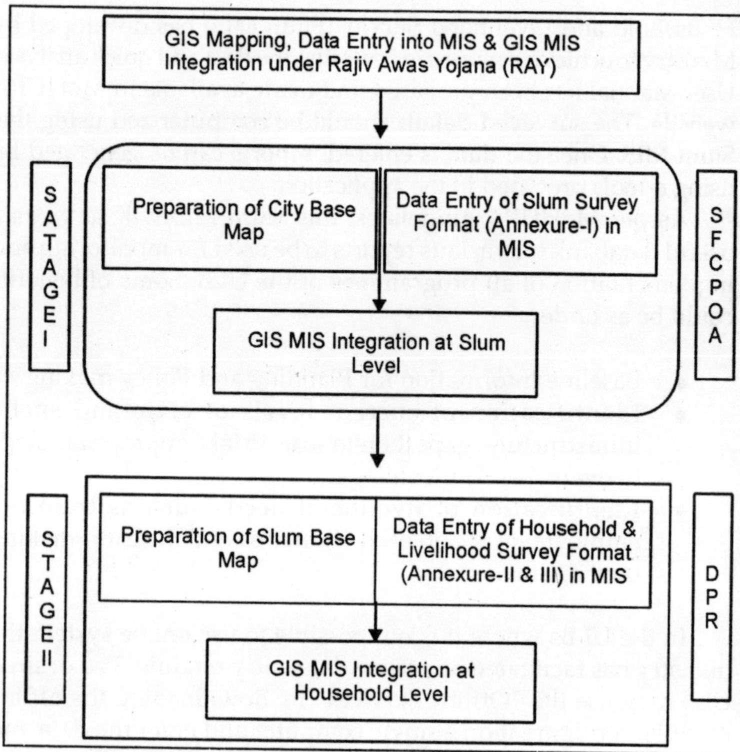

Source: Ray Guidelines, MoHUPA.

Fig. 11.5: *Flow Chart* GIUS-MIS integration

with MIS based common fields. This would enable the viewing of the integrated data and the preparation of the reports.

The survey formats encompasses data pertaining to slums level (Annexure I), Household (Annexure II) and Livelihood profile (Annexure III) of the slum dwellers. The unique id given to the slums during the delineation of slum boundaries are used as reference for integration of annexure I data (MIS) with slum boundaries in GIS. In the similar lines the unique id given to the foot prints/households/dwelling units are used for the integration of annexure II data with the footprint on slum level base map in GIS.

As per the guidelines of MoHUPA, the GIS enabled MIS data at household level will then be used for the preparation of following thematic layers during DPR stage:

Fig. 11.6: *Integration* of Spatial and Non-spatial data—-Bhavani Nagar slum, Gulbarga, Karnataka

- Existing Infrastructure Base Map of Slum.
- Digital Elevation Model (DEM), Relief and Slope Map of Slum.
- Socio-economic condition of Slum Households.
- Location and size of each dwelling Units.

Conclusion

The socio-economic surveys and base maps of city and slums are fundamental elements for the preparation of Plan of Action (PoA) reports towards achieving slum free cities. The survey data and base map preparation are managed significantly by using the technologies like MIS and GIS. The foremost aspects of using these technologies are storage of data, ease in accessing data and spatial analysis of data with respect to socio-economic surveys. The technologies also help in preparing a concurrent list of beneficiaries by out layering the duplication. Apart from these, MIS linked GIS databases of City base map will became fundamental datasets for ULBs for proceeding further. Therefore, the role of MIS and GIS technologies are of paramount importance towards slum free cities.

12

Role of Training and Research Institutions in Improving Urban Environment

Shri P. Gopal

'Cities and Towns' are fast growing haphazardly and abnormally increasing urbanization and the associated problems makes the planner as well as administrator to seek solution in an amicable way through their innovative and scientific study relating urban environment. 'Poverty' creates a danger to prosperity everywhere in the twenty-first century, Metropolitan cities as well as cities and towns of different sizes portray various problems, which are inter actively associated with population and settlement system. Government of India has established the Regional Centre for urban and environmental studies on Osmania University campus and its activities are varied and vivid to solve the problems of urban design and planning. In this chapter, RCUES—as a case study which presents the aspects; Such as:

> (1) Introduction, (2) Purpose, (3) Objectives, (4) RCUES—Successive Directors, (5) RCUES—Faculty, (6) Urban Poverty Alleviation Cell, (7) Areas of Training and Research of the RCUES, Hyderabad, (8) Training Programmes at a Glance, 2008-09—The Activities—Human Resource Development and Management—list of Research Modules—2008-09 to 2013-14—Research Publications, (9) Library and (10) Conclusion.

Individual to Institution

Introduction

Cities and towns are growing haphazardly and abnormally. The present increasing trend of urbanization is alarming the urban local bodies to cope-up with the enhanced demand for quality infrastructure and better delivery service within the limited financial resources. Varied nature of urban problems are existing and posing a great challenge. Unless systematic approach is adopted to deal with it, the nation may not achieve the desired goals of modernization and development of vibrant cities. Keeping in view of the above points in mind, Research and Training has assumed the importance World over. There is a greater need for taking up analytical studies and in depth, research on critical issues relating to Urban Development, Eradication of Urban Poverty and Slum Development. In the year 1970, the Ministry of Urban Employment, presently Ministry of Urban Development, Government of India has established the Regional Centre for Urban and Environmental Studies on the Osmania University Campus at Hyderabad to cater to the needs of Research and Training in South Indian Cities.

Purpose

1. The very purpose is to concentrate the Research and Training activities to be undertaken by the Regional Centre for Urban and Environmental Studies and also Policy initiatives that have been introduced by the Centre and State governments from time to time regarding urban development and poverty eradication besides forming the good work—done by NGOs and civil societies involved in this mission. The RCUES helps to prepare good policy makers, planners, other government functionaries and also train the trainers by academicians, administrators and potential resource persons to make the administrator as potential and excellent personnel in their respective field of specializations.
2. Though it is the duty of the urban local bodies to provide civic amenities and maintain such services in their respective areas including the slums and squatter settlements, they are not able to cope up with the increased demand for urban infrastructure due to their poor financial capacity. It is in this context, the staff working in urban local bodies—Municipalities, Municipal Corporations, Town planning, Revenue, Public Health Engineering, Sanitation,

Urban Community Development, staff need to be trained in the latest management techniques and conversant/ oriented with the rules and regulations which improve their capacity and formulation and effective implementation of programmes. Besides formar training, research also plays a crucial role in identifying the bottlenecks in the implementation of various schemes and also to suggest mid-term corrective measures for better implementation.

The major area of RCUES since its inception has been nothing but accepting the challenging terms in the area of research and training for promoting sustainable development of urban areas besides the above aspects, it is felt quite necessary to expand the horizon and determination to bring/culminate the latest research and training activities which are to be adopted as a strategy of its development programmes.

Personnal: Prof M.A. Muttalib was the founder, Director and the following are the objectives of the Centre.

Regional Centre for Urban and Environmental Studies—Its Objectives

- To undertake applied research identify and formulate action plans to resolve problems relating to urban development, administration and management
- To conceptualize and organize seminars, symposia, workshops, conferences etc. on the critical issues, constraints, problems and practices relating to the management and administration of urban development.
- To define and to organize access to demand responsive knowledge or skill transfer to the personal—elected as well as the cadres of civil servants involved in the management of the urban sector.
- To generate and disseminate information relating to policy planning, strategy formulation, action planning, programme implementation and management and
- To facilitate synergetic intervention between academics and professionals through project based retraining facilities and extension education programmes.

RCUES—Successive Directors

Since its inception, Regional Centre for Urban and Environmental Studies, Osmania University, is headed by a Director who is appointed among the Faculty Members of the University. The RCUES has seen several and severe ups and downs in its stability academic progress, administrative jargons, relationship with Osmania university, etc. However, the centre is functioning continuously with dedicated enthusiasm and without any interruption since 43 years. The Centre has a privilege to utilize the best and expertise services of 13 professors as its Directors and the details are stated below.

Table 12.1: List of Successive Director in RCUES

Sl. No.	*Name*	*From*	*To*
1.	Prof. M.A. Muttalib	01/01/1970	20/04/1986
2.	Prof. B. Hanumantha Rao, I/C	26/04/1986	20/08/1986
3.	Prof. D. Ravindra Prasad	21/08/1986	24/03/1997
4.	Prof. M. Bhagavanthaya Rao, I/C	25/03/1997	07/06/1997
5.	Prof. D. Ravindra Prasad	08/06/1997	19/11/2000
6.	Prof. V. Lakshmipathy, I/C	20/11/2000	02/04/2003
7.	Prof. M. Mutha Reddy, I/C	03/04/2003	08/07/2003
8.	Prof. D. Ravindra Prasad	24/01/2004	29/10/2004
9.	Prof. Bhupathi Rav, I/C	30/10/2004	08/05/2006
10.	Prof. Sofi Ali, I/C	08/05/2006	30/12/2006
11.	Prof. M. Mutha Reddy, I/C	30/12/2006	02/05/2008
12.	Prof. Bhupatthi Rav, I/C	02/05/2008	31/12/2014

RCUES—Faculty

The Regional Centre for Urban and Environmental Studies has a core faculty comprising two professors and the Director, I/C (Professor, in the Department of Public Administration, Osmania University). The Project Staff is engaged under different schemes and projects to meet the training and research needs from time to time. Faculty from other disciplines/Departments and other institutions of higher learning are drawn to meet the wide gap in current research and training needs. The core faculty and their academic achievements are mentioned as under.

Professor Bhupatthi Rav, M.A., M.Phil., Ph.D.

Professor (Dr.) Bhupatthi Rav is the Director of RCUES and had a wide experience and expertise of 38 years of teaching and research. He has specialized: (1) Public Administration, (2) Urban Affairs, and (3) Management Urban Local Bodies. Professor Bhupatthi Rav has guided 10 Ph.D's and 9 M.Phil. Scholars successfully, He was the member, Executive Council, Osmania university and chairman, Board of Studies, Department of Public Administration, Osmania University besides this, he held various positions in the university. He has published quite number of books and 30 papers in National Journals and also he is the member of eleven professional bodies. He has gated as seminar Director for four seminars.

Professor. A. Malla Reddy, M.A., M.Phil., Ph.D., Deputy Director, RCUES

Areas of specialization: Urban Slums, Urban Poverty Alleviation and Urban Development. Professor A. Malla Reddy has developed an excellent expertise in Urban Management and Urban Poverty Alleviation. He has nearly 30 years of teaching and research and conducted several training programmes. Professor Malla Reddy has Published two books and one dozen papers in National Journals. He has conducted various training workshops under Urban Poverty Alleviation and also conducted three National Evaluation Studies on IDSMT, EIUS and SJSRY.

Professor V. Gnaneshwar, M.A., Ph.D. has specialized in Urban Governance, Urban Policies and Urban Finance. Recently, he has attained the age of superannuation.

Professor N. Ashok Kumar, M.A., Ph.D. has specialized in Urban Infrastructure and Urban Environment.

Professor. Abdul Sameem Ansari, M.A., M.Phil, Ph.D. has specialized in Urban Renewal, Urban Management and Solid Waste Management.

Dr. Vasant Kumar Gonu, M.A., L.LB., Ph.D, has specialized in Reforms in Urban Governance—strategy and Change Management, Leadership, Team building, Urban issues etc. His area of interest lies on human trafficking, minimizing road traffic accidents, and empowerment of Urban Poor etc. At present, he is working as project coordinator.

Urban Poverty Alleviation Cell

The RCUES-Osmania University has been playing an important and significant role in the capacity building of the functionaries involved in all the slum improvement and Urban Poverty Alleviation Programmes, started by the Government of India over the years (i.e.) EIUS, UBSP, NRY and SJSRY. The RCUES is also recognized and identified as a National Training Institute (NTI) by the Ministry of Housing and Urban Poverty Alleviation, Government of India, for training functionaries and organizing regional and National Workshops on topical issues under SJSRY Scheme. A dedicated Urban Poverty Alleviation cell has been created in the RCUES, Osmania University to meet and mitigate the training and research requirements under the SJSRY and other Urban Poverty related programmes. The cell consists of the following members:

1. Professor (Retired) A.V. Satyanarayana Rao, M.A., Ph.D., Consultant. Professor (Dr.) A.V. Satyanarayana Rao was former Dean, Faculty of Management, Osmania University and has served this university in different positions. He held the positions, like, Head, Dean, officer on Special Duty, Convener of CETS, Director, ICSSR etc. He has published a number of books and guides the scholars for Ph.D. and M.Phil degrees.

Areas of Training and Research of RCUES, Hyderabad

The areas of research and training activities of this institute are being imparted to the requirement of the urban development and urban poverty alleviation programmes and schemes being launched by the Ministry of Urban Development and the Ministry of housing and Urban Poverty Alleviation, Government of India and the stakeholders State governments respectively which come under the jurisdiction of RCUES. The RCUES has organized 1424 training programme and trained 42,857 urban functionaries till 2007-08. In the earlier years, (i.e.) from 2001-02 to 2005-06, the RCUES, Osmania University, have organized 296 training programmes covering nearly over 10,000 urban functionaries. The focused areas of training and workshops are:

Urban Governance and Reforms

Awareness and orientation for municipal political representatives, women empowerment including gender budgeting, E-governance, in ULBS, Urban Governance Reforms, District Planning Committees, Ward Committees and Public-Private-Patnerships (PPP).

Urban Solid Waste Management

Garbage free cities and towns low cost and sustainable solid waste management strategies, Public-Private-Partnership in solid waste management and methods of waste treatment are important potential activities.

Urban Poverty Alleviation

Community Participation and Mobilization, Micro Finance and Marketing, Thrift and Credit Groups, Skill Development, Entrepreneurship Development, Public-Private-Partnerships, Local Institutional Development, Urban Informal Sector Development, etc.

Urban Financial Management

Revenue Management, Resource Mobilization Strategies including debt financing, Tax Administration including property tax, Financial Management Information System, Financial Reforms and S.F.C.'s and Financial Devolutions to ULBs.

Urban Transport and Traffic Management

Urban Transport Policy in India, Mobility and Traffic Issues, Effective Traffic Management, Methods, Sustainable Public Transport Systems, GIS and Traffic Management.

JNNURM

Integrated City Development plans, Implementation of UIDSSMT and IHSDP Programmes, Implementation of Reforms and City Level Networking.

Table 12.2: Training Programmes at a Glance: 2008-09

Sl. No.	*Programmes*	*No. of Programmes*	*No. of Participants*
1.	Management Development Programme	09	168
2.	National Level Workshops	02	155
3.	Urban Poverty Alleviation – SJSRY State Level Activities	24	816
4.	Extension Education Collaborative Programmes with MEPMA	18	1560
	TOTAL	53	2699

The Activities—Human Resource Development and Management

Human Resource Development and Management occupy an important role in the training agenda of RCUES. Diagnostics for Organization Re-Engineering, Capacity Building and Institutional Strengthening constitute a significant share of the applied research activities. The RCUES-Osmaina University shoulders the role of catalyst as well as facilities in re-engineering organization structures, systems and staffing including Training Need Analysis, Designing and Action planning relating to employee Training, Training of Trainers and implementation of the Training Action plans.

The Research Component involved most complex dimension of personnel management—job satisfactions, recommitment, placement, job-rotation, career planning and development. The training programme under the collaboration involved all cadres, in a wide band of topics—operations and maintenances of personal finance and accounts, consumer services etc.

- Hyderabad Metro Water Supply and Sewerage Board—Organization Re-Engineering and Diagnostics.
- Chennai Metropolitan Water Supply and Sewerage Board—Organizational Re-Engineering and Diagnostics.
- Maharashtra Jeevan Pradhikaran—Organizational Re-Engineering and Diagnostics.
- Andhra Pradesh State Co-operative Bank—Organizational Re-Engineering and Diagnostics.
- Andhra Pradesh State Trading Corporations Executive Development Programme

- Urban Police Administration—Improving interface with Public—Hyderabad City Police.
- Micro-level planning for Sustainable Development.

Swarna Jayanti Shahari Rojgar Yojana (SJSRY)

The Ministry of Urban Development and Poverty Alleviation, Government of India introduced SJSRY to provide gainful employment to the urban unemployees or under employed by integrating the earlier UBSP, NRY and PMIUPEP. The Government of India has identified the RCUES—Osmania University, as one of the National Training Institutes for organizing the training programmes to the municipal functionaries and the elected representatives of Andhra Pradesh, Tamil Nadu, Karnataka, Kerala, Madhya Pradesh and the Union Territories of Pondicherry and Andaman and Nicobar Islands.

Table 12.3: List of Research Studies and Modules—2008-2009 to 2013-2014

I. Action Oriented Research Projects: 2008-2009

Sl. No.	*Name of the Projects*	*Duration*	*Principal Investigator*
1.	Implementation of UIDSSMT in Andhra Pradesh	Feb-June, 2009	Prof. A. Malla Reddy
2.	Fund your city – A PPP Model – A case study of GHMC	Feb-June, 2009	Prof. V. Gnaneshwa
3.	Performance appraisal of Public Transport System in Hyderabad City	Feb-April, 2009	Prof. N. Ashok Kumai
4.	Garbage Free Campus – A study of Osmania University Campus	Feb-June, 2009	Prof. Abdul Sameem Ansari
5.	Anti-Human Trafficking in Urban Cities: Re-Socialization of Victims of Commercial Sexual Exploitation	March-May, 2009	Dr. G. Vasant Kumar
2009-2010			
1.	Innovative Approaches in Financial Resource Mobilization in ULBs- Fund Your City – A case study of Greater Hyderabad Municipal Corporation (GHMC)	Completed and Report was submitted	Prof. V. Gnaneshwar
2.	Institutional Frame Work for Implementation of UPA Programmes in Southern States	Completed and Report was submitted	Dr. Deepa Nair

(Contd.)

Table 12.3 (*Contd.*)

Sl. No.	*Name of the Projects*	*Duration*	*Principal Investigator*
3.	Women Empowerment – A study of Self-Help Groups in the State of Andhra Pradesh	Completed and Report submitted	Dr.Deepa Nair & Mr.Nanda Kishore
4.	PPP: Development of Neighborhood Community Centres	Work in Progress	Dr.Vasant Kumar
5.	Water SCADA in Vijayawada Municipal Corporation	Work in Progress	Prof.V.Gnaneshwar
6.	Exploitation of migrant women and children in Urban Areas	Completed & Report under preparation	Dr.G.Vasant Kumar
7.	Reforms in Solid Waste Management – A study of Greater Hyderabad Municipal Corporation (GHMC)	Work in Progress	Prof.A.S.Ansari
8.	Implementation of UIDSSMT in Kerala and Tamilnadu	Work in Progress	Prof.A.Malla Reddy

II. Training Modules: 2009-2010

Sl. No.	*Title of the Training Module*	*Duration*	*Faculty*
1.	Implementation of UIDSSMT Programme	Mar-April,2009	Prof. A.Malla Reddy
2.	Financial Resource Mobilization in ULBs	Mar-April,2009	Prof. V.Gnaneshwar
3.	Water Sustentation: Development Strategies	Mar-April,2009	Prof. N.Ashok Kumar
4.	Innovative Approaches in Solid Waste Management	Mar-April,2009	Prof. Abdul Sameem Anasari
5.	Role of Police in Urban Traffic Management	Mar-April,2009	Dr. G.Vasant Kumar

2010-2011

Sl. No.	*Title of the Training Module*	*Faculty*
1.	Financial Resource Mobilization in Urban Local Bodies	Urban Finance Cell Represented by Prof. V.Gnaneshwar
2.	Municipal Accounting Reforms	
3.	Property Tax Reforms in Urban Local Bodies	
4.	SJSRY–Community Mobilization & Development	Urban Poverty Alleviation Cell Represented by Dr. Vasant Kumar
5.	SJSRY–Revised Guidelines: Entrepreneurship Development & Self Employment	
6.	SJSRY–Skill Development: Step-by-Step Methodology	
7.	Street Vendor Policy: Identification of Beneficiaries and Development of Space in ULB's-Best Practices	

(*Contd.*)

(Contd.)

Sl. No.	*Title of the Training Module*	*Duration*	*Faculty*
8.	SJSRY: Skill Development Initiatives for the Empowerment of Urban Poor		Urban Poverty Alleviation Cell Represented by Dr. Vasant Kumar
9.	Resource Mobilization and Sustainability in Urban Poverty Alleviation		
10.	SJSRY Revised Guidelines: Microfinance and Entrepreneurship Development		
11.	SJSRY Revised Guidelines: Step-by-Step Operational Guidelines		
12.	Slum Free City Planning: Step-by-Step Methodology		Planning Wing-Represented by Shri M. Rama Rao
13.	Slum Free City Planning : GIS & MIS		
14.	SJSRY–Revised Guide Lines: Micro Finance and Entrepreneurship Development		Shri Briz Bhushan
15.	Elected Representative on Service Level Benchmarks for Urban Local Bodies		Solid Waste Management Cell Represented by Dr. Syeda Azeem Unnisa
16.	Solid Waste Management for Newly appointed Environmental Engineers		
17.	Innovative Approaches in Solid Waste Management		
18.	Bench Marking of Municipal Services : Sanitation		
19.	Bench Marking of Urban Water Supply and Sewerage		
20.	Service Level Benchmarks for Water Supply and Sewerage		Solid Waste Management Cell Represented by Dr. Syeda Azeem Unnisa

2011-2012

Sl. No.	*Title of the Training Module*	*Faculty*
1.	Financial Resource Mobilization in Urban Local Bodies	Urban Finance Cell Represented by Prof. V. Gnaneshwar*
2.	Development Control and Building Regulations for Sustainable Urban Development	
3.	Property Tax Reforms in Urban Local Bodies	
4.	SJSRY – Community Mobilization and Development of CBOs	Urban Poverty Alleviation Cell Represented by Dr. Vasant Kumar
5.	SJSRY – Revised Guidelines: Entrepreneurship Development and Self Employment	
6.	SJSRY – Skill Development: Step-by-Step Methodology	
7.	Street Vendor Policy : Identification of Beneficiaries and Development of Space in ULB's – Best Practices	

(Contd.)

(Contd.)

Sl. No.	Title of the Training Module	Faculty
8.	SJSRY: Skill Development Initiatives for the Empowerment of Urban Poor	
9.	Resource Mobilization and Sustainability in Urban Poverty Alleviation	
10.	SJSRY Revised Guidelines: Microfinance and Entrepreneurship Development	
11.	SJSRY Revised Guidelines: Step-by-Step Operational Guidelines	Urban Poverty Alleviation Cell Represented by Dr. Vasant Kumar
12.	Slum Free City Planning: Step-by-Step Methodology	Planning Wing- Represented by
13.	Slim Free City Planning: GIS and MIS	Shri M. Rama Rao
14.	SJSRY – Revised Guide Lines: Micro Finance and Entrepreneurship Development	Shri Briz Bhushan
15.	Quality Management in Municipal Water Supply	Water Supply & Solid Waste Management Cell Represented by Dr. Syeda Azeem Unnisa
16.	Water Supply & Sanitation in ULBs for Elected Representatives	
17.	Elected Representatives on Services Level Benchmarks for Urban Local Bodies	
18.	Solid Waste Management Rules 2000 Implementation Strategies in ULBs	
19.	Innovative Approaches in Solid Waste Management	
20.	Bench Marking of Municipal Services : Sanitation	
21.	Service Level Benchmarks for Water Supply & Sewerage	

2012-2013

Sl. No.	Title of the Training Module	Faculty
1.	Financial Resource Mobilization in Urban Local Bodies	Finance Cell Represented by Prof. V. Gnaneshwar
2.	Development Control and Building Regulations for Sustainable Urban Development	
3.	Property Tax Reforms in Urban Local Bodies	
4.	UPA-Social Mobiliztion and Institutional Development	Urban Poverty Alleviation Cell Represented by Dr. Vasant Kumar
5.	Slum Free City Planning : GIS & MIS	Planning Wing – Represented by Mr. M. Rama Rao

(Contd.)

(Contd.)

Sl. No.	*Title of the Training Module*	*Faculty*
6.	Quality Management in Municipal Water Supply	Water Supply & Solid Waste Management Cell Represented by Dr. Syeda Azeem Unnisa
7.	Solid Waste Management Rules 2000 Implementation Strategies in ULBs	
8.	Innovative Approaches in Solid Waste Management	
9.	Bench Marking of Municipal Services : Sanitation	
10.	Service Level Benchmarks for Water Supply & Sewerage	
11.	Urban Services for Elected Representatives	
12.	Urban Governance for Elected Representatives	
13.	Sustainable Urban Planning	
14.	GIS Based Property Tax	JNNURM cell Represented by Prof. V.Gnaneshwar & Dr. Syeda Azeem Unnisa
15.	Solid Waste Management	
16.	Water Quality Management	
17.	Delivery Management of Urban Services	

III. Research Studies and Modules: 2013-2014

Sl. No.	*Project*	*Type*	*Topic*	*Stage*
I	JNNURM	Modules	1. Orientation for Elected Representatives on Urban Services 2. Orientation for Elected Representative on Governance 3. Sustainable Urban Planning 4. GIS Based Property Tax 5. Solid Waste Management 6. Water Quality Management	Completed & Submitted
II	USHA	Modules	1. Collection of Housing and Building Construction Statistics and Building Material Prices, Wages of Labor 2. Slum/Slum Household/Livelihoods Survey in Cities/Towns 3. Slum Like Clusters Verifications 4. Development of Housing Start-up index (HUSI)- Collection of Building permits issued data-Methodology	Being Submitted
III	SJSRY	Module	Financial Inclusion – Bringing the Urban Poor into main Stream	Completed
		Research Study	Evaluation Study on the Process followed at the State level for selection of Skill Training Providers' (STPs) In the 6 States	Under Finalization
IV	UD	Research Studies/ Publications	1. Study on Clean and Dump Free Cities 2. Improving Urban Environment – Suryapet (AP) Experience 3. Implementation of UIDSSMT – AP Experience	Completed

Research Publications

Project specific research constitutes the bed rock of all the academic programmes at the RCUES-Osmania University, Hyderabad. Every training programme is proceeded by an in-depth study of the performance milieu, the practices, procedures, constraints and problems pertinent to the function under focus including the ways and means for transfer of appropriate knowledge and skills to ensure faculty response to the learning situations back at the centre.

The second dimension of research relates to critical and objective analysis of policies, strategies and action plans. The RCUES, Osmania University, Hyderabad has earned exceptionally high level of acceptance of its study procedures and the reliability of research output. Most of the research output in this category remain the property of the sponsors and therefore can be published only with their permission. In furtherance of the knowledge frontiers, scholars in the cognate subjects, however, are provided unhindered access to the available information base.

The faculty in addition to being involved in the institutional research also carry out research on their own initiative and subject of specialization with the proactive institutional support. The research output after due permission is published in the form of books, reports, occasional papers, articles in professional journals, etc.

Another feature of the research activity of the centre is the publication of urban statistics—These publications have proved very useful to scholars as well as practitioners of Urban and Environmental Studies.

Library

An unique library with an excellent collection of sector related literature over 12,000 books, reports, Ph.D. Theses and other Publications, is a hard earned asset of the Centre. Nearly 70 Journals, National as well as international are subscribed to assist the Faculty members, Research Scholars and also for the Trainees who are interested in furthering the frontiers of their knowledge.

Infrastructure

The Regional Centre for Urban and Environmental Studies (RCUES), Osmania University, is probably the first organization on the O.U. Campus, Where the faculties as well as the administrative staff are provided with access to computer systems individually. The office architecture is modeled on the Concept of Self-reliant work stations.

There are two large a/c conference halls equipped with state of art audio/video conference systems with a seating capacity of 85 and 60 separately. In addition to the above academic resources, the training infrastructure includes, 2 smaller rooms of a seating capacity of 25 each with audio/Video facilities for group discussion, a large classroom for 50 and a GIS laboratory.

Conclusion

It is concluded that to solve any problem relating to Urban Space/ Urban District/Cities and towns of various sizes have to find a solution to the present as well as future problems, eventually that may face. The administrator/economists/Geographer/Sociologists and Policy Specialists may be able to offer solution to a problem. To solve such problems, RCUES, Osmania University, Hyderabad may be able to impart good training for the five southern states of India, Teaching and Research Institute like RCUES should come to solve the Urban and Urban related problems.

13
Summary and Conclusions

K.L.N. Murty

"Urban environment study' is an important contribution to the field of urban environment related to concepts, methodology and approach to the problems for indepth study. It is highly desirable and useful not only to the beginners but also to the seasoned specialists of research studies. The important contributions are as follows:

1. It has been identified that in order to understand the patterns relating to urban space/urbanization, one has to identify, recognize, and analyse the urban environment.
2. It certainly provides an analysis of issues related to urban poverty, urban slums—government and also examine the problems at the urban spaces/cities those are facing problems due to their rapid growth.

   It has been further identified that in order to initiate the quality of life of urban dwellers, the government has to take initiatives by providing a number of facilities to lead a qualitative life. It is noted that qualitative life could be achieved, if we inject number of functions that are made accessible by the residents either urbanites/urban slum dwellers.
3. The dynamics of population leads to stress and strain of the residents because eventually they have to face the dearth of comforts and they have to lead a discomfort and discontented life in their settlements.
4. National Urban Livelihood Mission is a major body at the national level to augment the programmes to alleviate

urban poverty. It is further noted that the state level UPA programmes have to be synchronized along with NULM programmes in order to achieve maximum benefits within a period of five years.

5. It is tested that increasing population has its impact on the decreasing tendency of potential population (Ref. chapter 3)
6. It is further seen that increasing population leads to decreasing comfort in spite of the augmented urban poverty alleviation programmes. The picture is visible and presented in chapter 5.
7. It is visible that acknowledging is an important input for creating slum free cities in India. It could be seen from chapter entitled 'Role of technology in creating slum free cities' (chapter-11).
8. Institutional input for development could be seen in chapter "Environmental Impact Analysis (EIA)".
9. Various methods have been adopted for the elimination of poverty in urban areas over a period of time by the Government of India and other State governments respectively. The role of MEPMA, Government of A.P., Kudumbasree, Urban CVS, livelihood generation initiatives of Government of Gujarat (UMEED), Rajasthan Mission of Skill and Livelihoods have a positive impact on UPA. It is presented in chapter 5.
10. Reducing poverty "in urban India is an urgent task to government and mission mode approach is one and only one that could yield positive results over a period of time" It is seen from chapter 6, mission mode approaches focus on building community structures and integration of skills and livelihoods as central components of the programme.
11. It is presented that following the strategy of social mobilization, SHGs are created with a view to achieve savings mobilization, obtaining credit for employment requirements, mutual help and economic upliftment through income generating activities. It is seen from Aishwarya's article that more group can achieve development than a single individual. It is deduced that groups effort gives a total effect for development.
12. Slum dwellers constantly deal with issues such as lack of

clean water, constant migration at slums, no sewerage or waste disposal facilities, pollution and insanitary living conditions, high level of pollution, lack of basic needs and room crowding are some of the basic and important characteristics of slum housing. The answers to the above are; various programmes relating to UPA may bring development in a phased manner and its environmental impact assessment has been presented. Government of India is with a view to solve the problems at various levels and it tries to solve the problems that are straggling the entire population of Indian slums. It is presented in chapter 10.

13. It has been identified that there is every need to train the functionaries for the effective functioning of UPA programmes. Allocating meagre funds may not yield good results. Allocations of funds if they are properly made and wise planning or plan should be implemented to meet the objectives which may lead to achieve desired results in a metropolitan city. National level and state level training institutions should have to be established to train the trainers in a phased manner.

    In the light of the above scenario, our study suggested that the Ministry of Urban Affairs and Employment, Government of India has to establish at least one for each state RCUES to address the research and training needs of the constituent States.

14. It is further suggested that education may bring prosperity not only at the micro-level but also at the macro level. Through education, urban poverty alleviation is possible to achieve the targeted results. Otherwise, there will be a big gap between the investment and infrastructure requirements, which is a result of rapid growth of urban population. Due to this gap in resources, the urban population is deprived of the proper services and the poor may have to face even higher level of deprivation.

Finally, it is observed that Urban Centres are growing larger and become largest, urban governance becomes crucial because of the impact, it has on the life of innumerable urban poor dwellers. Cities are becoming development centrers, concentration of population and providers of specialized services and governance, their effective and well functioning becomes very important and crucial. It is a big problem for urban governance. Urban poverty could be eliminated or eradicated only by good governance through development programmes besides its mission mode approaches.

Annexure I

Poverty Estimates for 2011-12

New Delhi: 22 July, 2013

1. The Planning Commission has periodically estimated poverty lines and poverty ratios for each of the years for which Large Sample Surveys on Household Consumer Expenditure have been conducted by the National Sample Survey Office (NSSO) of the Ministry of Statistics and Programme Implementation. These surveys are normally conducted on quinquennial basis. The last quinquennial survey in this series was conducted in 2009-10 (NSS 66th round). However, since 2009-10 was not a normal year because of a severe drought, the NSSO repeated the large scale survey in 2011-12 (NSS 68th round). The summary results of this survey were released on 20th June, 2013.

Estimates for 2004-05 and 2009-10

2. The methodology for estimation of poverty followed by the Planning Commission has been based on the recommendations made by experts in the field from time to time. In December, 2005, Planning Commission constituted an Expert Group under the Chairmanship of Prof. Suresh D. Tendulkar to review the methodology for estimation of poverty. The Tendulkar Committee submitted its report in December 2009 and computed poverty lines and poverty ratios for 2004-05. For comparison they also computed poverty lines and poverty ratios for 1993-94 with identical methodology. These were accepted by the Planning Commission.

3. The next Large Sample Survey of Household Consumer Expenditure was conducted in 2009-10. Following the Tendulkar Committee methodology, Planning Commission made estimates of poverty for 2009-10 which were released through a Press Note

on 19th March, 2012.[1] Since several representations were made suggesting that the Tendulkar Poverty Line was too low, the Planning Commission, in June, 2012, constituted an Expert Group under the Chairmanship of Dr. C. Rangarajan to once again review the methodology for the measurement of poverty.

4. The Rangarajan Committee is deliberating on this issue and is expected to submit its report by middle of 2014. Since the data from the NSS 68th round (2011-12) of Household Consumer Expenditure Survey is now available, and the Rangarajan Committee recommendation will only be available a year later, the Planning Commission has updated the poverty estimates for the year 2011-12 as per the methodology recommended by Tendulkar Committee.

Estimates for 2011-12

5. The estimates of State-wise poverty lines for rural and urban areas for 2011-12 are given in **Table I.1**. The percentage and number of persons below poverty line for all States/UTs for rural areas, urban areas and combined are given in **Table I.2**. The all India poverty ratio is obtained as State-population weighted average poverty ratio, and the all India poverty line is the per capita per month expenditure that corresponds to the all India poverty ratio.

6. The NSSO tabulates expenditure of about 1.20 lakh households. Since these households have different number of members, the NSSO for purpose of comparison divides the household expenditure by the number of members to arrive at per capita consumption expenditure per month. This is called Monthly Per Capita Consumption Expenditure (MPCE) and is computed on the basis of three different concepts: Uniform Reference Period (URP), Mixed Reference Period (MRP), and Modified Mixed Reference Period (MMRP). As per Tendulkar Methodology, the poverty line has been expressed in terms of MPCE based on Mixed Reference Period. State-wise estimates of Average Monthly Per Capita Expenditure for rural and urban areas separately for the year 2011-12 are given in **Table I.3.**

7. For 2011-12, for rural areas the national poverty line using the Tendulkar methodology is estimated at Rs. 816 per capita per month and Rs. 1,000 per capita per month in urban areas. Thus, for a family of five, the all India poverty line in terms of

Table I.1: State specific Poverty Lines for 2011-12

Sl. No.	*States*	*Monthly per capita (Rs.)*	
		Rural	*Urban*
1.	Andhra Pradesh	860	1,009
2.	Arunachal Pradesh	930	1,060
3.	Assam	828	1,008
4.	Bihar	778	923
5.	Chhattisgarh	738	849
6.	Delhi	1,145	1,134
7.	Goa	1,090	1,134
8.	Gujarat	932	1,152
9.	Haryana	1,015	1,169
10.	Himachal Pradesh	913	1,064
11.	Jammu & Kashmir	891	988
12.	Jharkhand	748	974
13.	Karnataka	902	1,089
14.	Kerala	1,018	987
15.	Madhya Pradesh	771	897
16.	Maharashtra	967	1,126
17.	Manipur	1,118	1,170
18.	Meghalaya	888	1,154
19.	Mizoram	1,066	1,155
20.	Nagaland	1,270	1,302
21.	Odisha	695	861
22.	Punjab	1,054	1,155
23..	Rajasthan	905	1,002
24.	Sikkim	930	1,226
25.	Tamil Nadu	880	937
26.	Tripura	798	920
27.	Uttarakhand	880	1,082
28.	Uttar Pradesh	768	941
29.	West Bengal	783	981
30.	Puducherry	1,301	1,309
	All India	**816**	**1,000**

Note: Computed as per Tendulkar method on Mixed Reference Period (MRP).

consumption expenditure would amount to about Rs. 4,080 per month in rural areas and Rs. 5,000 per month in urban areas. These poverty lines would vary from State to State because of inter-State price differentials.

8. The national level poverty ratio based on comparable methodology (Tendulkar Method) for 1993-94, 2004-05 and 2011-12 estimated from Large Sample Survey of Household Consumer

Table I.2: Number and Percentage of Population below poverty line by States-2011-12 (Tendulkar Methodology)

Sl. No.	States	Rural		Urban		Total	
		%age of Persons	No. of Persons (lakhs)	%age of Persons	No. of Persons (lakhs)	%age of Persons	No. of Persons (lakhs)
1.	Andhra Pradesh	10.96	61.80	5.81	16.98	9.20	78.78
2.	Arunachal Pradesh	38.93	4.25	20.33	0.66	34.67	4.91
3.	Assam	33.89	92.06	20.49	9.21	31.98	101.27
4.	Bihar	34.06	320.40	31.23	37.75	33.74	358.15
5.	Chhattisgarh	44.61	88.90	24.75	15.22	39.93	104.11
6.	Delhi	12.92	0.50	9.84	16.46	9.91	16.96
7.	Goa	6.81	0.37	4.09	0.38	5.09	0.75
8.	Gujarat	21.54	75.35	10.14	26.88	16.63	102.23
9.	Haryana	11.64	19.42	10.28	9.41	11.16	28.83
10.	Himachal Pradesh	8.48	5.29	4.33	0.30	8.06	5.59
11.	Jammu & Kashmir	11.54	10.73	7.20	2.53	10.35	13.27
12.	Jharkhand	40.84	104.09	24.83	20.24	36.96	124.33
13.	Karnataka	24.53	92.80	15.25	36.96	20.91	129.76
14.	Kerala	9.14	15.48	4.97	8.46	7.05	23.95
15.	Madhya Pradesh	35.74	190.95	21.00	43.10	31.65	234.06
16.	Maharashtra	24.22	150.56	9.12	47.36	17.35	197.92
17.	Manipur	38.80	7.45	32.59	2.78	36.89	10.22
18.	Meghalaya	12.53	3.04	9.26	0.57	11.87	3.61
19.	Mizoram	35.43	1.91	6.36	0.37	20.40	2.27
20.	Nagaland	19.93	2.76	16.48	1.00	18.88	3.76
21.	Odisha	35.69	126.14	17.29	12.39	32.59	138.53
22.	Punjab	7.66	13.35	9.24	9.82	8.26	23.18
23.	Rajasthan	16.05	84.19	10.69	18.73	14.71	102.92
24.	Sikkim	9.85	0.45	3.66	0.06	8.19	0.51
25.	Tamil Nadu	15.83	59.23	6.54	23.40	11.28	82.63
26.	Tripura	16.53	4.49	7.42	0.75	14.05	5.24
27.	Uttarakhand	11.62	8.25	10.48	3.35	11.26	11.60
28.	Uttar Pradesh	30.40	479.35	26.06	118.84	29.43	598.19
29.	West Bengal	22.52	141.14	14.66	43.83	19.98	184.98
30.	Puducherry	17.06	0.69	6.30	0.55	9.69	1.24
31.	Andaman & Nicobar Islands	1.57	0.04	0.00	0.00	1.00	0.04
32.	Chandigarh	1.64	0.004	22.31	2.34	21.81	2.35
33.	Dadra & Nagar Haveli	62.59	1.15	15.38	0.28	39.31	1.43
34.	Daman & Diu	0.00	0.00	12.62	0.26	9.86	0.26
35.	Lakshadweep	0.00	0.00	3.44	0.02	2.77	0.02
	All India	**25.70**	**2166.58**	**13.70**	**531.25**	**21.92**	**2697.83**

Notes:
1. Population as on 1st March, 2012 has been used for estimating number of persons below poverty line. (2011 Census population extrapolated).
2. Poverty line of Tamil Nadu has been used for Andaman and Nicobar Island.
3. Urban Poverty Line of Punjab has been used for both rural and urban areas of Chandigarh.
4. Poverty Line of Maharashtra has been used for Dadra & Nagar Haveli.
5. Poverty line of Goa has been used for Daman & Diu.
6. Poverty Line of Kerala has been used for Lakshadweep.

Table I.3: State-wise estimates of Average Monthly Per Capita Expenditure (MPCE) as per Mixed Reference Period (MRP) for 2011-12

S.No.	*States/UTs*	*Rural*	*Urban*
1.	Andhra Pradesh	1563.21	2559.30
2.	Arunachal Pradesh	1455.87	2241.63
3.	Assam	1056.98	2090.18
4.	Bihar	970.41	1396.65
5.	Chhattisgarh	904.04	1776.21
6.	Delhi	2690.24	3160.76
7.	Goa	2460.77	2934.87
8.	Gujarat	1430.12	2472.49
9.	Haryana	1925.96	3346.32
10.	Himachal Pradesh	1800.62	3173.30
11.	Jammu & Kashmir	1601.51	2320.28
12.	Jharkhand	919.59	1894.41
13.	Karnataka	1395.10	2898.94
14.	Kerala	2355.53	3044.22
15.	Madhya Pradesh	1024.14	1842.35
16.	Maharashtra	1445.89	2937.06
17.	Manipur	1334.55	1448.91
18.	Meghalaya	1315.11	2293.82
19.	Mizoram	1384.44	2426.53
20.	Nagaland	1756.70	2279.42
21.	Odisha	904.78	1830.33
22.	Punjab	2136.39	2743.07
23.	Rajasthan	1445.74	2206.93
24.	Sikkim	1445.06	2528.11
25.	Tamil Nadu	1570.61	2534.32
26.	Tripura	1194.14	1996.66
27.	Uttarakhand	1551.42	2452.02
28.	Uttar Pradesh	1072.93	1942.25
29.	West Bengal	1170.11	2489.89
30.	A & N Island	2508.19	4439.03
31.	Chandigarh	2543.57	3000.27
32.	Dadra and Nagar	1094.20	2346.15
33.	Daman and Diu	2239.45	2163.94
34.	Lakshwadeep	2533.07	2666.49
35.	Puducherry	2309.92	2959.82
	ALL INDIA	**1287.17**	**2477.02**

Source: NSSO Report No. KI.(68/1.0) on Key Indicators of Household Consumer Expenditure in India 2011-12, NSS 68th round, National Sample Survey Office.

Expenditure data of 50th, 61st and 68th round respectively are given below.

Table I.4: Percentage and Number of Poor Estimated by Tendulkar method, using Mixed Reference Period (MRP)

	Poverty Ratio (%)			*Number of Poor (million)*		
	Rural	*Urban*	*Total*	*Rural*	*Urban*	*Total*
1. 1993-94	50.1	31.8	45.3	328.6	74.5	403.7
2. 2004-05	41.8	25.7	37.2	326.3	80.8	407.1
3. 2011-12	25.7	13.7	21.9	216.5	52.8	269.3
Annual Average Decline: 1993-94 to 2004-05 (percentage points per annum)	0.75	0.55	0.74			
Annual Average Decline: 2004-05 to 2011-12 (percentage points per annum)	2.32	1.69	2.18			

9. The percentage of persons below the Poverty Line in 2011-12 has been estimated as 25.7 per cent in rural areas, 13.7 per cent in urban areas and 21.9 per cent for the country as a whole. The respective ratios for the rural and urban areas were 41.8 per cent and 25.7 per cent and 37.2 per cent for the country as a whole in 2004-05. It was 50.1 per cent in rural areas, 31.8 per cent in urban areas and 45.3 per cent for the country as a whole in 1993-94. In 2011-12, India had 270 million persons below the Tendulkar Poverty Line as compared to 407 million in 2004-05, that is a reduction of 137 million persons over the seven year period.

10. During the 11-year period 1993-94 to 2004-05, the average decline in the poverty ratio was 0.74 percentage points per year. It accelerated to 2.18 percentage points per year during the 7-year period 2004-05 to 2011-12. Therefore, it can be concluded that the rate of decline in the poverty ratio during the most recent 7-year period 2004-05 to 2011-12 was about three times of that experienced in the 11-year period 1993-94 to 2004-05.

11. It is important to note that although the trend decline documented above is based on the Tendulkar poverty line which is being reviewed and may be revised by the Rangarajan

Committee, an increase in the poverty line will not alter the fact of a decline. While the absolute levels of poverty would be higher, the rate of decline would be similar. To illustrate the point, details about the magnitude of decline in poverty ratio at various levels above and below the Tendulkar Poverty Line are presented in **Chart I.1**.

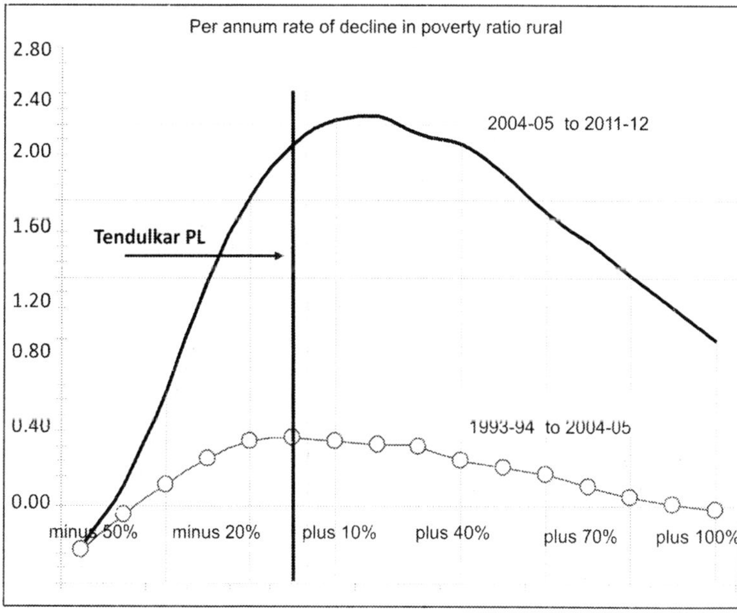

Chart I.1: Decline in poverty at various points above and below the Tendulkar Poverty Line (Annualized Rate of Decline on Y-axis and the variations from Tendulkar PL on X-axis)

12. The decline in poverty flows from the increase in real per capita consumption. The per annum increase in real MPCE for each of the ten deciles is presented at **Chart I.2**. The clear inference is that: (a) the real MPCE increased by much more in the second period (2004-05 to 2011-12) as compared to the first (1993-94 to 2004-05), (b) that the increase was fairly well distributed across all deciles of the population, and (c) the distribution was particularly equitable in rural areas.

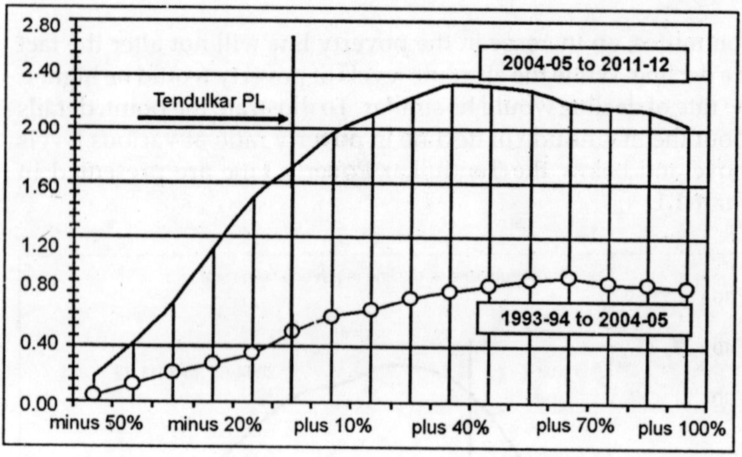

Chart I.2: Increase in Real Monthly Per Capita Consumption Expenditure (MPCE)—URP Annualized—for two periods (Rate of Increase in Real MPCE on Y-axis and Decile class on X-axis)

NOTE

1. Tendulkar methodology uses implicit prices derived from quantity and value data collected in household consumer expenditure surveys for computing and updating the poverty lines.

Maurile Schiff and L. Alam (2003), *Winters Regional International Development.* The International Bank for Reconstructions and Development, the World Bank.

Mayer, H.M. Kohn, C.F. (Eds) (1967), *Reading in Urban Geography,* Chicago.

Patwardhan, A.D. (2013), *Industrial Solid Waste,* New Delhi-Teri.

Pulla, Rao, D. (2012), *Urbanization and Economic Development,* ABD Publishers, Jaipur.

Rajie, K.V., (ED) (2006), *Elixir of Life, The Socio-Ecological Governance of Drinking Water,* Pub: Books for Change Bangalore.

Reidar Dale (1998), *Evaluating Development Progressive and Project,* Sage Publications.

Sai, Sujatha, D. (2012), *Growing Urbanization-Challenges & Strategies,* Discovery Publishing House, Pvt. Ltd, New Delhi.

Sai, Sujatha, D. (2012), *Water, Sanitation and Health in Urbanites,* Discovery Publishing House, Pvt. Ltd., New Delhi.

Sakunthala Narsimhan (1999), *Empowering Women: An Alternative, Strategy From Rural India,* Sage Publications.

Singh, J. (1984), *Geography and Environment Retrospect and Prospect* in Geography and Department of Geography, Pune University.

Singh, R.B. (2006), *Sustainable Urban Development,* Concept Publishing Company, New Delhi.

Singh, Savindra (2001), *Environmental Geography,* Prayag Pustak Bhawan, Allahabad.

Sinha, V.C. (1975), *Dynamics of India's Population Growth,* National Publishing House, New Delhi.

Subha, Singh (2014), *Concept in Urbanization,* ABD Publishers, Jaipur.

Suryakant (2004), *Reinventing Regional Development,* Festschrift to Honour Gopal Krishnan, Nina Singh, Rawat Publications Jaipur.

Thakur, Baleswar, (2005), *Urban and Regional Development in India,* Concept Publishing Company, New Delhi.

Vanita Pandey (2014), *Rethinking Urban Development,* Rawat Publication, Jaipur.

Virges, P. and Menon, G., *Slums Shelter and Environmental Improvement Programme,* Vol. 1 & 2 Published by Karnataka Slum Clearance Board.

Regional Work Shop

National Seminar on "Urban Poverty Alleviation", 25th-26th July, 2005 at RCUES Conference Hall, Osmania University, Hyderabad.

National Work Shop on "Urban Poverty Eradication Strategies", 25th-26th July, 2008 at RCUES Osmania University, Hyderabad.

National Seminar on "Management of Quality in Urban Services and City Infrastructure in Hyderabad", 12th-13th September, 2008 Organized by Matrusri Institute of P.G. Studies (Sponsored by Matrusri Education Society) Saidabad, Hyderabad.

Regional Work Shop on "Urban Poverty Alleviation. Plan Preparation and Implementation", 28th-29th November, 2008 at Tirupati.

Bibliography

Text Books

Abdul, Aziz (1989), *Development Programmes for Weaker Sections*, Print Well Publishers, Jaipur.

Ahluwalia (2013), *Environmental Studies—Basic Concepts*, Delhi-Teri.

Anindita Srivastav (2013), *Food Hygiene and Sanitation*, Axis Book Pvt. Ltd., New Delhi.

Baghel, C.L., Yogendra Kumar, (2006), *Good Governance Concept and Approaches*, Kanishka Publishers Distributors, New Delhi.

Bhatnager, Subhash (2004), *E-Government from Vision to Replacementation*, Sage Publications, New

Bhat, M., *Slum and Metropolis*, Rajata Publication, New Delhi.

Bose, Ashish (1978), India's Urbanization 1901-2001, Tata McGraw Publishing Co. Ltd., New Delhi.

Buch, M.N. (1993), *Environmental Consciousness and Urban Planning*, Orient Longman, Hyderabad.

Carter, H. (1979), *The Study of Urban Geography*, Trnold-Heinman, London.

Chandana, R.C. (1986), *A Geography Population*, Kalyani Publishers, New Delhi.

Clark, D. (1982), *Urban Geography*, Croom Helm London.

Coliver Brito/Aditya Singh (2014), *Understanding Urban Poverty in India*, Rawat Publications, Jaipur.

Cowling, T.M. and G.C. Steely (1973), *Sub-Regional Planning Studies*, Pentagon Press, Oxford.

Dalua, A.K. (1993), *Environmental Impact of Large Reservoir Projects on Human Settlements*, Ashish Publishing House, New Delhi.

Delhi.

Gore, M.S. (1968), *Urbanization and Family Change*, Popular Prakashan, Bombay.

Gupta, S.P. (1989), *Meaning and Development In India*, Allied Publishers Pvt. Ltd., New Delhi.

Joshi, Y.G. and D.K. Verma (2004), *Social Environment for Sustainable Development*, Rawat Publications, Jaipur.

Kumar, V.K. and Singh B.L., *A Study of Slum Environment* in Varanasi Environment Population and Development.

Index